Financial and Monetary Policy Studies

Volume 51

Series Editor

Ansgar Belke, Faculty of Business Administration and Economics, University of Duisburg-Essen, Essen, Germany

More information about this series at http://www.springer.com/series/5982

Frank Rövekamp · Moritz Bälz ·
Hanns Günther Hilpert
Editors

Monetary Policy Implementation in East Asia

Springer

Editors
Frank Rövekamp
East Asia Institute
Ludwigshafen University of Applied Sciences
Ludwigshafen, Germany

Moritz Bälz
Faculty of Law/Interdisciplinary Centre for East Asian Studies
Goethe University Frankfurt
Frankfurt am Main, Hessen, Germany

Hanns Günther Hilpert
German Institute for International and Security Affairs (SWP)
Berlin, Germany

ISSN 0921-8580 ISSN 2197-1889 (electronic)
Financial and Monetary Policy Studies
ISBN 978-3-030-50297-3 ISBN 978-3-030-50298-0 (eBook)
https://doi.org/10.1007/978-3-030-50298-0

This Springer imprint is published by the registered company Springer Nature Switzerland AG
The registered company address is: Gewerbestrasse 11, 6330 Cham, Switzerland

Preface and Acknowledgements

As central bankers would openly admit, implementation *does* matter in monetary politics. However, implementation issues are rather seldom the subject of serious academic research. To counteract both these deficits in perception *and* this research gap was the motive for the international conference entitled "Monetary Policy Execution in East Asia", which was organised by the East Asia Institute in Ludwigshafen in May 2018. The conference brought together leading experts from both academia and monetary authorities to explore the economic, legal and policy perspectives of monetary policy implementation in East Asia, complemented by a European perspective. The papers delivered at the conference formed the basis for this book.

The conference was made possible through the generous support of the *Deutsche Bundesbank*, the *Haniel Foundation* and the *Taipeh Representative Office* in Germany, which is gratefully acknowledged. Likewise, we wish to thank Springer International Publishing for accepting this volume into its series entitled *Financial and Monetary Policy Studies*. Finally, we are indebted to Chris Engert in Florence for his excellent work in the language revision and copy-editing of the manuscript.

Ludwigshafen am Rhein, Germany — Frank Rövekamp
Frankfurt am Main, Germany — Moritz Bälz
Berlin, Germany — Hanns Günther Hilpert

Contents

Contributors

Moritz Bälz Faculty of Law/Interdisciplinary Centre for East Asian Studies, Goethe University, Frankfurt am Main, Germany

Hwee Kwan Chow Singapore Management University, Singapore, Singapore

Patrick Hess European Central Bank, Frankfurt am Main, Germany

Hanns Günther Hilpert Research Division Asia, German Institute for International and Security Affairs (SWP), Berlin, Germany

Woosik Moon Graduate School of International Studies, Seoul National University, Gwanak-gu, Seoul, Korea

Frank Rövekamp East Asia Institute, Ludwigshafen University of Business and Society, Ludwigshafen, Germany

Sayuri Shirai Keio University, Fujisawa, Kanagawa, Japan

Helmut Siekmann Institute for Monetary and Financial Stability (IMFS), Goethe University, Frankfurt am Main, Germany

Ti-Jen Tsao Central Bank of the Republic of China (Taiwan), Taipei, Taiwan, R.O.C.

Ulrich Volz SOAS University of London, London, UK;
German Development Institute, Bonn, Germany

Fot Chyi Wong Singapore Management University, Singapore, Singapore

Abbreviations

ABC	Agricultural Bank of China
ABSPP	Asset-Backed Securities Purchase Programme
AG	Aktiengesellschaft
ANFA	Agreement on Net Financial Assets
APP	Asset Purchase Programmes
ASEAN	Association of Southeast Asian Nations
Bhd.	Berhad (Malaysian public limited company)
BIS	Bank for International Settlements
BoC	Bank of China
BoCOM	Bank of Communications
BoJ	Bank of Japan
BoK	Bank of Korea
Brexit	The Exit of the UK from the European Union
CBC	Central Bank of the Republic of China, Taiwan
CBIRC	China Banking and Insurance Regulatory Commission
CBP	Covered Bond Programmes
CBPP	Covered Bond Purchase Programmes
CBRC	China Banking Regulatory Commission
CCB	China Construction Bank
CCP	Chinese Communist Party
CIRC	China Insurance Regulatory Commission
CJEU	Court of Justice of the European Union (formerly ECJ)
CME	Comprehensive Monetary Easing
COFER	Current Composition of Official Foreign Exchange Reserves
CPF	Central Provident Fund
CPI	Consumer Price Index
CSPP	Corporate Sector Purchase Programme
CSRC	China Securities Regulatory Commission
DBS	Development Bank of Singapore Ltd
DSGE-VAR	Dynamic Stochastic General Equilibrium-Vector Autoregression

EAPP	Expanded (Extended) Asset Purchase Programme
EC	European Community/ies
ECB	European Central Bank
ECJ	European Court of Justice
EFSF	European Financial Stability Facility
EFSM	European Financial Stabilisation Mechanism
EFT	Exchange-Traded Funds
ELA	Emergency Liquidity Assistance
EMU	European Monetary Union
EPS	Earnings Per Share
ESCB	European System of Central Banks
ESM	European Stability Mechanism
ETFs	Exchange-Traded Funds
EU	European Union
EUR	European Monetary Unit
Fed	Federal Reserve
FOMC	Federal Open Market Committee
FSDC	Financial Stability and Development Commission
FX	Foreign Exchange
G-20	Group of Twenty: Argentina, Australia, Brazil, Canada, China, France, Germany, India, Indonesia, Italy, Japan, Republic of Korea, Mexico, Russia, Saudi Arabia, South Africa, Turkey, United Kingdom, United States and the European Union
GCEU	General Court of the European Union
GDP	Gross Domestic Product
GFCC	German Federal Constitutional Court
GPIF	Government Pension Investment Funds
GVC	Global Value Chain
HK$	Hong Kong Dollars
HKMA	Hong Kong Monetary Authority
ICBC	Industrial Bank of China
iDeCo	Individual-type Defined Contribution Pension Plan
IDE-JETRO	Institute of Developing Economies
IMF	International Monetary Fund
ISIN	International Security Identification Number
IT	Inflation Targeting
JGB	Japanese Government Bonds
JMoF	Japanese Ministry of Finance
JPY	Japanese Yen
J-REITs	Japan Real Estate Investment Trusts
KRW	South Korean Won
LB	Liabilities Box
LCU	Local Currency Unit
LTRO	Long-Term Refinancing Operations
M2	Money Supply

MA	Moving Average
MAS	Monetary Authority of Singapore
MCB	Minimum Cash Balance
MLF	Medium-Term Loan Rate Facility (rate)
MoF	Ministry of Finance
MPC	Monetary Policy Committee
MPS	Monetary Policy Statement
N.A.	National Association
NCB	National Central Bank
NEER	Nominal Effective Exchange Rate
NISA	Nippon Individual Savings Account
NPC	National People's Congress
NTD	New Taiwan Dollar
OECD	Organisation for Economic Co-operation and Development
OJ	Official Journal
OMO	Open Market Operations
OMT	Outright Monetary Transaction
P/E	Price–Earnings Ratio
PBC	People's Bank of China
PCE	Personal Consumption Expenditure (price index)
PDR	People's Democratic Republic
PRC	People's Republic of China
PSPP	Public Sector Asset Purchase Programme/Public Sector Purchase Programme
QE	Quantitative Easing
QQE	Quantitative and Qualitative (Monetary) Easing
R&D	Research and Development
Repo	Re-purchase Agreements
RMB	Renminbi
RRR	Reserve Requirement Ratio
S$NEER	Singapore Dollar Nominal Effective Exchange Rate
S&P	Standard & Poor's
SD	Standard Deviation
SDR	Special Drawing Right
SGD	Singapore Dollar
SGS	Singapore Government Securities
SME	Small- and Medium-sized Enterprise
SMP	Securities Market Programme
SNB	Swiss National Bank
SOAS	School of Oriental and African Studies
TAIEX	Taiwan Stock Exchange Weighted Index
TEU	Treaty on European Union/Treaty of Maastricht 1992, renewed by the Treaty of Lisbon in 2009
TFEU	Treaty on the Functioning of the European Union/Treaty of Lisbon in force 2009

TIVA	Trade in Value Added (OECD-WTO Database)
TLTRO	Targeted Longer Term Refinancing Operations
TMLF	Targeted Medium-Term Loan Facility
TOPIX	Tokyo Stock Price Index
UK	United Kingdom
UNCTAD	United Nation Conference on Trade and Development
US	United States (of America)
USA	United States of America
USD	United States Dollar
VA	Value Added
VAR	Vector Autoregression
WEO	World Economic Outlook (IMF)
WTO	World Trade Organization

Chapter 1
Monetary Policy in East Asia: Implementation Matters

Frank Rövekamp, Moritz Bälz, and Hanns Günther Hilpert

Abstract When monetary policy was still largely confined to the setting of interest rates and conventional open market operations, monetary policy implementation could be considered a technical issue beyond the scope for academic analysis. This has changed with the advent of the so-called unconventional monetary policies such as Quantitative Easing (QE). The exact way of conducting such policies has a huge influence not only on financial markets, but also on the real economy and on fiscal affairs. Meanwhile, central bank communication has proven to be a major factor for the efficiency of monetary policy paths, and in this field, too, success depends to a large degree on proper implementation.

The chapters in this book take a look at monetary implementation issues in various Asian economies. This widens the perspective for further areas, such as inflation targeting, exchange-rate policies and company-stock purchases by central banks. The case of the People's Bank of China demonstrates that the smooth implementation of monetary policy may be infringed by governance issues. Experiences from the Bank of Korea show that Inflation Targeting faces fundamental challenges in communication. Exchange-rate management remains very important for smaller and open economies, such as those of Singapore and Taiwan; here skilful implementation has to assure the control of short-term speculative capital movements without

F. Rövekamp (✉)
East Asia Institute, Ludwigshafen University of Business and Society, Rheinpromenade 12, 67061 Ludwigshafen, Germany
e-mail: roevekamp@oai.de

M. Bälz
Faculty of Law/Interdisciplinary Centre for East Asian Studies, Goethe University, Theodor-W.-Adorno-Platz 4, 60323 Frankfurt am Main, Germany
e-mail: baelz@jur.uni-frankfurt.de

H. G. Hilpert
Research Division Asia, German Institute for International and Security Affairs (SWP), Ludwigkirchplatz 3-4, 10719 Berlin, Germany
e-mail: hanns.hilpert@swp-berlin.org

F. Rövekamp et al. (eds.), *Monetary Policy Implementation in East Asia*, Financial and Monetary Policy Studies 51,
https://doi.org/10.1007/978-3-030-50298-0_1

negatively affecting trade and direct investments. The boundaries of QE are tested in Japan, where the central bank not only purchases government bonds but also company stock. The potential side effects on corporate governance and stock market volatility may still unfold. The cases presented in this book underline the importance of the implementation aspect of monetary policy and point to the need for further research in this area.

The achievement and preservation of price stability remain the primary goal of monetary policy. Ever since the global financial crisis of 2008/09, however, concerns about financial stability have also taken centre stage and the fighting of deflation, rather than inflation, has become the order of the day in the major economies. In this environment, traditional monetary policy tools, such as the setting of short-term interest rates and reserve policy quickly reached their limits and a range of largely untested measures, under the heading of "quantitative easing" (QE), emerged. With QE, central banks involved themselves in financial market dealings on an unprecedented scale. QE has also had strong effects on the global movement of capital, as investors faced rapidly decreasing opportunities for decent returns.

The strong side effects of QE have also brought the concrete implementation of monetary policy into focus. Differences in this regard potentially have huge repercussions on matters such as financing conditions and market volatility. In this connection, attention has been drawn to the question of what kind of collateral central banks accept in exchange for central bank money. In Europe, for example, more than 30,000 different securities are eligible as collateral for the European Central Bank, and Nyborg has shown that there has been a growth towards the usage of lower quality collateral over time. This, in the end, distorts market prices and thus affects the efficient allocation of resources not only in the financial markets, but also in the real economy.[1] Thus, the implementation details of QE, which are rarely in the spotlight, prove to be of the utmost importance.

Furthermore, the execution of monetary policy is a major concern not only for investors in finance and the real economy, but also for actors in the fields of fiscal and exchange-rate policy. Central bank communication and forward guidance is another field, in which success strongly depends on the precise implementation.

As the implementation aspect of monetary policy has not received much attention in academic research and literature, its practice has proven to be a somewhat evolutionary learning process.[2] Every step in this evolution is a kind of experiment, and central banks are learning from their successes and failures. In this way, spectacular monetary policy events are major concerns for the credibility of central banks and determine the monetary implementation path further down the road. Some prominent examples from Asia and Europe vividly illustrate the importance of implementation in the realms of communication:

Mario Draghi's magical words announcing the ECB's "Outright Monetary Transactions" (OMT) programme on 26 July 2012 can be considered as a brilliant masterpiece of successful central bank communication:

---

[1]Nyborg (2017).

[2]Bindseil (2016).

> Within our mandate, the ECB is ready to do whatever it takes to preserve the Euro. And believe me, it will be enough.[3]

Subsequently, the spread of French, Italian and Spanish government bonds declined and returned to their previous levels with yields slightly above that of German government bonds. Eventually, not a single Euro was spent for the OMT programme.

But there were also examples of mishaps, misjudgement and even impotence. Thus, the ECB has been less successful in its attempts to uphold prerogative sovereignty in the discussion about the significance and fiscal risks of target-2 balances.[4] In the Northern Eurozone countries, scepticism prevailed. To mention two further examples, the People's Bank of China's (PBC) surprising, uncommented decision of August 2016 to devaluate the RMB by 1.9% against the USD, let the stock markets tumble. Eventually, the PBC had to spend almost 500 billion USD to prevent the RMB from falling further. Similarly, the surprising announcement of the Indian government on 8 November 2016 to de-monetise all 500 and 1000 Rupee banknotes provoked an enduring cash shortage and created serious economic disruptions.

All these examples show that central bank communication faces a structural dilemma: to give credible forward guidance, precise and unambiguous information in sufficient quantity is called for. This, however, is accompanied by reduced possibilities to react flexibly in the face of surprising external developments. A central bank may face the unpleasant option of sticking to its forward guided course, even though it no longer constitutes the most appropriate choice, or of suddenly changing direction, which may come at the expense of credibility. In this way, there can be no fixed recipe for successful monetary policy communication; its implementation needs to be carefully gauged against the specific circumstances in which it finds itself.[5]

The contributions in this volume bear witness of the critical importance of monetary policy implementation mainly from the perspective of Asian economies, notwithstanding the major differences in their size and circumstances.

The conduct of monetary policy by the People's Bank of China is analysed by ***Patrick Hess*** in Chap. 2. In general, the PBC uses the same monetary policy tools as other central banks, namely, open market operations, standing facilities (*i.e.* borrowing and deposit facilities for commercial banks) and reserve requirements. It may also still rely on "window guidance" to informally advise the financial sector on the amounts of the banking loans to different sectors. Hess concludes that, despite its multiple objectives—price stability, promoting growth and employment, maintaining the balance of payments and financial stability—and despite a challenging and rapidly changing external environment, the PBC has, in fact, done reasonably well with its policies.

Hess' verdict, however, is less confident when it comes to transparency and accountability, which are conventional key demands on central bank policy to achieve

---

[3]Draghi (2012).

[4]Hellwig (2018).

[5]Weidmann (2018).

low inflation and manage inflation expectations. One reason for this is the fact that the PBC still lacks independence, as it needs to have its decisions approved by the State Council, China's government. But beyond this, a clear-cut communication policy is also hindered by the peculiar composition of the Monetary Policy Committee (MPC), the top decision-making organ of the PBC, and the position of the bank within the setting of other state institutions.

The MPC has many more external, than internal, members. The external members are vice-ministers or leaders of other economic and regulatory institutions. Already the process of decision-making is thus not only driven by the usual monetary indicators, but also by a complex balancing of interests with other institutions in the economic and the financial field. There is no "arm's length relationship" between the PBC and other important economic institutions in the Western sense.

After an episode of strong market volatility because of non-communication or miscommunication in the second half of 2015, the PBC's communication policy has improved, but, Hess concludes, transparency remains linked to independence, which is still clearly limited for the PBC as of today. The smooth implementation of monetary policy measures may, therefore, pose challenges, also in the future.

Woosik Moon, in Chap. 3, provides an inside view into the workings as well as the shortcomings of *Inflation Targeting* (IT) based on the Bank of Korea (BoK) experience. As IT has become the main monetary policy strategy for the major central banks of developed countries, the BoK also adopted it in the aftermath of the Asian crisis of 1997/98.

Under IT, a central bank focuses directly on achieving a specific inflation rate, instead of focusing on an intermediate target such as the money supply. This was first adopted by the Bank of New Zealand in 1990. Later the consensus emerged that, rather than 0%, a target of 2% was both appropriate and commensurate with price stability, considering price rigidities in the labour market. The 2% target was thus symmetric in the sense that undershooting it was as undesired as overshooting it.

However, given the history of high inflation in Korea, the BoK sets the target at 3% so as not to jeopardise its credibility. 3% was an asymmetric target, because a higher inflation rate was to be avoided, whereas an inflation rate of less than 3% was still welcome, even though it was considered unlikely. When, in the course of time, the BoK achieved inflation rates well below 3%, it was, however, widely criticised for not matching the goals that it had actually set for itself. It turned out that the workings of the fine points of inflation targeting are difficult to communicate, and, accordingly, are often not well understood. This resulted in credibility problems for the BoK.

Another issue with IT is that it needs to rely on inflation expectations, which the central bank tries to influence. This can be achieved comparatively well in a high inflation environment if the central bank communicates its willingness to use the well-proven monetary instruments to achieve the desired (lower) inflation rate in a credible manner. In a low inflation or even deflation environment, however, when inflation uncertainties are low, it is much more difficult to stimulate inflation expectations. In the case of Japan, for example, inflation expectations fail to reach the targeted 2% despite long-term efforts and unprecedented monetary easing by the

Bank of Japan. Thus, Moon concludes that the whole concept of inflation targeting may have reached its limits in an environment of low inflation.

Ulrich Volz, in Chap. 4, analyses the gap between declared monetary policy, often IT, as in Korea, and the actual behaviour of central banks in a range of East Asian countries. Traditionally, exchange-rate stability towards the US Dollar ranks high in importance for Asian economies, as many of them strongly depend on international trade and have a large share of their assets and liabilities denominated in US Dollars. Intervening in currency markets has, therefore, been a common feature for many central banks in the region. In this way, they try to control exchange-rate volatility and to avoid exchange-rate misalignments. Another goal of these interventions is the build-up of foreign currency reserves as a buffer against potential speculative attacks on their currency in the future.

On the other hand, a range of countries, namely, Japan, Indonesia, Korea, the Philippines and Thailand, have officially adopted an inflation-targeting strategy, which is incompatible with interventions in currency markets. Buying foreign currency to counter the appreciation of one's own currency, for example, increases the domestic money supply and may thus run counter to a targeted inflation rate. Volz shows, however, that, with the exception of Japan, the countries officially operating in an inflation-targeting framework have intervened significantly in the currency market in recent years, too. This is even more the case with countries which declare that they operate under a "managed exchange-rate regime", including China. Fear of being named a "currency manipulator" may be the most important reason for the deviation between officially declared and actually performed policy. This furthermore indicates that inflation targeting, despite its popularity, still lacks a clear operating framework or may even not be a suitable concept under certain circumstances.

Two central banks which officially put the exchange rate at the centre of their monetary policies are the Central Bank of the Republic of China, Taiwan (CBC) and the Monetary Authority of Singapore (MAS). Both are open economies that depend, to a very large degree, on foreign trade and, in principle, support the free flow of capital.

Ti-Jen Tsao analyses the case of Taiwan in Chap. 5. He emphasises that international capital movements are mostly driven by short-term financial speculation, and not by trade or long-term investment motives. This trend is reinforced by the massive quantitative easing strategies of major central banks in recent years, which drives capital to seek acceptable returns wherever it is still possible.

Taiwan's economy relies highly on international trade. Not only are exports of importance, but, because the export goods depend—to a large degree—on foreign value added, imports and exports are also strongly intertwined. A predictable and rather stable exchange rate without strong volatility is crucial in this environment. Notwithstanding this, less than 10% of the trade in New Taiwan Dollar (NTD) is now based on international trade, whereas more than 90% is for the purpose of short-term financial transactions, for example, in the Taiwanese stock market. Such short-term capital movements can be a source of considerable macroeconomic and financial instability, as is already evidenced by the Asian financial crisis of 1997/98.

The CBC, therefore, implements a range of measures to stabilise the exchange rate of the NTD. The strategy devised is that of "leaning against the wind", which means the central bank will not try to stem exchange-rate movements based on fundamental economic trends, but will try to avoid erratic movements based on the speculation and the short-term transactions of foreign investors. For this purpose, the CBC intervenes in the currency markets and has built a large pool of foreign currency reserves in order to give credibility to such interventions. Short-term capital movements are also restricted by regulations, such as prohibiting foreign investors from making NTD time deposits or the calling of cash collaterals in securities borrowing. *Tsao* considers the CBC monetary policy implementation to be successful, because the value of the NTD is less volatile than the currency of similar economies. This has helped Taiwan to maintain a current account surplus, low external debt and high financial liquidity.

Singapore is a small and open economy dependent on international transactions even to a higher degree than Taiwan. Also, Singapore bases its monetary policy on the stability of the exchange rate. As ***Hwee Kwan Chow*** and ***Fot Chyi Wong*** point out in Chap. 6, this simply makes sense, even for the purpose of inflation control, without even considering the potentially damaging effects of large short-term capital movements.

To achieve currency stability the Monetary Authority of Singapore (MAS) keeps the Singapore Dollar (SGD) stable against the value of a basket of currencies of important trading partners by currency market interventions. The exact composition of the basket is deliberately not made public in order to provide less attacking points for potential speculative movements. Otherwise, however, the MAS communicates in a very structured way to inform the market participants about its movements and the rationale behind them. Like the central bank in Taiwan, the MAS also deploys the strategy of "leaning against the wind", thereby allowing the gradual appreciation of the Singapore Dollar based on economic fundamentals, but keeping the short-term movements of the currency value within a defined band, which can be adjusted according to the prevailing economic situation. The MAS has been very successful in safeguarding the defined currency stability under various circumstances, such as the financial crisis of 2008/09 and in ensuring the recovery phase.

The focus on currency stabilisation has, however, the side effects that the MAS cannot directly control short-term domestic interest rates, because to do so might run counter to the exchange-rate targets. To avoid erratic movements of interest rates, the MAS has devised a range of measures in the domestic money market, such as providing credit and dealing in securities with selected participants. Chow and Wong conclude that the successful operations of the MAS over the years have also been due to the institutional framework in Singapore and the ethos of financial prudence on the part of the government.

Some fundamental issues in connection with monetary policy implementation come to light in connection with quantitative easing (QE) strategies, which gained popularity in major economies after the financial crisis of 2008/09 and also considerably affected the Asian financial and currency markets, as seen above. In order to obtain a deeper understanding of QE, the analysis of the case of Europe is particularly intriguing, as the QE policy of the ECB has been contested in the courts, where the potential problem areas have been clearly spelled out and argued about. ***Helmut Siekmann***'s Chap. 7 on "The Asset Purchase Programmes of the ECB in the Courts" thus offers valuable lessons and reference points for the Asian economies.

Siekmann analyses how two specific QE implementation lines of the ECB—the Outright Monetary Transaction (OMT) programme and the Public Sector Purchase Programme (PSPP)—have fared in the proceedings of the German Federal Constitutional Court (GFCC) and the Court of Justice of the European Union (CJEU). Both programmes have been challenged on the grounds that, because of their specific characteristics, they cross the realm of monetary policy. Rather than mainly influencing the general price level, they constitute acts of state financing and ease the financing conditions for certain financial institutions and other entities, so the claim. Thus, the central bank was not simply adhering to its legal mandate of conducting monetary policy, but was instead conducting economic and fiscal policy, which does not fall within its competencies.

None of the courts declared the programmes to be unlawful outright, but the GFCC, in particular, saw a clear potential for the ECB to overstep its monetary policy mandate and therefore sets out the conditions for the operation of the programmes, such as the following:

- Market operators must not know for certain that the ECB is going to purchase specific bonds.
- A minimum period must be observed between the issue of a security on the primary market and its purchase on the secondary market.
- Purchased bonds may only be held until maturity in exceptional cases.
- The purchases must be limited or suspended if the monetary policy goals are achieved.

The battle in the courts demonstrates the complexity of setting a clearly defined demarcation line between the theoretically separate realms of monetary and fiscal policy in the real world. It also shows that the implementation of monetary policy can have a huge effect not only on the desired outcome, but also on outcomes that are undesired.

Taking the QE policy even one step further than the ECB, the Bank of Japan (BoJ) has extended the range of assets that it purchases from bonds to stocks and other financial instruments.

Sayuri Shirai, in Chap. 8, analyses the purchases of company stock in the form of Exchange-Traded Funds (ETFs) by the Bank of Japan as an implementation tool of its so-called "Quantitative and Qualitative Easing" (QQE) monetary policy.

Stock purchases have been "off-limit" in conventional monetary policy and are forbidden outright for both the US Federal Reserve Board and the Bank of England. The reasons behind this are that a central bank is not positioned to take an active role as a shareholder, as, in this way, corporate governance can be compromised. The shareholder position may furthermore infringe upon necessary monetary policy measures in the event of rising inflationary pressure, as an increase in interest rates reduces the values of stocks and thus may cause a loss for the central bank. The same holds true for bonds, but these can at least be held until maturity, which limits the losses and keeps them within a predictable range.

Even before the QQE phase, which started in 2013, the Bank of Japan had bought the common stock of companies. But these were limited episodes which served the purpose of financial stability in the early 2000s and in the aftermath of the global financial crisis in 2008/09. The stocks were bought from commercial banks in order to allow them to write off bad loans and to clean their balance sheets.

The recent buying programme for stocks on a larger scale for monetary policy purposes started in 2013 in connection with the commencement of the QQE. The BoJ sets the goal to buy ETFs for 1 trillion Yen per year, which was later increased to 3 trillion and then to 6 trillion Yen. As of today (October 2019), it holds ETFs worth about 30 trillion Yen. The purpose of the programme has been to decrease the risk premiums for buying stocks, thereby inducing a portfolio re-balancing effect for investors towards more stocks. The increase in the Nikkei and TOPIX stock indices since 2013 is partly due to the ETF buying programme of the BoJ. The bank has become the largest shareholder in a number of companies and the effect on the corporate governance of these companies remains to be seen. It is furthermore unclear at this point how the BoJ will unwind its large position in the Japanese stock market without causing potentially massive disruptions.

All these cases show that implementation *does* matter in monetary policy. Consistent and sufficient communication is of critical importance, be it for the purpose of inflation targeting or for reaching the desired effects of intervention or for explaining the objectives of monetary policy. In the end, monetary policy must convince the general public and the financial markets that the central bank is rightly pursuing its stated goals, and that its deeds match its words. More than ever implementation failures undermine a central bank's credibility, which should be considered the key factor for successful monetary policy.[6] Implementation can thus not be considered to be merely a technical issue, but needs to take a prominent place in the research of monetary policy.

References

Bindseil, U. (2016). *Evaluating monetary policy operational frameworks*, 31 August 2016. Retrieved 10, Jan 2020, from https://www.kansascityfed.org/~/media/files/publicat/sympos/2016/econsymposium-bindseil-paper2.pdf?la=en.

Blinder, Alan S. (2000). Central bank credibility: Why do we care? How do we build it? *American Economic Review, 90*(5), 1421–1431.

Draghi, M. (2012). Speech at the Global Investor Conference in London, 26 July.

Hellwig, Martin. (2018). Target-Falle oder Empörungsfalle? Zur deutschen Diskussion über die Währungsunion. *Perspektiven der Wirtschaftspolitik, 19*(4), 345–382.

---

[6]Blinder (2000: 1422), Issing (2019: 22, 70).

Issing, Otmar. (2019). *The long journey of central bank communication, Karl Brunner Distinguished Lecture Series*. Cambridge MA and London: The MIT Press.

Nyborg, Kjell N. (2017). *Collateral frameworks—the open secret of central banks*. Cambridge: Cambridge University Press.

Weidmann, J. (2018). Central bank communication as an instrument of monetary policy. BIS Central bankers' speeches, 2 May 2018. Retrieved 10, Jan 2020, from https://www.bis.org/review/r180511a.htm.

Part I
The Framework of Monetary Policy Implementation

Chapter 2
China's Monetary Policy: Institutional Setting, Tools and Challenges

Patrick Hess

Abstract Understanding the monetary policy of China, the world's second largest economy, is more crucial today than ever, and yet it is not widely researched or well-understood outside of China. This chapter tries to narrow this gap by shedding light on the institutional setting of China's monetary policy, and by assessing its main tools and current challenges. It finds that, despite the progress and sophistication of Chinese monetary policy in recent years, for example, by moving from quantity-based to more price-based tools, its implementation suffers from shortcomings in communication and a lack of independence from political interference. Ultimately, it seems to be the Chinese Communist Party (CCP) that determines the "room for manoeuvre" that the People's Bank of China (PBC) has in order to maintain monetary and financial stability in the rapidly changing domestic and global environment. As a result, even in terms of communication, the PBC seems to deviate from today's central bank norm of taking transparency for granted for effectively managing inflation expectations.

The views expressed here are solely those of the author and do not necessarily reflect those of the European Central Bank. The author is grateful to Ulrich Bindseil, Claus Brand, Rodolfo Campos, Darrell Duffie, HOU Yue, William Lelieveldt, Li Xiang, Ana-Simona Manu, and the editors of this book for their valuable comments and suggestions. All mistakes are entirely his own.

P. Hess (✉)
European Central Bank, 60640 Frankfurt am Main, Germany
e-mail: patrick.hess@ecb.int

F. Rövekamp et al. (eds.), *Monetary Policy Implementation in East Asia*, Financial and Monetary Policy Studies 51,
https://doi.org/10.1007/978-3-030-50298-0_2

As interest rates become more market-based, we need a more authoritative and independent central bank to decide and implement monetary policy.

SHEN Jianguang, Mizuho Securities Asia, Hong Kong[1]

2.1 Introduction

In his lecture *On transparency* given at the Norwegian Academy of Science, the former Deputy Governor of *Norges Bank*, Jan F. Qvigstad, made the following remark:

> Simplifying somewhat, the former view was that monetary policy operated effectively by *surprising* economic agents. Today, economic theory posits that monetary policy works best if it is *predictable*.[2]

Gone are the days where central banks worked behind "thick walls"[3] and revealed as little as possible about their assessments and decisions. Today, central bank transparency and accountability are regarded as key to achieving low inflation and effectively managing inflation expectations. So starting from Qvigstad's observation that "transparency is now taken for granted among central banks" and that "most central banks are open about (i) the *objective* of monetary policy, (ii) its *strategy* for reaching the objective, and (iii) the *background* for and the *process* behind interest rate decisions",[4] this chapter tries to explore the extent to which this is also the case for China's central bank, the People's Bank of China (中国人民银行). Its independence, with regard to monetary policy, is the second question. And thirdly, the chapter attempts to assess the reasons for, and the relationship of, the answers to the first two questions. Insights into these key questions can help inform the general understanding of Chinese monetary policy, which seems to be under-researched, in particular, outside of China, but increasingly matters for, and hence receives the attention of, global markets, businesses and policy-makers.[5]

The analysis proceeds as follows: Section 2.2 looks into the institutional setting of monetary policy in China, namely, the dual mandate of the PBC, the role and members of its Monetary Policy Committee (MPC) and the positioning of the PBC

---

[1]Quoted in Bloomberg News (2016).

[2]Jan Fredrik Qvigstad, *On Central Banking*, 2016, p. 36. In his foreword, the economist and economic historian Michael Bordo notes that "Norges Bank has the best record in the world in transmitting its intentions, its forecasts, and the models it uses", so Qvigstad can count as a prime expert on the topic.

[3]In his lecture, Qvigstad recalls how, in 1780, fortified walls helped the Bank of England to protect successfully itself against riots, which afterwards led to the saying "safe as the Bank of England".

[4]Ibid., p. 34 and pp. 35–36, respectively.

[5]This includes the central bank of China's largest trading partners. In the 25 April 2019 issue of the ECB's *Economic Bulletin*, the word "China" appeared 67 times (not least due to the US–China trade war), while, in the previous eight issues (May 2018 to March 2019), it appeared on average only 25 times.

after the institutional reforms passed by the National People's Congress (NPC) in March 2018. Section 2.3 examines the targets and main tools of Chinese monetary policy, as well as its evolution and successes in recent years. Section 2.4 analyses the three research questions in more detail, and Section 2.5 concludes.

2.2 Institutional Setting of China's Monetary Policy

2.2.1 *The Mandate of the People's Bank of China (PBC)*

Established in 1948, it took the PBC 35 years to become a central bank, and another 12 years before this status was legally confirmed with the adoption of the Central Bank Law in March 1995.[6] In the 2003 amendment of that law,[7] Article 2, under the heading "General rules", lists the formulation and implementation of monetary policy as the primary task of the PBC, followed by financial stability tasks, and it also provides a first hint to the thorny issue of the PBC's independence:

> The People's Bank of China is the central bank of the People's Republic of China. The People's Bank of China, under the leadership of the State Council, formulates and implements monetary policy, guards against and eliminates financial risks, and maintains financial stability.[8]

Further key tasks are spelled out in Article 4, and include, *inter alia*, the issuance of Renminbi (RMB) and the administration of its circulation, the supervision and regulation of the inter-bank lending and bond markets, the execution of the foreign exchange (FX) administration, as well as the supervision and regulation of the inter-bank FX market, the maintenance of the normal operation of payment and settlement systems and—most importantly, as it gives the PBC regulatory powers—"the issuance and enforcement of regulations and rules concerning its tasks". Article 3 is crucial, as it contains the dual mandate of the PBC's monetary policy:

> The objective of monetary policy is to maintain the stability of the value of the currency, and thereby to promote economic growth.

---

[6]On the evolution and legal framework of the PBC, see Bell and Feng (2013), and Pißler (2015). Founded in December 1948, the PBC was, from 1953 to 1978, the sole bank of the People's Republic of China (PRC) and undertook all central and commercial banking functions. It assumed the role of a central bank only in 1983, and the "Big Four" state-owned commercial banks were established from 1979 to 1984. Despite a respective regulation issued in 1986, the PBC's central bank status was legally confirmed only in 1995 with the adoption of the *Law of the PRC on the PBC* (amendment in 2003).

[7]Until then, the PBC had also been responsible for banking supervision, which, after December 2013, was taken over by the China Banking Regulatory Commission (CBRC) established in March 2013.

[8]See Zhongguo Renmin Yinhang Tiaofa Si (2018), which is only available in Chinese. The translation of this and other quotations from this law, and from all other Chinese sources, were made by the author.

While, strictly speaking, the formulation leaves it open as to whether the internal (= price stability) or the external (= exchange-rate stability) "value of the currency" is meant here, one could argue that the word "thereby" suggests that price stability best supports economic growth. But, in an export-oriented economy, which China has become since opening up to the West 40 years ago, the exchange rate also has a huge impact on growth, and, over a long period, the central bank has indeed targeted its stability, and, to a certain extent, still continues to do so, as evidenced in recent speeches by the Governor of the PBC.[9] During the period from the mid-1990s to July 2005 (and again during the global financial crisis), when the RMB was (re-) pegged to the US dollar (USD), the nominal exchange rate was the main nominal anchor for China's monetary policy. Even if, in June 2010, the RMB exchange rate was allowed to float again, within a band that was further widened in April 2012, against the USD and a basket of other currencies, Chinese monetary policy was, until some years ago, still seen by some observers as being "heavily constrained" by China's exchange-rate policy (see, also, the contribution of Ulrich Volz, Chap. 4 in this volume).[10]

Within the PBC, the "Monetary Policy Department" (货币政策司) and the "Monetary Policy Department II" (货币政策二司) are responsible for monetary policy. The latter was established in 2009 and is also responsible for all tasks related to the exchange rate and to RMB internationalisation.

2.2.2 The Role of the Monetary Policy Committee (MPC)

Under the second heading "Organisational structure" of the revised Central Bank Law, Article 12 (previously Article 11) states that "the PBC sets up a Monetary Policy Committee" (货币政策委员会), and that its "tasks, composition and working procedures are determined by the State Council and reported to the Standing Committee of the NPC". Compared with the 1995 version, the amended article has an additional sentence which provides a clue as to the peculiar composition of the MPC, which, unlike those of other central banks, goes much beyond the PBC:

> The Monetary Policy Committee of the People's Bank of China shall have an important function within the macroeconomic management and the formulation and adjustment of monetary policy by the State.

While the monetary policy committees of other major central banks include no (ECB, Federal Reserve, Bank of Japan) or only a few (Bank of England) external

[9] See, for example, Yi (2018a), in which he states: "By ensuring basic stability of the value of RMB, we can help promote economic growth, and thereby meet the ultimate goal of monetary policy specified in the Law of the People's Bank of China". The statement is also relevant from another perspective as Yi Gang or the PBC, in general, seem to regard economic growth as taking priority over the first goal.

[10] See Prasad and Zhang (2014), who provide a summary of monetary policy until 2013, and Ma (2014). For the link between China's monetary policy and its RMB exchange-rate regime, see, also, Sun (2017).

members, the PBC's MPC comprises more external than internal members. Beyond the PBC Governor, who chairs the MPC (YI Gang), and three Deputy Governors (among them PAN Gongsheng, who also heads the State Administration of Foreign Exchange under the PBC), it includes ten non-PBC members: a Deputy Secretary-General of the State Council, a Vice Minister of the National Development and Reform Commission, a Vice Finance Minister, the Commissioner of the National Bureau of Statistics (NING Jizhe), the Chairmen of the newly merged China Banking Insurance Regulatory Commission (GUO Shuqing) and of the China Securities Regulatory Commission (YI Huiman), the President of the China Banking Association (TIAN Guoli, who is also Chairman of the China Construction Bank, one of the Big Four) and three academics, including MA Jun, the former Head of the PBC's Research Bureau and now the Director of Tsinghua University's Center for Finance and Development.[11]

The MPC's tasks, composition and working procedures are laid down in the *Provisions for the MPC of the PBC* first promulgated by the State Council in 1997 and available on the PBC website.[12] Article 2 of the Provisions stipulates that the MPC is only a "consultative body (咨询议事机构) for the formulation of monetary policy by the PBC".[13] Article 3 further details the role of the MPC:

> The MPC shall, upon the basis of comprehensive research on the macroeconomic condition, and in accordance with the targets of the State for macroeconomic management, discuss and advise on the following monetary policy items: the formulation and adaptation of monetary policy, the intermediate monetary policy targets, the use of different monetary policy tools, important monetary policy-related measures, and the co-ordination between monetary and other macroeconomic policies.

In particular, the last point explains the high number of non-PBC representatives on the MPC, which is not a coincidence but intentional. To put a positive spin on this arrangement, this multiplicity of actors can allow more diverse views[14] on monetary policy to be taken into account, considering, for example, the impact of monetary policy decisions from the perspectives of fiscal policy, financial sector policy and even real economic policies. The downside is, however, a risk of interference by

---

[11]For the full member list of the current MPC (only in Chinese), see 中国人民银行货币政策委员会委员 Zhongguo Renmin Yinhang Huobi Zhengce Ersi (2019). Guo is, strictly speaking, also Deputy Governor of the PBC, but he sits on the MPC as CBIRC Chairman.

[12]See Zhongguo Renmin Yinhang Huobi Zhengce Ersi (2010). Article 20 stipulates that the MPC meets "in the middle of the first month of each quarter", and can hold ad-hoc meetings upon request by the Chairman or more than one-third of its members.

[13]The MPC of the Eurosystem (the central bank system of the euro area) also has an advisory role, as it only prepares monetary policy decisions, which are taken by the ECB's Governing Council (consisting of the Executive Board of the ECB and the Governors of all euro area central banks). On the other hand, the Federal Open Market Committee (FOMC) of the US, the Policy Board of the Bank of Japan, and the MPC of the Bank of England do have exclusive decision-making power on monetary policy.

[14]In terms of gender diversity, the PBC's MPC scores worst among the major central banks, as there are currently no women (although in the past there were), while the ECB's Governing Council, the BoJ's Policy Board and the Bank of England's MPC all have one female member, and the FOMC even has three.

other government agencies or even a subordination of monetary policy under other economic policies or the political agenda of the country's leadership. The Bank of Japan (BoJ) provides an interesting comparison in this respect, as six of the nine members of its Policy Board also have diverse backgrounds from the financial sector and beyond,[15] but, during their tenure, they are BoJ executives, who are there solely to adopt the perspective of the central bank.

2.2.3 The PBC in the Post-March 2018 Institutional Setup

Big decisions in China follow a 5-year cycle. After Xi Jinping's rise to power at the 18th Party Congress in October 2012, he was inaugurated by the NPC in March 2013, and, in March 2018, the NPC made similarly important decisions for China's future: not only was "Xi Jinping Thought" enshrined in the Constitution and the President's term-limit abolished, but China's parliament also blessed far-reaching institutional reforms, which, in the financial realm, included (1) the merger of the CBRC and CIRC into the China Banking and Insurance Regulatory Commission (CBIRC), (2) a transfer of regulatory and macro-prudential powers to the PBC in the field of banking and insurance and (3) the nomination of LIU He, who had been elevated to the Politburo by the 19th Party Congress in October 2017, as Vice Premier and Chairman of the State Council's Financial Stability and Development Commission (FSDC). Other key changes included the appointment of Yi Gang as PBC Governor succeeding ZHOU Xiaochuan, of LIU Kun as new Minister of Finance, and of Guo Shuqing as new CBIRC Chairman (see Fig. 2.1).[16]

Important in the context of monetary policy is also the fact that, in addition, Guo was made Deputy Governor and Party Secretary of the PBC. His latter role is both unusual—previous Governors had always also been PBC Party Secretaries—and significant, as will be seen.[17] So the reforms have not only strengthened the institutional power of the PBC, but, by elevating Guo Shuqing and Liu He, they also have a crucial personal dimension, as in China individuals tend to matter in the policy-making process even more than institutions. In Fig. 2.1, the FSDC is depicted under the State Council, but in fact it sits above the PBC, the CBIRC and the China Securities Regulatory Commission (CSRC). The FSDC had been established in November 2017 after the 19th Party Congress[18] to oversee and coordinate the policies of these regulators in order to avoid, as had happened in the past, regulatory inconsistency and arbitrage. The fact that Liu, Xi Jinping's most trusted economic

---

[15]For their backgrounds, see https://www.boj.or.jp/en/about/organization/policyboard/index.htm.

[16]Later, the otherwise untouched CSRC also received a new Chairman with the appointment of YI Huiman.

[17]On the meaning and implications of the Chinese institutional reforms of spring 2018, see, also, Hess (2018).

[18]On the FSDC and other economic policy measures after the 19th Party Congress, see Naughton (2018).

Fig. 2.1 Who leads which institution under the new setup?
Source: Xinhuanet and the institutions' websites

aide, chairs the FSDC and is Vice Premier in charge of economic and financial affairs, makes him the dominant leader, perhaps even more powerful than Premier LI Keqiang, in this area.

2.3 Targets, Tools and Track Record of Chinese Monetary Policy

2.3.1 Monetary Policy Targets and Main Tools

In monetary policy, it is common to distinguish between operational and intermediate targets. While operational targets "can sufficiently be controlled by the central bank"[19] and effectively influence the ultimate goals of monetary policy (such as price stability and economic growth), intermediate targets are not under the direct control of the central bank.

The PBC has been referring to three intermediate targets: quantity-based money supply (M2), bank lending and price-based market interest rates. Traditionally, the focus had been on intermediate quantitative targets, and target values were defined for monetary or credit aggregates (such as new loan growth). But, due to "financial innovation and a rapidly changing financial system structure" and the fact that "M2 is correlated less and less with inflation and growth", and that "M2 outturn has

[19]Ulrich Bindseil, *Monetary Policy Operations and the Financial System*, 2014, p. 10.

deviated from the target over the past couple of years",[20] the emphasis is now more on price-based variables. In a speech in 2018, Governor Yi expressed it as follows[21]:

> As the correlation between quantitative indicators and economy gradually declines, the monetary policies of major developed countries and market economies are principally aimed at regulating price indicators. Reforms in China were also focused on nurturing a market-based interest rate system and enhancing a price-oriented regulation and transmission mechanism.

In line with this development, the PBC now focuses, as its operational target, on short-term money-market rates. This applies, in particular, to the 7-day reverse repo rate, which is a weighted average of participating banks (= deposit institutions; hence, its name "DR007") and which is closely watched by the market, even if the PBC has not yet confirmed this rate as its target interest rate.[22]

Like most other central banks, the PBC uses three main monetary policy tools to ensure that the envisaged level of its operational target is reached in financial markets: open market operations (OMO), standing facilities and reserve requirements. *Open market operations* are "central bank transactions with banks at the central bank's initiative", and usually take the form of lending operations, but can also consist of outright purchases or sales of financial assets.[23]

Standing facilities are "central bank operations at the initiative of banks", and can be sub-divided into overnight borrowing facilities, in which banks can borrow from the central bank against collateral, deposit facilities, in which they can deposit funds at the central bank, and discount facilities, in which they can sell short-term paper (typically drafts) at a discount to the central bank.

Reserve requirements "oblige banks to hold a certain minimum level of sight deposits on their account with the central banks" and "may apply to single day-ends, or to an average over e.g. a one-month period".[24]

Unlike other central banks, the PBC has three more tools at its disposal, which it has used and continues to use at times to varying degrees: the issuance of central bank bills ("sterilisation bonds"), the administrative setting of deposit and lending benchmark rates and the so-called "window guidance". The PBC widely used the first one in the context of its exchange-rate policy until China's foreign reserves reached their peak of almost 4 trillion USD in June 2014; in order to keep the exchange rate

[20]McMahon et al. (2018), p. 6. As further evidenced, the authors note that the *2018 Government Work Report* did no longer specify any target value for the monetary aggregate and credit aggregates.

[21]Yi (2018a).

[22]See McMahon et al. (2018).

[23]Unlike other major central banks, the PBC has not yet used quantitative easing, *i.e.* asset purchases, as it still has "policy space" with short-term interest rates not having reached zero yet. But, in January 2019, it introduced a targeted medium-term loan facility (TMLF, 定向中期借贷便利) at a rate of 40 basis points below the standard 1-year MLF rate, to boost lending to small- and medium-sized enterprises (SMEs), and banks with a "potential to step up support to SMEs" may use the facility. See J.P. Morgan (2019).

[24]All quotations are from Bindseil (2014), pp. 9–10.

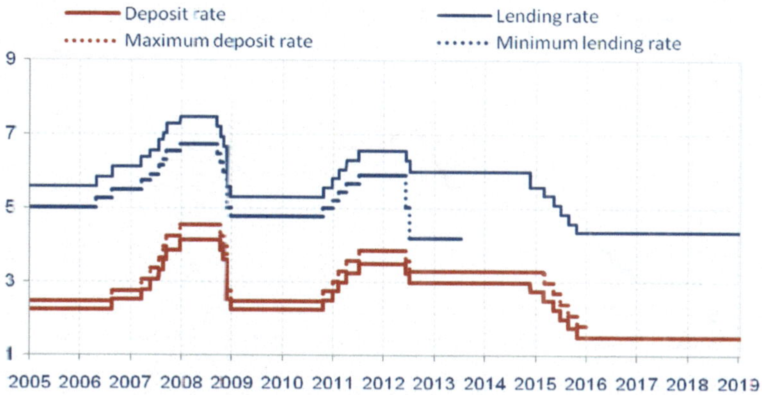

Fig. 2.2 Benchmark interest rates of the PBC in per cent.
Source: CEIC Data, PBC

low, the PBC bought USD against RMB, and, in order to "sterilise" the liquidity injections stemming from this foreign-reserve accumulation, it issued central bank bills. The second tool has been of lesser importance, since the remaining ceiling on deposit rates was eliminated in 2015, thereby fully removing interest-rate controls.[25] But the benchmark interest rates (Fig. 2.2) still matter for the borrowing costs of the corporate and household sectors, as "banks tend to set their lending rates in line with the benchmark lending rate".[26]

The third tool, window guidance, can take the form of setting a quarterly quota for the state-owned banks on the total value of their loans, and "guiding" them, regarding which amounts to lend to which sectors.[27] It works not only because of the discretionary power of the central bank, but also because of the fact that China's banks are pre-dominantly state-owned, which gives the government, or, more precisely, the Chinese Communist Party (CCP), huge leverage over their lending. And window guidance, which usually takes place behind closed doors,[28] also has a large influence

[25] Caps on lending rates had already been eliminated 2 years earlier, in 2013. See Hess (2014), footnote 18.

[26] J.P. Morgan (2018a), p. 2.

[27] And the third tool is also linked to the second tool, as, despite the official removal of the deposit-rate ceiling in 2015, there is still informal guidance by the PBC on the upper limits of bank deposit rates.

[28] A rare exception was the PBC's announcement of a "discussion" on 15 November 2018 between its Governor Yi, the CBIRC Deputy Chairman WANG Zhaoxing and the heads or deputy heads, which may be a sign that the meeting was called at very short notice, of several share-holding commercial banks and all "Big Five" (ICBC, BoC, CCB, ABC and BoCOM), and the Party Secretary of China Development Bank (see Zhongguo Renmin Yinhang 2018). According to the announcement, Governor Yi stressed in the meeting that banks should increase their efforts to provide loans to private firms and SMEs facing financing difficulties, in line with Xi's call that the financial industry should support the real economy.

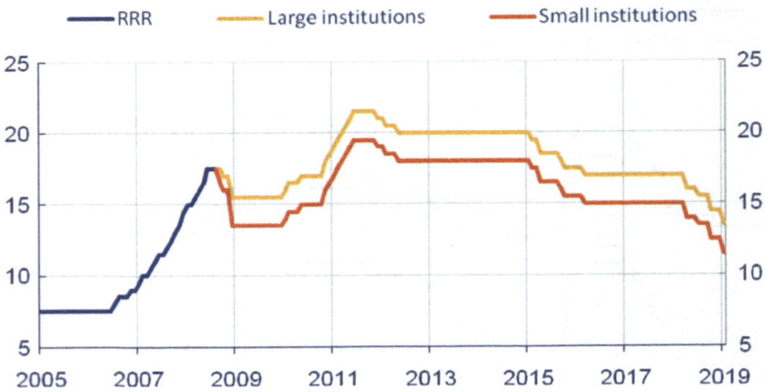

Fig. 2.3 Reserve requirement ratios (RRR) in per cent.
Source: CEIC Data, PBC

on the non-state-owned banks. It depends on the economic and financial conditions, and happens whenever the PBC considers it necessary.

2.3.2 Evolution and Successes in Recent Years

China's use of its large array of monetary policy instruments has evolved in recent years in a way that can be characterised as a shift from quantity-based to more price-based tools. The PBC now relies much less on central bank bills and increasingly uses OMOs and liquidity facilities.[29] In 2015, the PBC introduced an interest-rate corridor mechanism, in which market-based policy rates such as its OMO 7-day reverse repo rate and standing and marginal lending facilities at different maturities are used to affect money-market rates in the desired direction. This has resulted in a big increase in the net liquidity provided by the PBC to banks since 2015. On the other hand, quantitative tools and, in particular, reserve requirements also continue to play a role, as relatively high reserve requirement ratios (RRR) are still considered necessary to prevent systemic financial risks, and, at the same time, decreasing them is a convenient tool for the PBC to inject liquidity, and this has been widely used as a stimulus recently (Fig. 2.3).

Since April 2018, the PBC has implemented four targeted RRR cuts to boost economic growth, lowering the ratio to 13.5 per cent for large and 11.5 per cent for small institutions, and, in early May 2019, it announced further cuts "aimed at helping small- and medium-sized banks to serve small and private enterprises better,

[29]This has also been publicly stated by the PBC. See Yi (2018b), where he made the following statement: "At present, the focus of China's monetary policy is gradually shifting from quantity control to price control". On China's evolving monetary policy framework, see, also, Girardin et al. (2017).

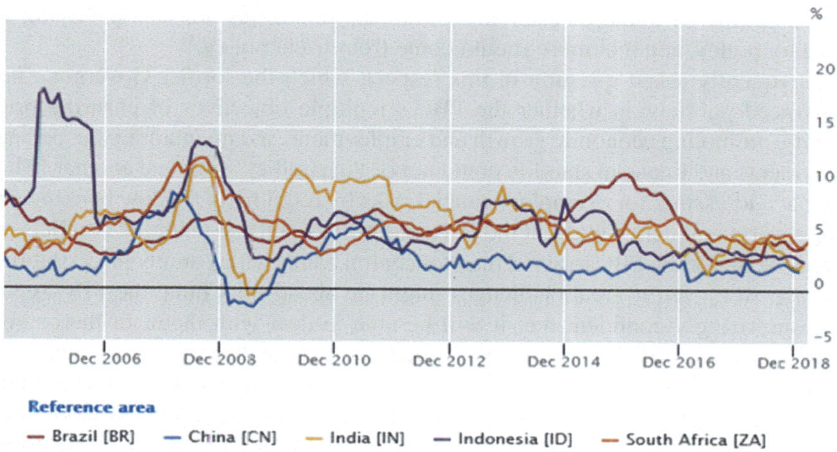

Fig. 2.4 Comparison of CPI inflation in China and other countries. Source: BIS

Fig. 2.5 Chinese real GDP growth in per cent (target and outcome). Source: CEIC Data, PBC

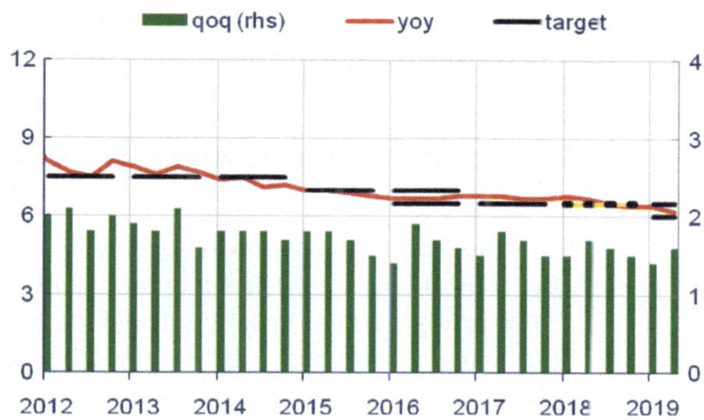

which will, in turn, support the overall economy".[30] RRR cuts are effective, as they release central bank money, against which banks can then take additional deposits, thus allowing more loans. So what has been the track record of China's monetary policy in recent years? Despite a challenging and rapidly changing domestic and international environment, the PBC has, with its monetary policy, managed relatively well to contain inflation, in particular, in comparison with its emerging market peers (Fig. 2.4), and, to some extent, also to support growth (Fig. 2.5). The PBC is proud of the success of the former and communicates it externally, but it also acknowledges

[30]See Reuters (2019b). The original PBC announcement has "small and micro enterprises" (小微企业).

that, especially in terms of economic stimulus, authorities are overly relying on monetary policy, and that more should come from fiscal policy.[31]

A frequently asked question in this respect, which the former Governor Zhou also voiced publicly, is whether the PBC's multiple objectives of ensuring price stability, promoting economic growth and employment, and maintaining the balance of payments and financial stability could not be "in conflict" with one another.[32] It is true that addressing, for example, financial risks by reigning in shadow banking and local government debt[33] come at the price of lower growth, so potential conflicts are more difficult for the PBC to avoid than for central banks with a purely price-stability mandate. But, even if great challenges might lie ahead for China, the PBC seems to be surprisingly confident that it will be able to deal with them. In the context of the recent re-escalation of the US–China trade (and technology) war, the above-mentioned MPC member Ma Jun, for example, has been quoted by Reuters with the statement that the Chinese central bank had "sufficient monetary policy tools to cope with current internal and external uncertainties", and would look to fine-tune policy according to changes in the country's economic situation.[34]

2.4 Challenges in Terms of Transparency and Independence

2.4.1 How Transparent is China's Monetary Policy?

The PBC's communication is also evolving, and, today, it comprises five main channels: First, the central bank publishes a quarterly Monetary Policy Report (货币政策执行报告) covering monetary policy decisions and assessments of the relevant economic and financial developments. Released between 2 and 3 months after each quarter in Chinese, and another month later in English, the reports are "generally backward looking", but increasingly also include some forward-looking information.[35] Second, the PBC publishes short press releases within 1 or 2 days after each quarterly MPC meeting, but, unlike the Fed, the BoJ and the ECB, does not release meeting minutes or accounts, nor are the MPC meeting dates announced in advance. These regular press releases have been complemented by *ad hoc* press releases to explain specific monetary policy measures such as the various RRR cuts since early

[31]This was informally stated by a PBC representative in late 2018, but Yi (2018b) holds a similar view: "Fiscal policy should focus on rebuilding buffers while accommodating growth needs" (p. 2).

[32]See Zhou (2016). In an internal presentation in October 2016, the former MPC member HUANG Yiping from Peking University called it a "complicated relationship among these objectives".

[33]With an overall leverage in the economy of around 260% of GDP, J.P. Morgan's observation that "curbing credit growth" is China's "Achilles heel" seems to be very true. See J.P. Morgan (2018b).

[34]Quoted in Reuters (2019a).

[35]McMahon et al. (2018), p. 10. Earlier analyses of the effectiveness of the PBC's monetary policy and the transmission of its interest policy can be found in Sun (2013), Ma et al. (2015), respectively.

2018. Third, press conferences are regularly held by the PBC, for example, on the occasion of the annual NPC sessions, and fourth, official speeches are regularly given by PBC representatives. While these four forms of written and oral communication are not new, an interesting innovation is provided by the fifth channel; since January 2016, the PBC has published daily OMO notices to explain the rationale for conducting (or not conducting) open market operations. This could be seen as a reaction to episodes of severe mis-communication by the central bank on its measures in mid-2015 and January 2016, which had increased market volatility and led to calls for improved clarity by the PBC from global policy-makers including the IMF.[36] A recent analytical IMF paper devoted to PBC communication also found that, in particular, the "OMO information notices, for example, reduced volatility and improved monetary policy effectiveness". But, on the other hand, the IMF paper concluded that "the empirical analysis highlights that communication can have important benefits and that greater central bank transparency and independence would help further improve PBC's effectiveness, including through forward guidance".[37] One specific piece of advice by the authors on how the PBC could improve its communication has already been implemented: in January 2019, China's central bank launched a new English website, which is much more user-friendly and allows for easier and more timely access to monetary policy-related (and other) information in English.

2.4.2 *How Independent is the PBC with Regard to Monetary Policy?*

To assess the PBC's independence in performing its monetary policy function, it is helpful to distinguish four dimensions: institutional, personal, financial and functional independence.[38] Bälz and Heckel (2015) define institutional independence as the "overall independence of a given institution within the set-up of the various organs of government". Looking at Article 7 of the Central Bank Law, *de jure*, the PBC seems to be independent, both at an overall institutional level and with regard to its monetary policy implementation:

> The People's Bank of China shall, under the leadership of the State Council, independently implement monetary policy, perform its functions and carry out its business operations according to the law, and be free from interference by local governments, government departments at various levels, non-governmental organisations, and individuals.

---

[36] In a note prepared for the G-20 Finance Ministers and Central Bank Governors' Meetings in February 2016, the IMF stated that "in China, [...] the authorities should ensure clear communication of their exchange rate policies". See IMF (2016), p. 8.

[37] McMahon et al. (2018), p. 23. Lo (2015) reaches a similar conclusion by noting in his chapter *China's Future Monetary Policy*, p. 185, that the PBC "will have to adopt some form of forward guidance as a communication strategy to provide information to the public on future monetary policy stance".

[38] Bälz and Heckel (2015) have analysed the four main aspects of central bank independence for the BoJ.

But the addition of "under the leadership of the State Council", which is also made in Article 2 quoted above, already undermines the PBC's independence, and Article 5 makes the limits of its ability to decide "independently" on monetary policy matters much clearer:

> The People's Bank of China shall report its decisions concerning annual money supply, interest rates, foreign exchange rates and other important matters specified by the State Council, to the State Council for approval before they are implemented.

The personal independence of the PBC from the State Council, China's government, is also not given, as both the PBC Governor and the Deputy Governors are appointed or removed by the Premier. This requires the approval by the NPC, which is formally China's legislature but has no independent powers as it *de facto* depends—as does the State Council itself—on the CCP.

The criterion of financial independence is not fulfilled, either, as the PBC budget also depends on the government. Article 38 of the Central Bank Law specifies that "the People's Bank of China shall have an independent budget arrangement", "its budget shall be reviewed by the fiscal authority (*i.e.*, the MoF) and become part of the central government budget" and the use of its budget "is subject to the supervision of the fiscal authority under the State Council". This is an issue in relation to monetary policy, as it means that the PBC is not free from the government in the use of its manpower and financial resources in order to fulfil its respective mandate.[39]

Functional independence is partly given as, on the one hand, changing monetary policy tools, targets or even goals require State Council approval, while, on the other hand, the PBC enjoys at least a *de jure* freedom in the use of its tools (instruments), which are listed in Article 23:

> To implement monetary policy, the People's Bank of China may apply the following monetary policy instruments:
>
> 1. Require banking institutions to place deposit reserves at a given ratio;
> 2. Determine the benchmark interest rate of the central bank;
> 3. Conduct rediscount for banking financial institutions with accounts at the People's Bank of China;
> 4. Provide lending to commercial banks;
> 5. Trade treasury bonds, other government securities, financial bonds and foreign exchange on the open market;
> 6. Other monetary policy instruments specified by the State Council.
>
> When applying the above-mentioned monetary policy instruments to implement monetary policy, the People's Bank of China may formulate detailed conditions and procedures.

[39] Japan's Ministry of Finance (JMoF) also controls the budget of the BoJ, and expenses related to monetary policy are carved out with the approval of the JMoF, in sharp contrast with the PBC, where they are not, as it is not as financially independent as the former. See Bälz and Heckel (2015), p. 32.

De facto, however, the use of the tools is also not fully up to the PBC, as all "monetary-policy decisions are the result of consensus-building among various stakeholders",[40] *i.e.* those represented in the MPC analysed above. It is also for this reason that the authors of the IMF paper concede the PBC "only limited operational independence at the monetary policy instrument level".[41]

2.4.3 Relationship Between Transparency and Independence

Thus, clearly, the PBC is not independent with regard to its monetary policy, and the answer to the first guiding question is only mixed at best: despite some progress in recent years, partly under foreign pressure it seems, China's central bank still lags behind in terms of transparency, compared to other major central banks, on several scores, such as publishing minutes and the future dates of MPC meetings, and holding press conferences after each meeting. Why is this, and is there a relationship between the two? The answer may be found in the peculiar post-March 2018 setup with Guo as the PBC's Party Secretary, instead of the PBC Governor, as used to be the case before. This is a significant change. Before Yi Gang was appointed, it was actually rumoured that Liu He would succeed Zhou Xiaochuan as PBC Governor,[42] because of the increasing importance of monetary policy in coping with China's current challenges (such as the growth slowdown and mounting financial risks), and because Liu was seen as having much more political capital and experience than Yi. In the end, the CCP decided otherwise and made Liu Vice Premier and FSDC Chairman, and Yi PBC Governor, but apparently with Guo "behind" him. The impression that Guo Shuqing plays an important role in the background is corroborated by the fact that it was Guo, not Yi, who, in November 2018, first announced the "125 Target" (一二五目标) for bank lending to private sector firms after Xi pledged to help them gain better access to credit: this policy stipulates that "as a minimum, big banks should lend ***one*** *third*, and small and medium banks ***two*** *thirds* of their total new lending to private firms, and, within three years, credit to private sector firms should amount to at least ***50*** *per cent* of total new loans", hence, its name.[43] After its announcement, both Party Secretary Guo and Governor Yi were vocal about the "125 policy", which reflects the Party's concerns about the serious challenges being faced by the private sector. And it is too early to say whether the threefold target will finally be met. However, not only will the new policy in the first instance remain associated with Guo, but it also shows the limits of monetary policy independence and communication in situations in which the larger political agenda of the day overrides their respective exigencies. In other words, the relationship between the PBC's transparency and independence is

[40]McMahon et al. (2018), p. 5.

[41]Ibid., p. 4.

[42]Cf., Reuters (2018). ZHU Rongji had also been both Vice Premier and PBC Governor in the early 1990s.

[43]Hou (2019), p. 4.

such that the central bank can only be as transparent as its rather limited independence allows.

2.5 Conclusion

Despite the undisputed success and sophistication of Chinese monetary policy in recent years, for example, by gradually moving from quantity-based tools to more price-based tools and improving communication, the PBC cannot take transparency "for granted" as other major central banks can. Because the larger political objectives of the Communist Party always prevail, it is ultimately the CCP that seems to determine the PBC's room for manoeuvre and tasks it to maintain monetary and financial stability in the rapidly changing domestic and global environment. To sum up, one can say that the PBC's lack of transparency is contingent on its lack of independence. This conclusion was already nicely summarised in August 2016 by Louis Kuijs, the Head of Asia economics at Oxford Economics in Hong Kong:

> While there's a trend toward more messaging and communication, there's still quite some way to go. Unlike other central banks that can lay out their thinking, that's harder for the PBC because the winds can shift if the leadership change their minds. The best they can do is explain the line of the moment.[44]

References

Bälz, M., & Heckel, M. (2015). The Independence of the Bank of Japan in the Light of Statutory Rules and Central Bank Independence Indices. In F. Rövekamp, M. Bälz, & H. G. Hilpert (Eds.), *Central banking and financial stability in East Asia*. Cham et al: Springer.

Bell, S., & Feng, H. (2013). *The rise of the People's Bank of China: The politics of institutional change*. Cambridge MA: Harvard University Press.

Bindseil, U. (2014). *Monetary policy operations and the financial system*. Oxford: Oxford University Press.

Bloomberg News (2016). China's Opaque Central Bank Tries Something New: Communication [available at: https://www.bloomberg.com/news/articles/2016-08-16/china-s-opaque-central-bank-finds-new-policy-tool-communication]. 16 August 2016.

Girardin, E., Lunven, S., & Ma, G. (2017). China's evolving monetary policy rule: From inflation-accommodating policy to anti-inflation policy [available at: https://www.bis.org/publ/work641.pdf]. BIS Working Papers, May 2017.

Hess, P. (2018). What China's recent shake up means for the economy [available at: https://thediplomat.com/2018/03/what-chinas-recent-shake-up-means-for-the-economy]. The Diplomat, 23 March 2018.

Hess, P. (2014). China's Financial System: Past Reforms, Future Ambitions and Current State. In F. Rövekamp & H. G. Hilpert (Eds.), *Currency cooperation in east Asia*. Heidelberg: Springer.

---

[44]Cited in Bloomberg News (2016). Kuijs had been the World Bank's Senior Economist on China before.

Hou, Y. (2019). The Private Sector: Challenges and Opportunities During Xi's Second Term [available at: https://www.prcleader.org/hou]. China Leadership Monitor, 1 March 2019.
Huang, Y. (2016). China's Monetary Policy in Transition. Unpublished presentation, October 2016.
International Monetary Fund (2016). Global Prospects and Policy Challenges [available at: https://www.imf.org/external/np/g20/pdf/2016/022616.pdf]. Group of Twenty IMF Note—Finance Ministers and Central Bank Governors' Meetings, 26–27 February 2016.
Lo, C. (2015). *China's impossible trinity: The structural challenges to the "Chinese Dream"*. Basingstoke: Palgrave Macmillan.
Ma, J. (current MPC member) (2015). 马骏, Shi K 施康, Wang HL 王红林, Wang LS 王立升. Lilü zhuandao jizhi de dongtai yanjiu 利率传导机制的动态研究. Dynamic analysis of the interest rate transmission mechanism. 中国人民银行工作论文 PBC Working Paper, November 2015.
Ma, J. (2014). Interest Rate Transmission under China's New Monetary Policy Framework. In *Financial Liberalization, Innovation, and Stability: International Experience and Relevance for China* [available at: https://www.imf.org/external/np/seminars/eng/2015/PBC/ebook.pdf]. *PBC-IMF Joint Conference*, March 2014.
McMahon, M., Schipke, A., & Li, X. (2018). China's Monetary Policy Communication: Frameworks, Impact, and Recommendations [available at: https://www.imf.org/en/Publications/WP/Issues/2018/11/17/Chinas-Monetary-Policy-Communication-Frameworks-Impact-and-Recommendations-46375]. IMF Working Paper, November 2018.
J. P. Morgan (2019). A Guide to China's Local Bond Market: An In-depth Overview of China's $13tn Local Bondmarket, Opportunities and Recent Developments, 30 May 2019.
J. P. Morgan (2018a). China The Limits of Monetary Policy in this Trade War, 17 July 2018.
J. P. Morgan (2018b). China: The Future of Monetary and Financial Stability Policies, 19 March 2018.
Naughton, B. (2018). Economic Policy in the Aftermath of the 19th Party Congress [available at: https://www.hoover.org/sites/default/files/research/docs/clm55-bn-final.pdf]. China Leadership Monitor, 23 January 2018.
Pißler, K. B. (2015). History and Legal Framework of the People's Bank of China. In F. Rövekamp, M. Bälz, & H. G. Hilpert (Eds.), *Central banking and financial stability in East Asia*. Cham: Springer.
Prasad, E., & Zhang, B. (2014). Monetary Policy in China. In S. Fan, K. Ravi, S. Wei, & X. Zhang (Eds.), *The oxford companion to the economics of China*. Oxford: Oxford University Press.
Qvigstad, J. F. (2016). *On Central Banking*. Cambridge: Cambridge University Press.
Reuters (2019a). China's Central Bank Adviser Says U.S. Tariffs could Cut GDP Growth by 0.3 Percentage Points, [available at: https://www.reuters.com/article/us-usa-trade-china-pboc/chinas-central-bank-adviser-says-u-s-tariffs-could-cut-gdp-growth-by-0-3-percentage-points-idUSKCN1SG014]. 10 May 2019.
Reuters (2019b). China Gives Modest Boost to Economy with RRR Cut amid Renewed Trade Tensions, [available at: https://www.reuters.com/article/us-china-economy/china-gives-modest-boost-to-economy-with-rrr-cut-amid-renewed-trade-tensions-idUSKCN1SC02D]. 6 May 2019.
Reuters (2018). Exclusive: Xi Confidant Emerges as Front Runner to Head China's Central Bank—Sources, [available at: https://www.reuters.com/article/us-china-economy-pboc-exclusive/exclusive-xi-confidant-emerges-as-front-runner-to-head-chinas-central-bank-sources-idUSKCN1G719L]. 23 February 2018.
Sun, G. (2017). Reforms in China's Monetary Policy: A Frontbencher's Perspective. New York, 2015 (cf., also, Vox China, China's Monetary Policy and Its RMB Exchange Rate Regime, [available at: http://www.voxchina.org/show-3-45.html]. September 2017).
Sun, R. R. (2013). Does monetary policy matter in China? *A Narrative Approach. China Economic Review, 26*(2), 56–74.
Yi, G. (2018a). China's monetary policy framework: supporting the real economy and striking a balance between internal and external equilibrium [available at: https://www.bis.org/review/r190130b.pdf]. Lecture given at Chang'an Forum held by Chinese Economists 50 Forum, Tsinghua University, 13 December 2018.

Yi, G. (2018b). Statement at the 38th Meeting of the International Monetary and Financial Committee (IMFC) [available at: https://meetings.imf.org/~/media/AMSM/Files/AM2018/IMFC/chn.ashx], 12–13 October 2018.

Zhongguo Renmin Yinhang 中国人民银行 (2018), Renmin Yinhang zhaokai jinrong jigou huobi xindai xingshi fenxi zuotanhui 人民银行召开金融机构货币信贷形势分析座谈会 The People's Bank opened a discussion to analyse the loan situation of financial institutions, [available at: http://www.pbc.gov.cn/goutongjiaoliu/113456/113469/3664582/index.html]. 16 November 2018.

Zhongguo Renmin Yinhang Huobi Zhengce Ersi 中国人民银行货币政策二司 (2019) Monetary Policy Department II of the People's Bank of China, Zhongguo renmin yinhang huobi zhengce weiyuanhui weiyuan 中国人民银行货币政策委员会委员 Members of the Monetary Policy Committee of the People's Bank of China, [available at: http://www.pbc.gov.cn/huobizhengceersi/214481/214543/218247/2859033/index.html]. 26 June 2019.

Zhongguo Renmin Yinhang Huobi Zhengce Ersi 中国人民银行货币政策二司 (2010) Monetary Policy Department II of the People's Bank of China, Zhongguo renmin yinhang huobi zhengce weiyuanhui tiaoli 国人民银行货币政策委员会条例 Provisions for the Monetary Policy Committee of the People's Bank of China, [available at: http://www.pbc.gov.cn/huobizhengceersi/214481/214543/214782/2847827/index.html]. 14 September 2010.

Zhongguo Renmin Yinhang Tiaofa Si 中国人民银行条法司 (2018) Legal Affairs Department of the People's Bank of China, Zhonghua renmin gongheguo Zhongguo renmin yinhang fa (xiuzheng) 中华人民共和国中国人民银行法(修正)Amended Law of the People's Republic of China on the People's Bank of China [2003], [available at: http://www.pbc.gov.cn/tiaofasi/144941/144951/2817256/index.html]. 24 April 2018.

Zhou, X. (2016). Managing Multi-Objective Monetary Policy: From the Perspective of Transitioning Chinese Economy [available at: http://www.imf.org/en/News/Articles/2016/07/06/17/45/SP062416-Xiaochuan-Zhou-Michel-Camdessus-Central-Banking-Lecture]. Michel Camdessus Central Banking Lecture given at IMF, 24 June 2016.

Chapter 3
Inflation Targeting in Korea

Woosik Moon

Abstract The implementation of inflation targeting in Korea highlights the importance of distinguishing between its symmetric and asymmetric operations. When Korea suffered from high inflation, the Bank of Korea set the inflation target at 3%, instead of 2%. Given its underlying intention to lower the inflation rate to below 3%, rather than to maintain it centred at around 3%, its operation of inflation targeting was not necessarily a failure even when the inflation rate fell below 2%. In contrast, it would be a complete failure if the inflation rate rose above 4%. Clearly, this asymmetry cannot be applied to the operation of many advanced economies which, by adopting a target set at 2%, have endeavoured to insure that inflation is neither running persistently above nor below this target.

3.1 Introduction

In December 2015, the Bank of Korea (hereinafter BoK) decided to lower its inflation target to 2%, from the target range of 2.5–3.5% put in place during the period 2013–15. This decision was a landmark event in the sense that, as the BoK attempted to fulfil its mandate for price stability faithfully, its operation of inflation targeting (hereinafter IT) was also shifted from an asymmetric one to a symmetric one. Notwithstanding this, many people, including the BoK staff, failed to take sufficient notice of this change. For instance, if the BoK sets the target (or the average of the target range) at 3%, it was simply because this target was considered to be the minimum attainable inflation rate, not because it was a long-term inflation rate compatible with the mandate of price stability, which might be 2% or below. Thus, when the target was set at 3%, it should be stressed, the main intention of policymakers was to lower the inflation rate to below 3%, rather than to maintain the inflation rate centred at

W. Moon (✉)
Graduate School of International Studies, Seoul National University, 1, Gwanak-ro, Gwanak-gu, Seoul 08826, Korea
e-mail: mwoosik@snu.ac.kr

F. Rövekamp et al. (eds.), *Monetary Policy Implementation in East Asia*, Financial and Monetary Policy Studies 51,
https://doi.org/10.1007/978-3-030-50298-0_3

around 3%. Clearly, this operation of IT could not be identical with that of many of the advanced economies that adopt a symmetric target set at 2%.

The ignorance of this difference created much unnecessary criticism that the monetary policy of the BoK was not expansionary enough to increase the inflation rate around its target rate of 3%, and thus failed to accomplish its mission. But even if the inflation rate was very low, hovering below 2%, it does not necessarily mean that the monetary policy was a failure. Rather, it could be a successful operation towards the long-term goal of price stability, unless real output or employment falls below its potential or neutral level.

The Korean case highlights the importance of distinguishing between symmetric and asymmetric operations with regard to the assessment of IT. This distinction has remained blurred, although, unlike most of the countries which set their target inflation rates at around 2% and hence took a symmetric operation for granted, Korea maintained an asymmetric operation framework until 2015. Symmetry emerged as being important for the first time in 2016, when the Federal Open Market Committee in the US referred to its inflation objective as a "symmetric inflation goal" rather than just a simple "inflation goal" in its "Statement on Longer-Run Goals and Monetary Policy Strategy", first published in 2012 (Federal Open Market Committee 2016). What it means by this is that the central bank will endeavour to insure that inflation is neither running persistently above nor below its target. In contrast, the asymmetry refers to running inflation persistently low, which would constitute the conventional stabilisation policy necessary for many high inflation developing countries, or persistently high, which was recommended to cope with the Global Recession by economists such as Blanchard et al. (2010), for example. Based on Moon (2015, 2018), who explained past Korean IT from an asymmetric point of view, this chapter intends to conduct a comprehensive assessment of the IT that Korea has experienced in the aftermath of the Global Financial Crisis.

The organisation of this chapter is as follows. In Sect. 3.2, an overview of the operation of IT since its introduction in Korea is given, while in Sect. 3.3, the theoretical foundation for evaluating the performance of Korea's IT operation is examined. Then, Sect. 3.4 looks at concrete examples of both symmetric and asymmetric operations. Section 3.5 concludes the chapter by throwing some light on the future prospects of the usefulness of IT.

3.2 A Brief History of IT in Korea

Inflation targeting is a monetary policy framework which focuses on inflation itself as the ultimate goal, and aims to achieve this goal over the mid-term horizon. First adopted by New Zealand in 1990,[1] this framework of monetary policy was introduced to Korea through the recommendation of the International Monetary Fund (IMF)

[1] For a general assessment and review of IT, see Svensson (2011, 2013).

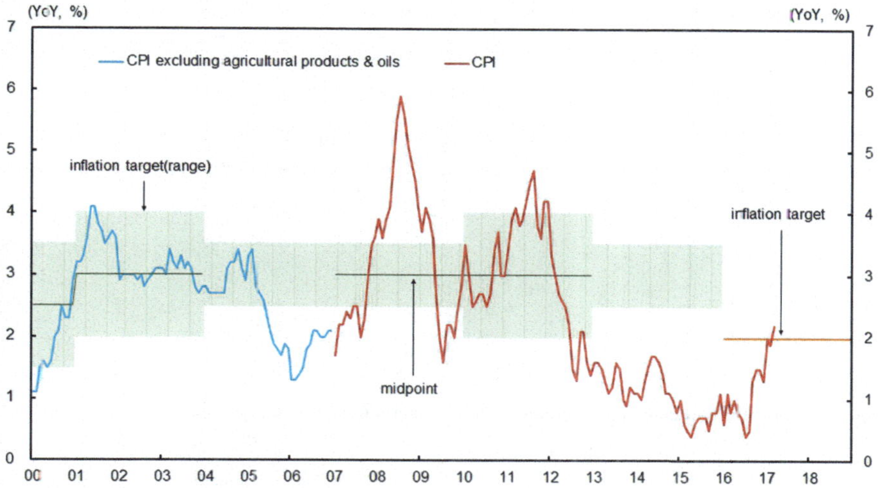

Fig. 3.1 The inflation target and the performance of inflation rates in Korea. *Source* BoK (2017)

immediately after the 1997 currency crisis when the macroeconomic policy of Korea was under the IMF surveillance and BoK law had to be revised.

Based on Article 6, Clause 1 of the Bank of Korea Act, therefore, the BoK currently sets the inflation target in consultation with the Ministry of Economy and Strategy. Currently, the consumer price index (CPI) inflation rate is used to measure the inflation rate, replacing the core CPI inflation rate, which was used up to 2007. Under this framework, the BoK is requested to adjust its policy rate in order to maintain the annual rate of CPI inflation near the target rate over a mid-term time horizon of 3 years. Figure 3.1 shows the movement of the CPI and the performance of IT in Korea since the year 2000, 1 year after its adoption in 1999.

In the early stage of IT, the core CPI inflation rate was used as a target indicator and the target inflation rate was set at 3 ± 1%, except for the period between 2000 and 2001 (set at 2.5 ± 1%). Since 2007, the target indicator has changed to the CPI inflation rate and the target rate has remained set at 3%. During the period 2010-12, however, the band of fluctuation, which was narrow with ± 0.5%, was extended to ± 1%. From 2013 to 2015, targeting a point changed to setting a target range with 2.5-3.5%. During this period, the CPI inflation rate fell substantially, remaining far short of its targeted range. After reaching its peak at 4% in 2011, for instance, the CPI inflation rate fell to 1.2% in 2013, and remained around 1% until 2016, although the BoK reacted to this fall through an expansionary monetary policy. As a result, the BoK came to miss its inflation target, set at the target range of 2.5-3.5%, for the whole 3 years until 2015, leading to harsh criticism of the BoK's monetary stance.

One criticism was related to the concern that Korea, like Japan, was entering into a deflation trap. But this criticism was ill-founded because, first of all, it misunderstood the IT operation of the BoK. It pre-supposed that the operation of IT with a target rate of 3%, which Korea was adopting, should be symmetric, like that of the advanced

Fig. 3.2 The inflation expectations measured by general public and experts. *Source* BoK database

economies, with a target rate of 2%. Thus, according to this criticism, the BoK should be as much concerned about a fall in the inflation rate as it should about a rise. The BoK's IT—which had a target inflation rate at 3%—was asymmetric, which meant that the priority of the policy was to lower the inflation rate below the target, and, therefore, missing the target from below could not be interpreted as an IT failure. Furthermore, despite the sustained low inflation rate, the inflation expectation, as shown in Fig. 3.2, did not drop to a significant extent below 2%, which was compatible with the BoK's long-term price stability.

It is, however, true that consistent deviation from the target range could raise a credibility problem for the monetary policy. For this reason, the target was ultimately lowered in December 2015 to 2%, on the grounds that the Korean economy's underlying inflation had dropped to around 2%. This meant that the operation of IT should thereafter shift to symmetric operation, giving equal weight to the drop as well as to the rise in the CPI inflation rate.

Since 2016, the method of presenting the inflation target has also been changed from the target range of 2.5–3.5% to the target point. It was pointed out that, even though the target range system gave the central bank a broad degree of discretion in its policy operation, it might be unsuitable for anchoring inflation expectations (BoK 2016).

3.3 A Tool for Assessing IT in Korea

It is worthwhile examining the operation mechanism of IT in detail in order to assess the actual performance of the IT in Korea. Generally speaking, IT is characterised by three elements: the setting of price stability as a primary goal of the central bank, the announcement of the target and accountability. Unfortunately, there was no rigorous economic theory about how IT—centred on these three elements—could stabilise the inflation rate.[2]

However, some important implications can be inferred from the work of Kahneman and Tversky (1974), who investigated the mechanism of decision-making under conditions of uncertainty, in particular, the relation between uncertainty and anchoring. For instance, it can be argued that

(1) announcing the target explicitly is an important element of anchoring[3];
(2) band is less effective for anchoring than point target;
(3) credibility is counted as paramount with regard to the operation of IT. To secure credibility, however, the central bank needs as much speech and communication as action. Indeed, concerning the choice between words and deeds, J. Alfred Broaddus, Jr, made the following remark at the meeting of the Federal Open Market Committee in 1996: "I think a few well-chosen words stemming from the right source, backed up by deeds, can be a powerful credibility builder over time" (Federal Open Market Committee 1996, p. 48);
(4) the effect of anchoring will be stronger when uncertainties are greater, and weaker in the inverse case. Usually, it seems that there are more uncertainties when the inflation rate is high than when inflation rate is very low. Thus, it is very likely that IT works better as an instrument to reduce the inflation rate rather than to raise it.

Thus, how could the actual performance of IT be assessed? In this regard, we follow Demertzis et al. (2009) and the International Monetary Fund (IMF 2013) and assume that the inflationary expectation is formed as follows:

$$\pi_{t+1}^{e} = \lambda\pi^{T} + (1-\lambda)\pi_{t}$$

where π_{t+1}^{e} is the expected inflation rate in period t + 1, π^{T} the target rate and π_t, the current realised inflation rate.

This equation means that the inflationary expectation of private agents π_{t+1}^{e} is affected by the announcement of the target π^{T} made by the central bank and by the actual performance of the realised inflation rate π_t, while the size of λ determines the effectiveness of the IT. If the value of λ is near 1, for instance, the IT is fully operative. In contrast, if λ is near 0, then the IT is not operative at all, and the inflation expectation depends solely on the past inflation performance of private agents. Usually, if the inflation expectation is short term, it is known to be more influenced by past inflation rates. Based on the IMF (2013), Fig. 3.3 shows the trend of coefficient λ estimated for 12 advanced countries during the period 1990–2012.

Thus, the IT turns out to have worked very successfully, especially since the year 2000. By announcing the target itself, the central bank contributes to making

[2]The widespread use of IT was rather empirical, in the sense that the IT adoption countries were supposed to stabilise their inflation successfully. For instance, the first adoption of IT by New Zealand was achieved on political grounds, rather than on economic logic.

[3]From this perspective, the implicit target system, as was the case for the US before 2012, was not as effective as the explicit target system that most IT countries have adopted.

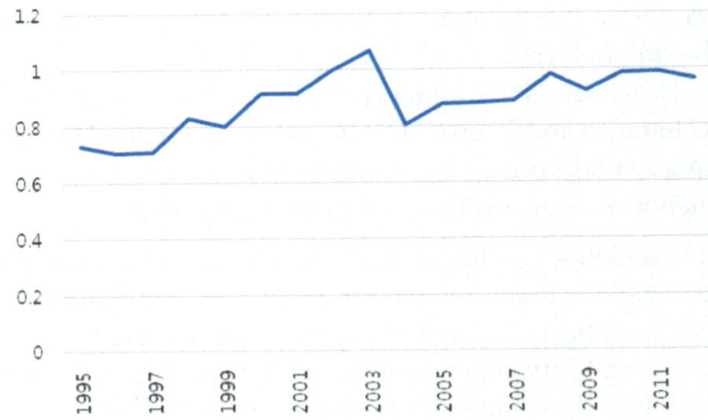

Fig. 3.3 Trend of λ for 12 advanced economies. *Note* The IMF ran the regression over 5-year rolling windows for the equation $\pi^e_{t+1} - \pi^T = \gamma + \theta\,(\pi_t - \pi^T)$ where π^e_{t+1} is the expected inflation, π^T the inflation target, π_t is the realised inflation rate and γ and θ are constants. The coefficient λ is obtained from $\lambda = (1-\theta)$. *Source* IMF (2013)

the diverse inflationary expectations of private agents converge towards the target and thus to providing "an anchor" to inflationary expectations. The problem for the assessment of the IT, however, is that the inflationary expectation is not an observable variable, although central banks do try to estimate it. Thus, what people observe is only the variables π^T and π_t, and people tend to assess the performance of the IT based on the comparison of these two variables. For instance, if π_t deviates widely from π^T, then people are likely to consider the operation of the IT to be a failure, although there are no grounds for it. The operation should be assessed in the light of the comparison between π^e_{t+1} and π^T. The deviation between π^T and π_t just reflects the loss of the central bank's reputation and credibility, as emphasised by Kydland and Prescott (1977), Barro and Gorden (1983).

3.4 Assessing the Operation of IT in Korea

What inflation rate does society consider to be desirable for price stability? Although the European Central Bank (ECB) focuses on an inflation rate which is slightly below 2%, there seems to be a consensus that an inflation rate of 2% will be compatible with the price stability mandated to the central bank, in particular, thanks to Janet Yellen, who first proposed it at the 1996 Federal Open Market Committee Meeting (Federal Open Market Committee 1996).[4]

Following this consensus, let us consider that the target for the desirable level of price stability is set at 2%. If the target was set up at 2%—as it is indeed set in many

[4]In 1996, Janet Yellen, as a Federal Reserve governor, had an extensive exchange regarding the definition of price stability with the then Federal Reserve Chairman Alan Greenspan. Greenspan defined it as "the state in which expected changes in the general price level do not effectively alter business and household decisions" and said that zero inflation would guarantee it. In response to this remark, Yellen emphasised the need to "grease the wheels of the labor market", allowing real wage adjustment through rising prices to cope with rigid nominal wages. It led her to propose 2% inflation rate as compatible with the mandate of price stability. In 2012, the Federal Open Market Committee adopted, for the first time, an explicit longer run inflation objective of 2 per cent as measured by the PCE price index. See Federal Open Market Committee (1996).

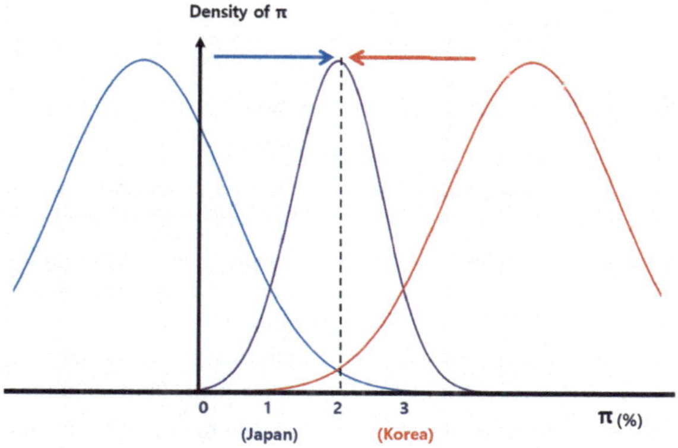

Fig. 3.4 Probability density of inflation and the setting of the inflation target.

advanced countries—then symmetric interpretation of IT can be applied, and both overshooting and undershooting of the target should equally be a cause for concern. However, some countries can temporarily set the target at a higher level than the desirable long-term level, let us say at 3%, or at lower level than the desirable level, let us say 1%. (3% as a ceiling and 1% as a floor[5]). For example, Korea set the target at 3% because it suffered from quite a high inflation rate before the introduction of IT. It was clear that the implicit operational goal of this target was to stabilise the inflation rate below 3%, not to maintain it around 3%. In contrast, when the target was temporarily set at 1%, as in Japan, the implicit aspiration of policymakers was to raise the inflation rate above 1% until it could be stabilised at around 2%. Then, the operation of the IT could not be symmetric. Figure 3.4 distinguishes three cases of IT operation depending on the level of the inflation target.

(1) IT under $\pi^T = 2\%$

Let us suppose, first, that the target is set at 2%. This is the case for most of the central banks in advanced countries. In this case, the central bank should pay equal heed to the lower and upper limits of the target. As a matter of fact, the US Federal Reserve (hereinafter the Fed) emphasised that the 2% inflation target was a symmetric goal (Federal Open Market Committee 2016). Then, depending on the position of the actual inflation rate π_t, three cases, one, where π_t is near the target of 2%, two, when it rises above the upper limit, let us say 3% and three, when it falls below the lower limit, let us say 2%, can be distinguished. Also, depending on whether the expected inflation rate π^e_{t+1} coincides with the target rate $\pi^T = 2\%$, the following six cases can be obtained (Table 3.1).

Let us assess the performance of the IT in each of these cases. The first case is where $\pi_t = 2\%$ and π^e_{t+1} remain near the target of 2%. Clearly, the IT is a big success here. The second case is where $\pi_t = 2\%$ and π^e_{t+1} fall below 1% or rise above 3%.

[5]J. Alfred Broaddus, Jr, had already suggested that 3% would be the ceiling. See, also, the Federal Open Market Committee (1996).

Table 3.1 The operation of IT under $\pi^T = 2\%$

	π^T	π_t	π^e_{t+1}	Performance assessment
Case 1	2	2	2	Success
Case 2	2	2	1 or 3	Unrealistic
Case 3	2	3 (above)	2	Credibility is hurt but anchoring effect works well. No need to be concerned about inflation
Case 4	2	3 (above)	3	Complete failure. Through the continuous missing of the target, inflationary expectation is upwardly adjusted. Concern about inflation
Case 5	2	1 (below)	2	Credibility is hurt but anchoring effect works well. No need to be concerned about deflation
Case 6	2	1 (below)	1	Complete failure. Through the continuous missing of the target, inflationary expectation is downwardly adjusted. Concern about deflation

Given that the target was set at 2% and the actual inflation rate also remained at the same level, it would not be realistic to imagine a sudden abrupt change in the inflation expectation, and thus this case will be counted as being unrealistic. The third case is where π_t deviates from the upper limit of the target, rising above 3%. On the surface, the operation of the IT appears to be a failure, but, given that the inflation expectation is still anchored around 2%, it may not necessarily be so. In the sense that the actual inflation is well above the target, it is true that it can do harm to the credibility of the monetary policy. But, because the anchoring mechanism is in place, the IT can still work. The fourth case is where both π_t and π^e_{t+1} are deviating above the upper limit. This operation of the IT can be counted as a complete failure. The fifth case is where π_t falls below 2%. As in the third case, the operation of the IT appears to be failure, but, given that π^e_{t+1} remains around 2%, the anchoring is working and the operation of the IT is not a failure. Only the credibility of the IT operation will be hurt. Finally, the sixth case is where both π_t and π^e_{t+1} are deviating from the lower limit of the target, let us say 1%, and, in this case, the IT turns out to be a complete failure.

(2) **IT under π^T= 3%**

Let us now consider the case in which the target was set at 3%, instead of 2%, as in Korea before 2016. Here, clearly, the objective of the IT is to lower the inflationary expectation below 2% because the price stability defined by the BoK Act is not necessarily at 2%. Thus, the operation of the IT is not symmetric, as in the case of the inflation target of 2%. That is to say, two cases in which inflation rises above the upper limit, let us say, to 4%, and in which inflation falls below the lower limit, let us say, to 2%, are not equally perceived. If the inflation rate rises above 4% and misses the target, there is no doubt that the IT is a complete failure. But, even if inflation drops below 2%, this cannot be considered to be a serious policy failure because the price stability goal specified as the mandate of the independent central bank is

Table 3.2 IT under $\pi^T = 3\%$

	π^T	π_t	π^e_{t+1}	Performance assessment
Case 1	3	3 (around)	3	Failure. The actual inflation is equal to the target inflation but the inflationary expectation is not anchored to 2%, so that additional measures are needed to lower the inflationary expectation
Case 2	3	3 (around)	2 or 4	Unrealistic
Case 3	3	4 (above)	3	Because of the anchoring effect, the inflationary expectation is not changed, but the credibility of central bank is damaged due to missing the target
Case 4	3	4 (above)	4	Complete failure. Neither anchoring, nor credibility. Concern about inflation
Case 5	3	2 (below)	3	Despite the drop of the actual inflation rate below 2%, anchoring is working and inflationary expectation cannot be downwardly adjusted. There is a need to lower inflationary expectation
Case 6	3	2 (below)	2	Successful stabilisation. Through the drop of the actual inflation rate to below the 2%, the inflationary expectation is downwardly adjusted. But, given the big divergence between the target and the expectation, anchoring does not work and needs the target to be reset

to maintain the inflation rate below 2% unless it is too excessive. (For instance, in the case of the ECB, price stability is interpreted as achieving 2% or a little below). Indeed, the reason why the BoK set the target around 3% for so long was not just because this 3% target was considered desirable, but because stabilising the inflation rate sufficiently below 3% was thought too unlikely to be attained. Thus, when the central bank has a target of 3%, then it should make more efforts to prevent inflation from rising above 4% than to stopping inflation from falling below 2%. Against this backdrop, the performance of the IT for the following six cases can be assessed (Table 3.2).

The first case is where $\pi_t = 3\%$ and π^e_{t+1} remain near the target of 3%. On the surface, it seems that the operation of the IT is successful, but, in reality, it may be close to a failure in the sense that it failed to lower the inflationary expectation down to almost 2%. Indeed, there should be an additional tight monetary policy to bring the inflationary expectation down towards 2%. The second case is where $\pi_t = 3\%$ but π^e_{t+1} rises sufficiently above or falls sufficiently below the target of 3%. But this case is not likely to occur in the real world because the inflation expectation could not be formed independently of the target and the realised inflation rates. The third and fourth cases are where the inflation rate rises above the upper bound by 1%. In the third case, however, the inflation expectation is maintained around the target of 3% probably thanks to the anchoring effect of the IT. The operation of the IT is not bad except for its putting the credibility of the monetary policy at risk. In the fourth case, the operation is a complete failure because neither the realised inflation rate nor the inflation expectation met the target. The fifth and sixth cases are when the inflation rate falls below the 2% lower limit. In the fifth case, the inflation rate falls below 2%, but, as long as the anchoring effect holds, the inflationary expectation fails to drop. Additional effort will be needed to lower the inflationary expectation below 3%. Against this backdrop, the BoK decided to take the band approach of the IT in 2012 in order to de-anchor the inflationary expectation. Instead of a point target at 3%, the BoK took the range or band between 2.5 and 3.5% for the operation of the IT.

The sixth case is where the inflationary expectation fell along with the actual inflation rate, despite the setting of the target at 3%. In the sense that both the actual and the expected inflation missed the target, the operation of the IT can be said to be a failure. Indeed, there were many criticisms against the BoK's operation of the IT, but they were, for the most part, groundless due to mis-interpreting the operation of the IT as a symmetric operation, like those of the IT in the advanced countries. Although the operation of the IT was not satisfactory enough, the BoK nonetheless achieved its goal of stabilisation successfully.[6] The only problem is that the divergence between the target and expected inflation rate might do harm to the credibility of the monetary policy and therefore suggests the resetting of the target. As already pointed out, this has led the BoK to adopt an inflation target of 2% since 2016.

(3) IT under $\pi^T = 1\%$

Another interesting asymmetric operation of IT is carried out when the target inflation rate is set at 1%, as in the case of Bank of Japan (hereinafter BoJ). The BoJ had a target set at 1% before the launch of the Quantitative and Qualitative Easing in 2013. Clearly, the principal goal of the BoJ was to escape from the deflationary spiral that Japan was in by raising the inflation rate above the target. That is to say, the operational aim of the IT was to raise the inflation rate above 1%, not to maintain it around 1%. If the BoJ could raise the inflation rate near to 2%, it could be counted as a successful operation, but if it had an inflation rate near 0%, it is clear that the operation would be seen as a failure. Indeed, because the assessments of IT under $\pi^T = 1\%$ and under $\pi^T = 3\%$ will be very similar to each other, detailed assessment will not be carried out in order to avoid repetition. But, concerning the effect of anchoring, there is another important asymmetry between these two cases. In the former, the central bank attempts to raise the inflationary expectation in a deflationary situation, while in the latter, the central bank tries to lower it in inflationary circumstances. It is taken for granted that lowering inflation in an inflationary situation has the same effect as increasing the inflationary expectation in order to fight deflation if the country in question is trapped in a deflationary situation. But, as pointed out, the anchoring effect can be very weak in a situation in which the inflation rate and consequently the inflation uncertainties are very low. Thus, when the actual inflation rate widely misses the target from below, the validity of the IT in establishing the inflationary expectation can be called into question.

[6]However, there were no worries about deflation, as shown in the inflationary expectation, which remained between 2 and 3% even though the actual inflation rate fell below 1%.

To see it more clearly, let us go back to the model. Here, λ measures the extent to which the inflation target anchors the inflation expectation of the people. It is very likely that the size of λ will be different, depending on the situation in which the economy finds itself. For instance, if the economy is characterised by high inflation and therefore high inflation volatility, then the value of λ is likely to be higher, whereas if it is characterised by lower inflation and lower inflation volatility, the value of λ will be smaller. That is to say, during a high inflation period λ will be higher than it would be during a low inflation period. This is why it is difficult for the Japanese IT to be successful. Few people believe that the 2% inflation rate will be achieved.

In this regard, Blanchard's proposal to set the inflation target intentionally higher than is actually appropriate may be erroneous (Blanchard et al. 2010). Indeed Ehrmann (2014) shows that the effect of IT is weaker in a low inflation environment. Apart from this empirical study, the recent IT experience of the BoJ also provides further strong evidence that a continuous expansionary policy fails to produce an increase in inflation. This evidence suggests that the argument of Blanchard and even the relevance of the IT as an instrument to increase inflation rate could be doubted.

3.5 Conclusion and the Future Prospects for IT

Inflation targeting was a very important operation tool in stabilising the inflation rate in many countries when the inflation rate was running high. Korea was not an exception. In the past, Korea suffered from relatively high inflation rates and the introduction of IT contributed to stabilising inflation through the anchoring of the inflation expectations of private agents to 3%. Given that this target was still ambitious relative to its long-run price stability, the focus of the operation was to reduce the inflation below the target and therefore the operation of the IT carried out by the BoK could not be considered inappropriate even when the actual inflation rate fell far below 2%. When this happened, the BoK simply decided to move its target down to 2%.

Since the year 2012, however, inflation has become more subdued throughout the world. In some countries and regions, there is even increasing concern about deflation. This is reflected into the flattening Phillips curve. As made clear by the IMF (2013), for instance, the Phillips curve has flattened in almost all countries throughout the world, and the inflation rate has been determined independently of the growth rate or unemployment rate, and thus there is no guarantee at all that a high inflation rate necessarily leads to a higher growth rate and lower unemployment.

Is IT still a relevant operation framework for central banks? So far, it seems that the answer has been positive, highlighting the flexibility of IT when faced with the flattening Phillips curve (Svensson 2011). But low inflation or deflation throws more fundamental questions about the usefulness of IT, because there is no guarantee that raising inflationary expectations under conditions of low inflation works as well as lowering them under conditions of high inflation does. If this is the case, it is very likely that the anchoring mechanism itself will break down, and that central banks need to find an operation framework alternative to IT, no matter what it may be.

References

Bank of Korea. (2016). *Monetary Policy Report.*

Bank of Korea. (2017). *Monetary Policy Report.*

Barro, R., & Gordon, D. (1983). Rules, Discretion and reputation in a model of monetary policy. *Journal of Monetary Economics*, 12.

Blanchard, O., Dell'Ariccia, G., & Mauro, P. (2010). Rethinking macroeconomic policy. *IMF Staff Position Note.*

Demertzis, M., et al. (2009). Anchors for inflation expectations. De Nederlandsche Bank Working Paper No. 229.

Ehrmann, M. (2014). Targeting inflation from below-how do inflation expectations behave?" Bank of Canada Working Paper 2014–52.

Federal Open Market Committee. (1996). Meeting Transcripts 2–3 July 1996, available at: https://www.federalreserve.gov/monetarypolicy/fomchistorical1996.htm.

Federal Open Market Committee. (2016). Statement on Longer-Run Goals and Monetary Policy Strategy, available at: https://www.federalreserve.gov/monetarypolicy/files/FOMC_LongerRunGoals_20160126.pdf.

IMF. (2013). The Dog that didn't Bark: Has Inflation been Muzzled or was it just Sleeping? *World Economic Outlook.*

Kahneman, D., & Tversky, A. (1974). A Judgement under the Uncertainty: Heuristics and Biases. *Sciences, 185.*

Kydland, F. E., & Prescott, E. C. (1977). Rules rather than discretion: the inconsistency of optimal plans. *Journal of Political Economy*, *85*(3).

Moon, W. (2015). Three issues regarding the operation of monetary Policy in Korea. A comment made at the conference on Macroeconomic Policy and Price Measurement Issues in a Low Inflation Environment held by the Bank of Korea in August 2015.

Moon, W. (2018). *A study on monetary policy*, Yougok Press (In Korean).

Svensson, L. E. O. (2011). Inflation targeting. In B. Friedman & M. Woodford (eds.), *Handbook of Monetary Economics*, vol. 38, chap 22.

Svensson, L. E. O. (2013). Some lessons from six years of practical inflation targeting. *Sveriges Riksbank Economic Review, 3.*

Part II
Central Banks in Foreign Exchange Markets

Chapter 4
Exchange-Rate Management in East Asia: Words and Deeds

Ulrich Volz

Abstract This chapter discusses the declared exchange-rate policies of East Asian central banks and compares these with the de facto policies. Central banks that officially proclaim a fixed or managed exchange rate tend to intervene more in foreign exchange markets than central banks which officially follow a floating regime. However, even central banks that have implemented inflation-targeting frameworks with floating rates appear to carry out interventions. Several countries that self-describe their exchange-rate regime as "managed floating" appear to have been heavily engaged in foreign exchange-market interventions.

> *... other countries take advantage of us with their money and their money supply and devaluation. ... We know nothing about devaluation. Every other country lives on devaluation. You look at what China is doing, you look at what Japan has done over the years. They play the money market, they play the devaluation market. And we sit there like a bunch of dummies.*
>
> US President Donald Trump in a press conference on 31 January 2017.

4.1 Introduction

As a global trade war is unfolding, exchange-rate policies are increasingly coming into focus. US President Donald Trump has persistently complained about the

This chapter is based upon a presentation delivered at a conference on "Monetary Policy Execution in East Asia" at the East Asia Institute in Ludwigshafen. I thank Simon Dikau for providing excellent research assistance and conference participants for helpful feedback. I also thank the editors of this book for very helpful comments and suggestions as well as their patience. The usual disclaimer applies.

U. Volz (✉)
SOAS University of London, London, UK
e-mail: uv1@soas.ac.uk

German Development Institute, Bonn, Germany

F. Rövekamp et al. (eds.), *Monetary Policy Implementation in East Asia*, Financial and Monetary Policy Studies 51,
https://doi.org/10.1007/978-3-030-50298-0_4

supposedly "unfair" exchange-rate practices of trading partners and accused them of artificially lowering the value of their currencies to boost the competitiveness of their export industries—supposedly to the harm of the US economy. The Trump administration even proposed punitive duties for countries that allegedly manipulate currencies.[1] Unsurprisingly, China has been singled out as the main culprit, but other East Asian economies, including Japan, and the Republic of Korea (hereinafter Korea), have also become the targets of Trump's accusations of currency manipulation, along with the Europeans, the Canadians and the Mexicans.

US complaints about the alleged currency manipulations of trading partners are nothing new. Germany and Japan were heavily criticised by the US in the 1980s for supposedly undervaluing their currencies, giving way to the Plaza Accord in 1985,[2] which caused a fall of the value of the dollar by 40% over the period 1985–87.[3] Resembling the accusation faced by Japan since the 1980s, China has been heavily under fire from the US for alleged currency manipulation since the early 2000s.[4]

According to Article IV, Section 1 (iii) of the International Monetary Fund (IMF)'s Articles of Agreement, IMF member countries should "avoid manipulating exchange rates or the international monetary system in order to prevent effective balance of payments adjustment or to gain an unfair competitive advantage over other members".[5] The fund is tasked to "oversee the compliance of each member" and "exercise firm surveillance over the exchange rate policies of members".[6] What exactly constitutes exchange-rate manipulation, however, is not that straightforward to determine. The fund's 1977 decision on "Surveillance over Exchange Rate Policies"[7] puts forward a set of indicators that are to be used in assessing whether IMF members are abiding by the Principles for the Guidance of Members' Exchange Rate Policies, including: "(i) protracted large-scale intervention, (ii) undue official or quasi-official borrowing or short-term lending for balance of payments purposes, (iii) a change, for balance of payments purposes, of restrictions on, or incentives for, current transactions and capital flows, (iv) the pursuit, for balance of payments purposes, of monetary and other domestic policies that abnormally encourage/discourage capital flows, (v) behavior of the exchange rate unrelated to underlying economic and financial conditions, (vi) unsustainable flows of private capital".[8]

---

[1] See Politi (2019).

[2] The Plaza Accord was a joint agreement between France, West Germany, Japan, the United States and the United Kingdom, to depreciate the US dollar in relation to the Japanese yen and the German Deutsche mark by intervening in currency markets, signed at the Plaza Hotel, New York, on 22 September 1985.

[3] For a recent assessment of the Plaza Accord, see Bergsten and Green (2016).

[4] See, for example, Preeg (2003).

[5] IMF (2016), Article IV, Section 1.

[6] IMF (2016), Article IV, Section 3.

[7] Decision No. 5392-77/63, 29 April 1977.

[8] IMF (2006, p. 9).

When countries are faced with accusations of currency under-valuation or manipulation, they usually refute these claims and provide all sorts of (more or less convincing) explanations as to why they should not be branded as currency manipulators. While it is beyond the scope of this chapter to carry out a comprehensive assessment of whether countries are, in truth, under-valuing their currencies, and should be labelled as currency manipulators, it does seek to address a related and equally important question: to wit, are central banks in East Asia doing what they say they are doing in their exchange-rate policies, and is this reflected in their degree of intervention in the foreign exchange market?[9] In particular, the chapter analyses whether central banks "walk the talk", that is, do what they say, as opposed to making empty promises, and whether their actual policies are in line with official monetary frameworks. To this end, the chapter reviews the exchange-rate policies of East Asian countries and discusses the role of foreign exchange interventions.

The remainder of this chapter is organised as follows. Section 4.2 will briefly review the exchange-rate policies of East Asian central banks. Section 4.3 will look into the alleged currency manipulation of the East Asian economies. Section 4.4 will then discuss the role of interventions, and how these align with the chosen monetary and exchange-rate regime. Section 4.5 concludes.

4.2 Exchange-Rate Policies of East Asian Countries

The currency regimes of East Asian economies have been characterised by McKinnon as the East Asian dollar standard,[10] basically describing a situation in which the East Asian economies—with the notable exception of Japan—maintained fixed or managed exchange rates against the US dollar. The East Asian dollar standard evolved as an informal system which, due to the fact that almost all countries stabilised their currencies against the same external anchor, provided a relatively high degree of intra-regional exchange-rate stability for East Asia.

Figure 4.1 shows the exchange rates of East Asian currencies against the US dollar for the period 1993–2017. An upward movement implies a devaluation against the US dollar. The bars depict a 5% change in the value for each data point in the exchange-rate data series. As can be seen in Fig. 4.1, Indonesia, Korea, Laos, Malaysia, the Philippines, Thailand, and Vietnam had their currencies pegged firmly against the US dollar up to the Asian crisis in 1997. Since the forced depreciation during the crisis, these countries have all introduced more flexibility to their exchange rates, albeit to different degrees. Taiwan has been operating a managed floating system since 1978, but, in practice, the new Taiwan dollar has been kept within a rather narrow range against the US dollar. While Hong Kong and Macao have maintained their currency

[9]Under East Asia, we comprise China, Hong Kong, Macao, Taiwan, Japan, Korea and the ten Southeast Asian nations that form the Association of Southeast Asian Nations (ASEAN), namely Brunei, Cambodia, Indonesia, Lao PDR (Laos), Malaysia, Myanmar, the Philippines, Singapore, Thailand and Vietnam.

[10]See McKinnon (2005).

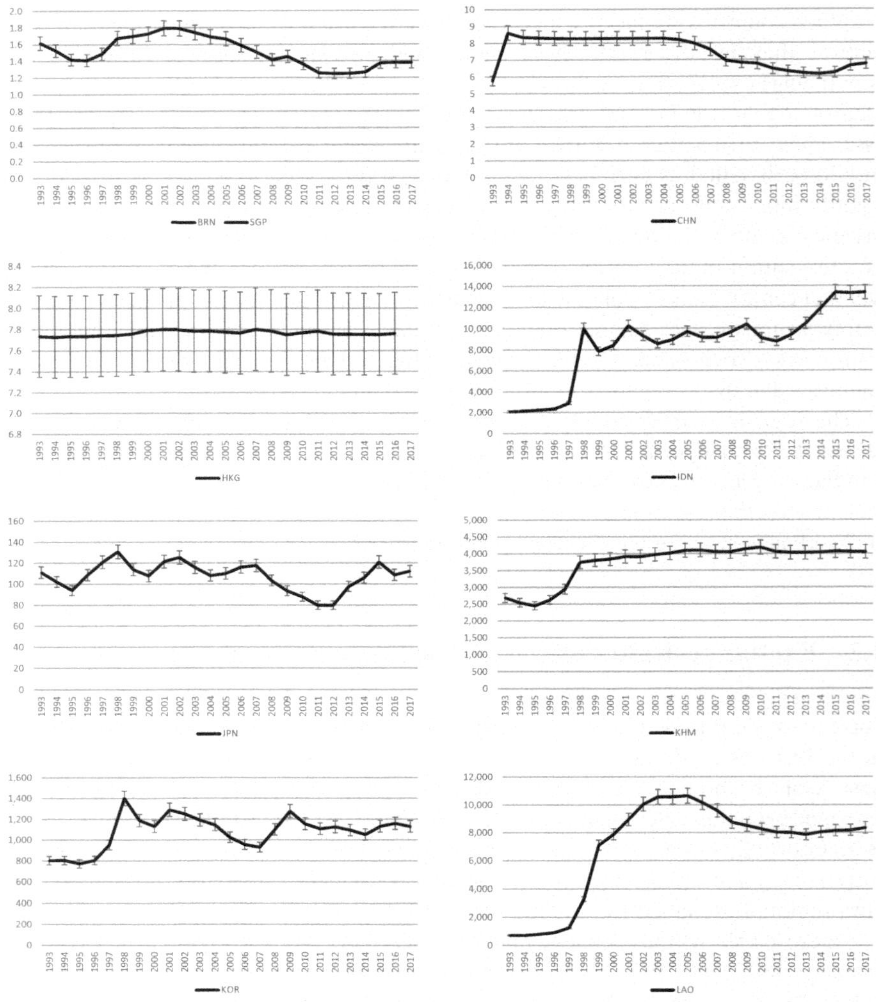

Fig. 4.1 Official exchange rate against the US dollar (local currency unit per USD), 1993–2017. *Source* Compiled with data from the IMF's Monetary and Financial Statistics. *Note* Bars depict 5% changes. BRN = Brunei, SGP = Singapore, CHN = China, HKG = Hong Kong, IDN = Indonesia, JPN = Japan, KHM = Cambodia, KOR = Korea, LAO = Laos PDR, MAC = Macao, MMR = Myanmar, MYS = Malaysia, PHL = Philippines, THA = Thailand, TWN = Taiwan, VNM = Vietnam

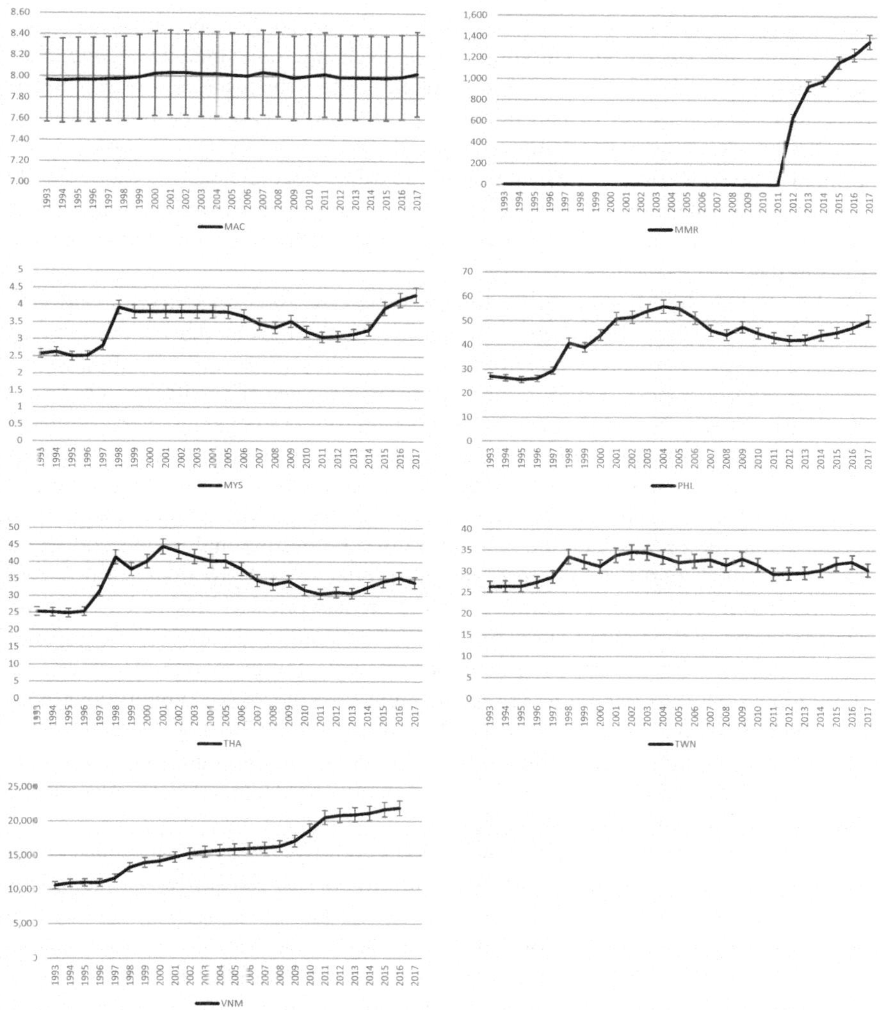

Fig. 4.1 (continued)

board arrangements throughout, China, which had a firm dollar peg until July 2005, has gradually introduced more flexibility in its exchange rate since then. Singapore has maintained a currency basket arrangement, while Brunei has a currency board arrangement that pegs the Brunei dollar at par to the Singapore dollar. Japan has had a flexible exchange rate for the yen since the end of the Bretton Woods system. Myanmar, which used to peg the kyat against the IMF's Special Drawing Right (SDR) basket of major international currencies at 8.51 kyat per SDR, moved to a floating exchange-rate regime in April 2012 and has since seen a dramatic devaluation against the US dollar.

As highlighted by McKinnon,[11] although most East Asian countries abandoned hard dollar pegs and allowed more flexibility in their exchange rates to avoid becoming the targets of renewed currency attacks, they continued to stabilise their exchange rates against the dollar, with different degrees of flexibility. There are various reasons why East Asian countries have continued to manage their exchange rates against the US dollar.[12] First, a large share of the financial assets and liabilities of the East Asian economies has been denominated in US dollars, making financial markets sensitive to exchange-rate changes against the dollar. Second, since 1980, the East Asian region has seen the emergence of a broad regional trade–production network, in which parts and components are produced and processed in different locations across the region. This trade–production network was only able to develop in environments with relatively low exchange-rate volatility. Thirdly, the economies of East Asia have been competing as exporters, with the exchange-rate decisions of individual countries having a significant impact on the trade competitiveness of their neighbours. And, last, but not least, the emergence of China,—which has been stabilising the renminbi against the dollar since 1994—as the region's most important economy, has reinforced the rationale of managing exchange rates against the dollar—or the renminbi, as some suggest.[13]

Table 4.1 provides an overview of the exchange-rate regimes of East Asian central banks for 2017, according to the IMF's *Annual Report on Exchange Arrangements and Exchange Restrictions*.[14] Column 2 lists the de jure exchange-rate regime that countries report to the IMF. Column 3 lists the de facto exchange-rate regime classification that the IMF provides. Lastly, column 4 provides the IMF's assessment of the de facto monetary-policy framework classifications for each country. Out of the 14 East Asian countries listed, there are 4 countries with discrepancies between the self-declared de jure exchange-rate regime and what the IMF considers the de facto exchange-rate regime. Cambodia, China and Laos self-describe their exchange-rate arrangement as "managed floating", whereas the IMF classifies it as "other managed arrangement" and "stabilised arrangement", respectively. Malaysia describes its exchange-rate regime as "managed floating", whereas the IMF considers it as "floating".

[11] Ibid.

[12] See Volz (2010, 2011, 2012, 2014).

[13] See, for example, Henning (2013).

[14] IMF (2018).

Table 4.1 Exchange-rate regime as declared by the central bank and IMF classification of de facto exchange-rate arrangements and monetary-policy frameworks, 2017

Country	Exchange-rate regime (de jure)	Exchange-rate regime (de facto)	Monetary-policy framework (de facto)
Brunei	Currency board	Currency board	Exchange-rate anchor (SGD)
Cambodia	Managed floating	Other managed arrangement	Exchange-rate anchor (US Dollar)
China	Managed floating	Stabilised arrangement	Monetary-aggregate targeting
Japan	Free-floating	Free floating	Inflation-targeting framework
Hong Kong	Currency board	Currency board	Exchange-rate anchor (US Dollar)
Indonesia	Floating	Floating	Inflation-targeting framework
Korea	Floating	Floating	Inflation-targeting framework
Laos PDR	Managed floating	Stabilised arrangement	Other
Malaysia	Managed floating	Floating	Other
Myanmar	Other managed arrangement	Other managed arrangement	Monetary-aggregate targeting
Philippines	Floating	Floating	Inflation-targeting framework
Singapore	Stabilised arrangement	Stabilised arrangement	Exchange-rate anchor (composite)
Thailand	Floating	Floating	Inflation-targeting framework
Vietnam	Stabilised arrangement	Stabilised arrangement	Exchange-rate anchor (composite)

Source Compiled with data from IMF (2018). *Note* Macao and Taiwan are not covered by IMF (2018)

The central banks of Japan, Indonesia, Korea, the Philippines and Thailand have all adopted an inflation-targeting framework which is, strictly speaking, incompatible with targeting any other indicator than inflation, be it wages, level of employment, or the exchange rate.[15] And indeed, both the de jure and de facto exchange-rate regimes of these countries are listed by the IMF as floating (free floating in the case of Japan). While not having adopted an inflation-targeting regime, Malaysia is also operating a floating regime (self-described as managed floating).[16] Virtually, all other East Asian economies have some kind of fixed or managed exchange-rate regime.

[15] Jahan (2017), Volz (2015).

[16] Although price stability has been an important target for East Asian central banks, it has been only one out of several targets, besides exchange-rate stability, the current account, employment and financial sector stability. For a critique of the inflation targeting approach in East Asia, see Volz (2015).

Table 4.2 List of East Asian "currency manipulators" according to Bergsten & Gagnon

	Years of manipulation in 2016–18	2018 net official assets		Net official flows (billions of US dollars)			2016–18 average net official flows (% of GDP)	2016–18 average current account (% of GDP)
		Billions of US dollars	% of GDP	2016	2017	2018		
China	0	3,252	24	−452	45	−3	−1	1
Hong Kong	1	417	115	−7	32	2	3	4
Japan	0	1,449	29	4	17	29	0	4
Macao	3	83	153					
Malaysia	0	92	26	0	5	−18	−1	3
Korea	0	461	38	6	27	23	1	6
Singapore	3	833	231	49	100	63	21	17
Thailand	2	199	41	25	31	−1	4	10
Taiwan	1	462	78	8	17	10	2	13

Source Compiled with data from Collins and Gagnon (2019)

4.3 Currency Manipulation in East Asia?

According to Bergsten & Gagnon,[17] who conducted a comprehensive analysis of currency manipulation, "[a]t least 20 economies actively manipulated their currencies during the first 15 years of this century".[18] They concluded that "China was by far the most active manipulator", and that "[s]everal other Asian economies—most notably Hong Kong, Korea, Singapore, and Taiwan—behaved similarly at least some of this time, partly to emulate China and avoid losing competitive position to it".[19] Bergsten & Gagnon point to the problem of "competitive non appreciation" in which countries "block adequate (or any) upward revaluation of a fixed rate or resist market-driven appreciation of a flexible rate".[20]

Using the same methodology as Bergsten & Gagnon,[21] Collins & Gagnon present an updated list of currency manipulators (Table 4.2).[22] According to their analysis,

[17]Bergsten and Gagnon (2017, p. 171).

[18]Bergsten and Gagnon (2017) define a "currency manipulator" as a country that meets all of the following criteria in a given calendar year: recording a current account surplus larger than 3% of GDP; net acquisitions of official foreign-currency assets exceeding 2% of GDP; foreign exchange reserves and other official foreign assets exceeding three months of imports; foreign exchange reserves and other official foreign assets exceeding 100% of short-term external debt; net official flows exceeding 65% of oil exports minus production cost; and being classified by the World Bank as a upper middle-income or high-income country.

[19]Bergsten and Gagnon (2017, p. 171).

[20]Ibid., p. 2.

[21]Ibid.

[22]Collins and Gagnon (2019).

currency manipulation fell to its lowest level since 2001, with only three economies meeting all the criteria for currency manipulation in the year 2018: Singapore, Norway and Macao. Over the period 2016–2018, both Singapore and Macao meet the criteria for all 3 years, while Thailand meets it twice, and Hong Kong and Taiwan only once. China has not met the criteria for currency manipulation since 2014.

In its semi-annual report to Congress in May 2019, the US Treasury did not designate any country as a currency manipulator.[23] However, it listed six East Asian economies—China, Japan, Korea, Singapore, Malaysia and Vietnam—on its "Monitoring List of major trading partners that merit close attention to their currency practices and macroeconomic policies".[24] Unsurprisingly, all of them refute the notion that they may be currency manipulators.

4.4 Foreign Exchange Interventions and the Exchange Rate

East Asian central banks have a long history of intervening in the foreign exchange market to stabilise their currencies. Figure 4.2 illustrates the increase in the foreign exchange holdings of East Asian countries. Reserves have risen multi-fold: in China, they increased from 23 billion USD in 1993: Q4 to 3.4 trillion USD in 2018: Q1. In Japan, the country with the second largest reserves, they rose from 100 billion USD in 1993: Q4 to 1.3 trillion USD in 2018: Q1. In Korea, they rose from 20 billion USD in 1993: Q1 to 389 billion USD in 2017: Q4.

The literature on central bank interventions has identified four principal motivations for foreign exchange market intervention:[25]

(i) *Leaning against the wind*: Surveys conducted by the Bank for International Settlements (BIS) have shown that the most prominent reason for central banks in emerging market economies to intervene in foreign exchange markets is to constrain exchange-rate volatility and smoothen the trend movement of the exchange rate.[26] To this end, central banks "systematically interven[e] against the direction that the exchange rate is moving".[27]

(ii) *Reducing exchange-rate misalignment*: A second major reason for central banks to intervene in foreign exchange markets is to address concerns about exchange-rate misalignments. An over-valued exchange rate may cause problems for the economy's export sector and current account, while an under-valued exchange rate could lead to a surge in capital inflows, imported inflation and an overheating of the economy.

---

[23]US Treasury, *Macroeconomic and Foreign Exchange Policies of Major Trading Partners of the United States*, Report to Congress, May, Washington, DC (2019, p. 6).

[24]Ibid., p. 6. The only other three economies named on this list are Germany, Italy and Ireland, which are all members of the Eurozone.

[25]Adler and Tovar (2011), Basu and Varoudakis (2013), Chutasripanich and Yetman (2015).

[26]BIS (2005, 2013).

[27]Chutasripanich and Yetman (2015, p. 3).

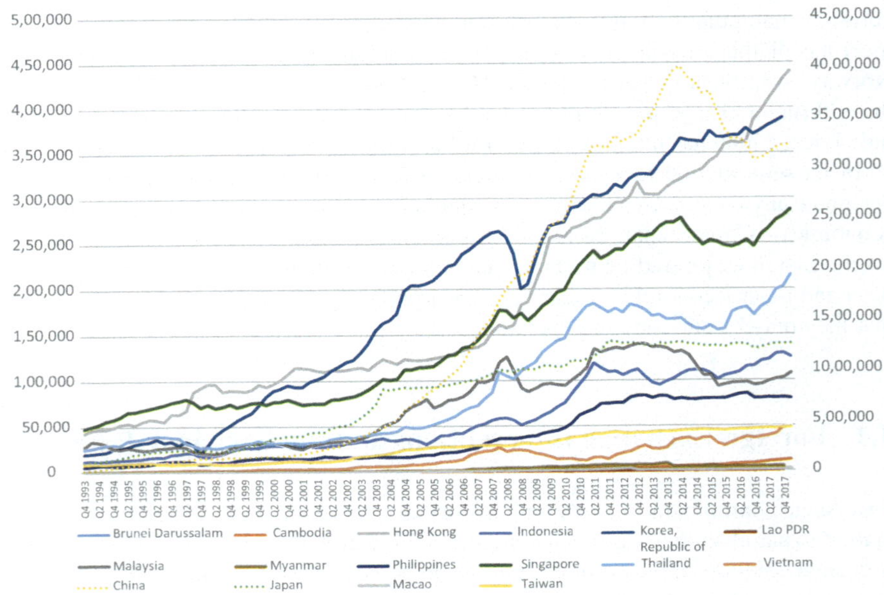

Fig. 4.2 International reserves, official reserve assets (in US dollars), 1993–2018. *Source* Compiled with data from IMF Monetary and Financial Statistics. *Note* Values for China and Japan are displayed on the right axis

(iii) *Managing foreign exchange reserves*: As a lesson of the emerging market crises of the 1990s, the central banks of developing and emerging market economies started to build up foreign exchange reserves as the first line of defence against speculative currency attacks. According to Adler & Tovar,[28] half of the central banks intervening in foreign exchange markets over the period 2004–2010 sought to build up foreign exchange reserves.

(iv) *Ensuring liquidity*: Finally, central banks may conduct foreign exchange market interventions to provide sufficient liquidity to domestic financial institutions to avoid financial market distress. This may be necessary for economies with less developed financial markets.

Most central banks remain silent on the reasons for, and frequency of, foreign exchange intervention, not least out of fear of being branded as currency manipulators. Unfortunately, very few central banks actually publish their intervention data.[29] To gauge whether the level of a central bank's intervention in the foreign exchange market corresponds to their officially declared exchange-rate regime, we analyse the relationship between the annual change in international reserves (as a proxy for a central bank's activity in the foreign exchange market) and annual exchange-rate

[28]Adler and Tovar (2011).

[29]Fratzscher et al. (2019).

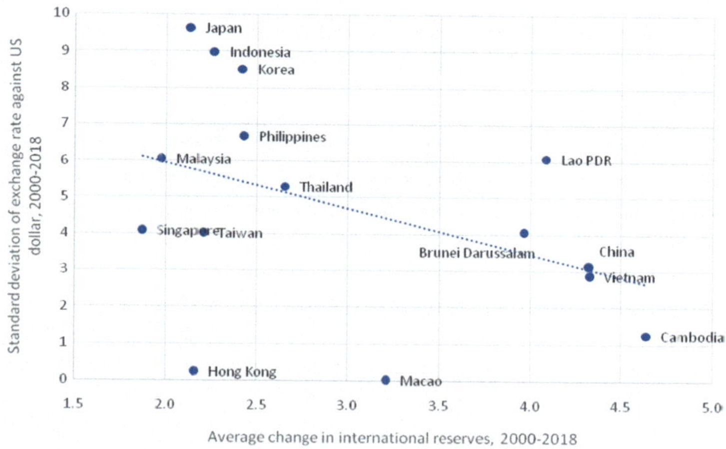

Fig. 4.3 Average change in international reserves and standard deviation of the exchange rate against the US dollar, 2000–2018.
Source Compiled with data from IMF COFER and IMF Monetary and Financial Statistics.
Note Myanmar is not included in this figure as the SD of its exchange rate is too large

volatility. Admittedly, this is a very blunt approach, but large changes in foreign exchange reserve holdings are arguably the best indicator of active exchange-rate management and a central bank's attempt at influencing not only the volatility but also the level of the exchange rate. Figure 4.3 plots the average change in international reserves and the standard deviation of the local currency exchange rate against the US dollar for the East Asian economies for the period 2000–2018. The graph shows a clear, negative relationship between exchange-rate volatility against the US dollar and the average change in reserves.

The figure shows that central banks that officially declare a fixed or managed exchange-rate regime intervene more in foreign exchange markets than central banks that officially have a floating regime. As discussed earlier, the central banks of Japan, Indonesia, Korea, the Philippines and Thailand have all adopted an inflation-targeting framework and have declared their exchange-rate regimes as floating (free floating in the case of Japan). Japan, Indonesia, Korea and the Philippines are indeed the countries with the highest degree of exchange-rate variability against the US dollar, while at the same time showing comparatively low changes in international reserves. This suggests that their level of intervention in the foreign-exchange markets has been broadly in line with their self-declared monetary and exchange-rate regime. However, even these central banks appear to conduct substantial interventions.[30] Thailand, for example, the other inflation targeter, recorded somewhat less exchange-rate volatility and greater changes in foreign reserves over this period.

[30]It should be noted that Japan has not intervened in the foreign-exchange market since November 2011.

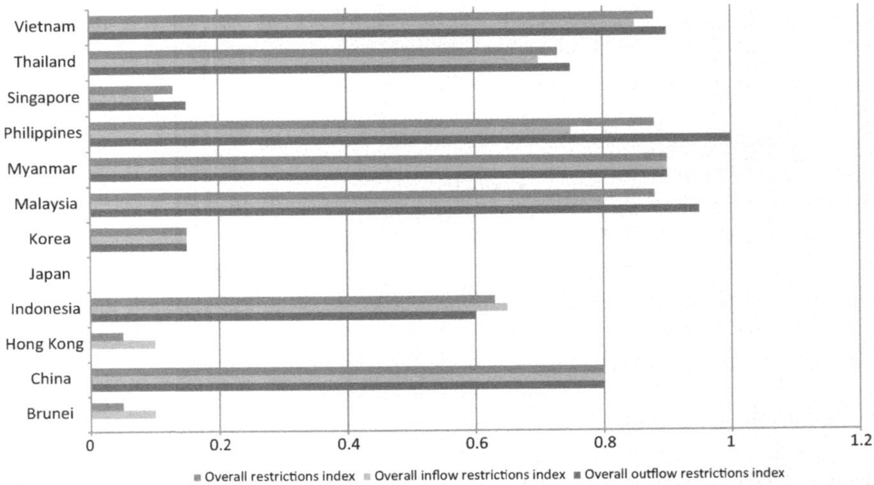

Fig. 4.4 Capital inflow and outflow restrictions of East Asian countries, 2017.
Source Compiled with updated data from Fernandez et al. (2016). *Note* A higher value indicates more restrictions. A value of 0 indicates a completely liberalised capital account. Data for Macao and Taiwan are not available

On the right side of the figure are those countries with a relatively high level of changes in foreign reserves over the observed period. Vietnam displays a large average change in international reserves year-on-year, as may be expected for a country with a stabilised exchange-rate arrangement. However, Cambodia, China and Laos, which more recently have self-described their exchange-rate regime as "managed floating", appear to have been heavily engaged in foreign exchange market interventions too.

Currency stabilisation has been facilitated in China, Indonesia, Malaysia, Myanmar, the Philippines, Thailand and Vietnam by relatively high degrees of capital inflow and outflow restrictions (Fig. 4.4). In contrast, Brunei, Hong Kong, Korea and Singapore have very few restrictions, while Japan has none.

4.5 Conclusions

East Asian central banks that officially declare a fixed or managed exchange rate tend to intervene more in foreign exchange markets than central banks that officially have a floating regime. Nonetheless, central banks that have officially implemented inflation targeting frameworks with floating rates also appear to carry out interventions. Moreover, several countries that describe their exchange-rate regimes as "managed floating", most notably Cambodia, China and Laos, appear to have been heavily engaged in foreign exchange market interventions. This does not necessarily suggest that these countries are currency manipulators, but it admits questions regarding the accuracy of their policy reporting. Apparently, not all central banks in East Asia are fully transparent about their actual exchange-rate policies.

It should be pointed out that the proxy used for foreign-exchange intervention, the average net year-on-year change in official reserves, is a very blunt one, which does not fully capture central bank interventions aimed at smoothening the exchange rate, as these will involve the buying and selling of the domestic currency. Moreover, the analysis has not discussed the role of verbal interventions, which, in some cases, maybe more important than actual foreign exchange market interventions. The analysis presented here is therefore *by no means* comprehensive. Deep-going analysis of the frequency and extent of foreign-exchange intervention (including verbal interventions) is needed, for which better data are needed.

The discussion here should not give the impression that exchange-rate management and foreign-exchange interventions as such are negative. Indeed, exchange-rate management has been an integral part of the East Asian economic development model that has helped to improve living conditions across the region significantly. Exchange-rate management and foreign-exchange interventions may be particularly relevant at times when developing and emerging economies face large and volatile capital flows because of unconventional monetary policies in advanced countries.[31] The example of Japan, which has largely abstained from foreign-exchange intervention over the last decades—in sharp contrast to heavy-handed interventions in earlier periods—shows how rapid and large-scale exchange-rate appreciations can harm the domestic manufacturing industry.[32] Hence, the exchange rate should play an important role in any central bank's monetary-policy framework, and particularly so in developing and emerging economies. Acknowledging the importance of the exchange rate for the conduct of monetary policy is crucial. However, to integrate the exchange rate adequately into the monetary framework, central banks have to be transparent about it.

References

Adler, G., & Tovar, C. E. (2011). *Foreign exchange intervention: A shield against appreciation winds?* (IMF Working Paper No. 11/165). Washington DC: International Monetary Fund.

Basu, K., & Varoudakis, A. (2013). *How to move the exchange rate if you must: The diverse practice of foreign exchange intervention by central banks and a proposal for doing it better* (World Bank Policy Research Working Paper No. 6460) Washington DC: World Bank.

Belke, A., & Volz, U. (2019). Flows to emerging market and developing economies—Global liquidity and uncertainty versus country-specific pull factors. *Review of Development Finance, 9*(1), 32–50.

[31] Belke and Volz (2019).

[32] Belke and Volz, forthcoming.

Belke, A., & Volz, U. (forthcoming). The Yen exchange rate and the hollowing out of the Japanese industry. *Open Economies Review*.

Bergsten, C. F., & Gagnon, J. E. (2017). *Currency conflict and trade policy: A new strategy for the united States*. Washington, DC: Peterson Institute for International Economics.

Bergsten, C. F., & Green, R. (Eds.). (2016). *International monetary cooperation: Lessons from the Plaza accord after thirty years*. Washington, DC: Peterson Institute for International Economics.

BIS. (2005). Foreign exchange market intervention in emerging markets: Motives, techniques and implications (BIS Paper No 24). Basel: Bank for International Settlements.

BIS. (2013). *Market volatility and foreign exchange intervention in emes: What has changed?* (BIS Paper No 73). Basel: Bank for International Settlements.

Chutasripanich, N., & Yetman, J. (2015). Foreign exchange intervention: strategies and effectiveness (BIS Working Paper No. 499). Basel: Bank for International Settlements.

Collins, C. G., & Gagnon, J. E. (2019, June 6). Currency manipulation continues to decline (PIIE Trade and Investment Policy Watch). Washington DC: Peterson Institute for International Economics. https://piie.com/blogs/trade-investment-policy-watch/currency-manipulation-continues-decline.

Fernandez, A., Klein, M., Rebucci, A., Schindler, M., & Uribe, M. (2016). Capital control measures: A new dataset. *IMF Economic Review, 64*(3), 548–574.

Fratzscher, M., Gloede, O., Menkhoff, L., Sarno, L., & Stöhr, T. (2019). When is foreign exchange intervention effective? Evidence from 33 countries. *American Economic Journal: Macroeconomics, 11*(1), 132–156.

Henning, C. R. (2013). Choice and coercion in East Asian exchange rate regimes. In B. J. Cohen & E. M. P. Chiu (Eds.), *Power in a changing world economy lessons from East Asia* (pp. 89–110). New York: Routledge.

IMF. (2006, July 19). Review of the 1977 decision on surveillance over exchange rate policies. In *Preliminary Considerations, Background Information, and Summing Up of the Board Meeting*. https://www.imf.org/external/np/pp/eng/2006/pc.pdf.

IMF. (2016, April). *Articles of agreement of the international monetary fund*. https://www.imf.org/external/pubs/ft/aa/pdf/aa.pdf.

IMF. (2018). *Annual report on exchange arrangements and exchange restrictions 2017*. Washington, DC: International Monetary Fund.

Jahan, S. (2017). Inflation targeting: Holding the line. *Finance & Development* (Back to Basics), 72–73.

McKinnon, R. I. (2005). *Exchange rates under the East Asian dollar standard: Living with conflicted virtue*. Cambridge, MA: The MIT Press.

Politi, J. (2019, May 24). US proposes punishment for countries that manipulate currencies. *Financial Times*. https://www.ft.com/content/ff06fdca-7db4-11e9-81d2-f785092ab560.

Preeg, E. H. (2003). Exchange rate manipulation to gain an unfair competitive advantage: The case against Japan and China. In: C. Fred Bergsten & J. Williamson (Eds.), *Dollar overvaluation and the world economy*. Special Report No. 16 (pp. 267–284). Washington DC: Institute for International Economics.

Treasury, U. S. (2019, May). *Macroeconomic and foreign exchange policies of major trading partners of the United States*, Report to Congress. Washington, DC: U.S. Department of the Treasury Office of International Affairs. Retrieved from https://home.treasury.gov/system/files/206/2019-05-28-May-2019-FX-Report.pdf.

Volz, U. (2010). *Prospects for monetary cooperation and integration in East Asia*. Cambridge, MA: The MIT Press.

Volz, U. (2011). On the choice of exchange-rate regimes for East Asia. In Y.-W. Cheung, V. Kakkar, & G. Ma (Eds.), *The evolving role of Asia in global finance* (pp. 123–156). Emerald Group Publishing: Bingley.

Volz, U. (2012). Financial regionalism in East Asia. *International Spectator, 47*(4), 95–109.
Volz, U. (2014). RMB internationalisation and currency co-operation in East Asia. In H. G. Hilpert & F. Rövekamp (Eds.), *Currency cooperation in East Asia* (pp. 57–81). Heidelberg and New York: Springer.
Volz, U. (2015). On the future of inflation targeting in East Asia. *Review of Development Economics, 19*(3), 638–652.

Chapter 5
Taiwan's Exchange-Rate Policy and Its Current Challenges

Ti-Jen Tsao

Abstract Cross-border capital flows account for a significant share of Taiwan's interbank foreign exchange transactions, and some active foreign investors play a key role in the total of foreign capital flows. Large and frequent short-term capital movements pose one of the major threats to financial stability in Taiwan. Confronted with this challenge, the Central Bank of the Republic of China (Taiwan), or CBC, employs a range of measures to manage the foreign exchange market and capital movements. This practice fulfils the CBC's legal mandate of maintaining the stable value of the new Taiwan dollar (NTD) to underpin economic growth in Taiwan. Because of great dependency on imported energy, high foreign portfolio investment, the lack of International monetary Fund (IMF) membership and reserve currency status, Taiwan's reserve holdings stay at a relatively high level, which provides a necessary buffer to reduce excess volatility in the NTD exchange rate, instead of any attempt at competitive depreciation.

5.1 Introduction

Before the global financial crisis of 2008, the advocates of free cross-border capital flows argued that capital-poor economies could accelerate their productivity growth if they permitted capital to flow freely in from capital-rich economies. In addition to the lasting benefit of capital inflows on investment, capital-poor economies are able to smooth their business cycles via cross-border capital flows. However, the global financial crisis of 2008 gave us a different lesson to that which the supporters of free cross-border capital flows had advocated. Dadush and Stancil (2011) found that

The views expressed are those solely of the author and do not necessarily reflect those of the Central Bank of the Republic of China (Taiwan).

T.-J. Tsao (✉)
Central Bank of the Republic of China (Taiwan), 2, Sec. 1, Roosevelt Rd., Taipei 10066, Taiwan, R.O.C.
e-mail: tjtsao@mail.cbc.gov.tw

F. Rövekamp et al. (eds.), *Monetary Policy Implementation in East Asia*, Financial and Monetary Policy Studies 51,
https://doi.org/10.1007/978-3-030-50298-0_5

international capital did not flow from capital-rich economies to capital-poor ones; instead, it mainly flowed into capital-rich economies. The reason behind this is that the savings rate is usually higher in the developing economies than in the developed economies, but investment opportunities are fewer in the former than in the latter.

According to the 2013 Trade and Development Report of the United Nations Conference on Trade and Development (UNCTAD), growing unrestricted international capital flows do not necessarily stimulate real investment or bring higher and more stable GDP growth rates. It usually attracts short-term capital flows to speculate on financial assets across countries. While the financial market is known not to be perfectly efficient, it comes as no surprise to find prices being seriously distorted by market failure, for example, by herding behaviour in foreign exchange markets. This market inefficiency could further harm economic development and international trade. The United Nations Development Programme, in one of its 2009 reports, claimed that international capital flows had become the main driver of exchange-rate variation, in place of international trade or economic fundamentals.

In some recent literature, unregulated international capital flows are believed to be an unstable factor in the global economy. Bluedorn et al. (2013) showed that, since 1980, for a sample of nearly 150 countries, private capital flows are typically volatile for all these countries, advanced or emerging, across all points in time. This holds true across most types of flows, including bank, portfolio debt and equity flows. Rey (2015) highlighted that gains to international capital flows have proved elusive, be it in calibrated models or in the data. Large gross capital flows derived from the easy monetary policies of major central banks disrupt asset markets and financial intermediation, which results in the harmful side effects. Chen et al. (2015) pointed out that the estimated effects of US quantitative easing on emerging economies are generally larger than those found for the United States and other advanced economies. The estimates suggest that US monetary policy spillovers contributed to overheating in emerging economies and corresponding exchange-rate appreciation pressure. Therefore, cross-border monetary policy spillovers, via international capital flows, can be important sources of global macroeconomic and financial instability.

It is observed that short-term international capital flows have dominated the fluctuations of the exchange rate of the New Taiwan Dollar (NTD). When foreign investors remit money in Taiwan, the NTD exchange rate usually appreciates and vice versa. The latest statistics indicate that foreign capital flows have accounted for a major share of Taiwan's interbank foreign exchange transactions. Meanwhile, several active foreign investors play a key role in foreign capital flows. Beyond the NTD exchange rate, Taiwan's stock market performance is also skewed in the direction of short-term foreign capital flow. Data show that the local stock market usually booms with the NTD appreciation when cross-border capital flows in and vice versa.

As a small and highly open economy, Taiwan relies heavily on international trade for its economic development, but this kind of economic structure usually attracts short-term cross-border capital to take advantage of its thin market, which undermines not only the stability of Taiwan's financial market but also its domestic economy. The thinness of Taiwan's local financial market can be perceived from the following numbers: the total market value of the NTD assets owned by foreign investors, including stocks, bonds and deposits, reached 392 billion USD, around 87% of Taiwan's foreign exchange reserves, at the end of 2017. Fortunately, Taiwan has been able to maintain a current account surplus, low external debt, high financial liquidity, etc., so that its economy is less vulnerable to external shocks, compared with that of other emerging market economies.

The rest of the chapter is organised as follows. Section 5.2 presents the impact of short-term capital flows on the financial market in Taiwan. The policy measures to address the aforementioned issue are presented in Sect. 5.3. The foreign exchange policy of the Central Bank of the Republic of China (Taiwan), or CBC, is discussed in Sect. 5.4. Finally, Sect. 5.5 concludes the findings and assesses the policy implications.

5.2 The Impact of Short-Term Capital Flows on Taiwan's Financial Market

As the financial account of Taiwan continues to open up, capital flow management inevitably becomes a tougher task for the domestic authorities. Activities involving foreign portfolio investment have increased largely in the local currency market. On the other hand, the share of international trade was down to less than 10% of the NTD spot transaction from more than 40% in the 1990s. Increasing foreign portfolio investment usually carries more fickle capital flows. Especially after the 2008 global financial crisis, the volatility of international capital flows in Taiwan has nearly doubled relative to the level depicted in Fig. 5.1. This phenomenon is not only for capital inflows but also for capital outflows.

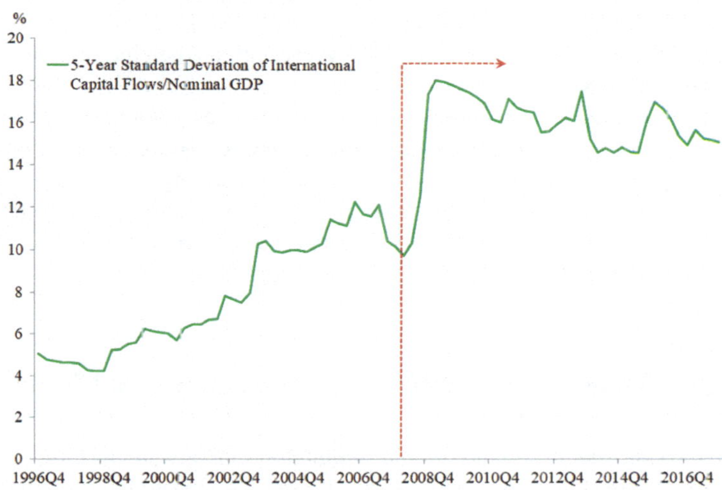

Fig. 5.1 International capital flow volatility in Taiwan.
Source Central Bank of the Republic of China (Taiwan)

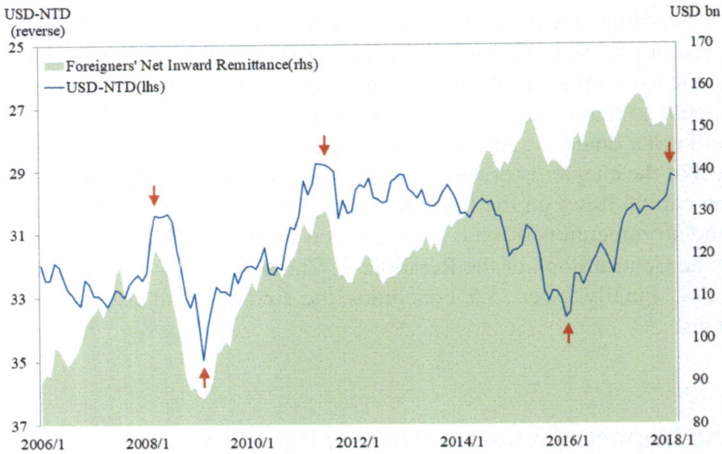

Fig. 5.2 Foreigners' net inward remittance and exchange rate of US dollar against NT dollar. *Source* Financial Supervisory Commission (Taiwan), Bloomberg

According to current statistics, foreign capital inflows and outflows accounted for more than 40% of Taiwan's interbank foreign exchange transactions for the last 3 years, while the 20 most active foreign investors accounted for around 40% of the total foreign capital flows. Moreover, foreign capital flows have been one of the main factors that have influenced not only the directions of the NTD exchange rate but also the Taiwan Stock Exchange Weighted Index (TAIEX). According to the data released by the Financial Supervisory Committee (Taiwan), foreign investors owned 32% of locally listed companies by market value at the end of 2017, which could be up to 39% if a foreign direct investment was included. Figures 5.2 and 5.3 show that the TAIEX normally rises with the NTD appreciation when international capital flows in and vice versa.

It is not unusual in Asian economies for local exchange rates and stock markets to be driven by foreigners' remittances, rather than economic fundamentals. Figures 5.4 and 5.5 show that the correlation between Asian exchange rates reflected less domestic economic growth after the 2008 global financial crisis. Conversely, they have exhibited high co-movement for the recent decade. This situation has greatly challenged the financial stability of these Asian economies.

5.3 Policy Measures to Address the Aforementioned Issue

To reduce the side effects of international capital flows in Taiwan, the CBC has taken long-term measures and employed short-term tools. The objective of the long-term policy measures is to maintain sufficient flexibility of the NTD exchange rate to

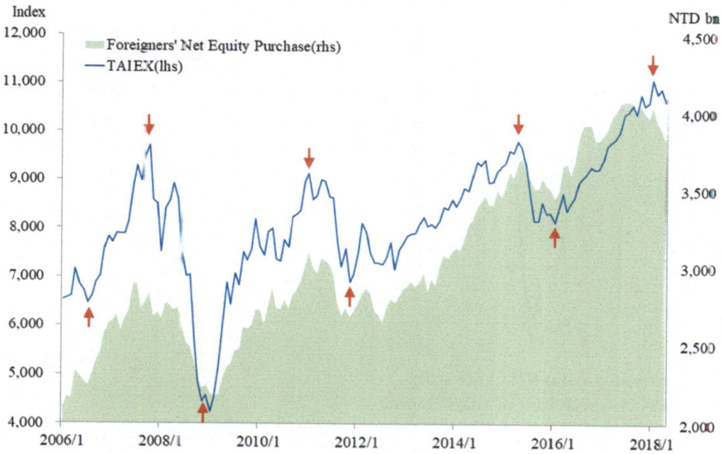

Fig. 5.3 Foreigners' net equity purchase and Taiwan Stock Exchange Weighted Index. *Source* Financial Supervisory Commission (Taiwan), Bloomberg

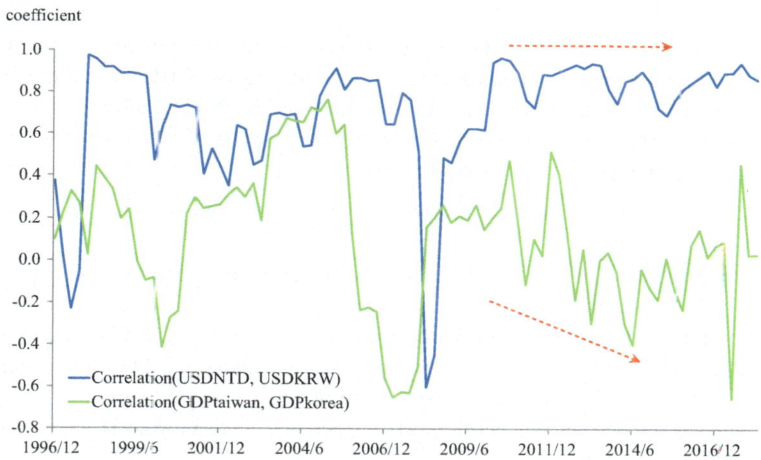

Fig. 5.4 Exchange rate correlation between NT dollar and Korea won, and GDP growth correlation between Taiwan and South Korea.
Source Bloomberg

reflect the actual economic situation of Taiwan. Thus, it is easy to observe the two-way fluctuations of the NTD exchange rate over longer periods of time, instead of one-direction NTD appreciation or depreciation. Moreover, Taiwan has been moving towards more balanced international trade, and providing domestic residents with wider access to overseas investment.

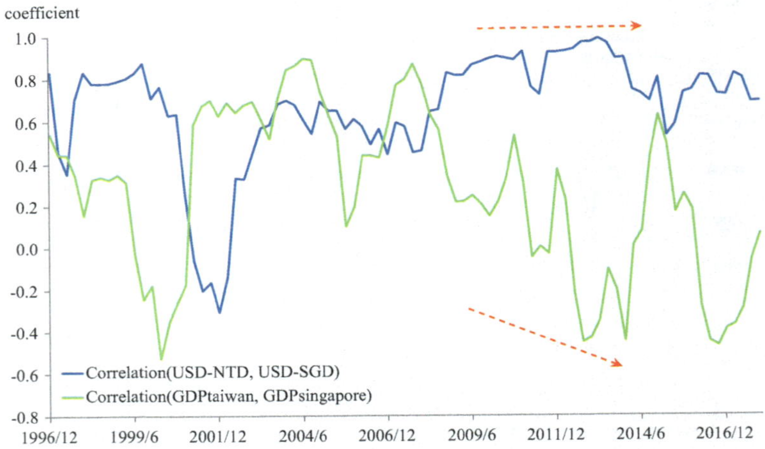

Fig. 5.5 Exchange rate correlation between NT dollar and Singapore dollar, and GDP growth correlation between Taiwan and Singapore.
Source Bloomberg

Taiwan welcomes cross-border capital flows for direct investment or portfolio investment but not currency speculation. In consequence, the CBC has adopted short-term policy tools to reduce speculation activities on the NTD exchange rate, especially after the 2008 global financial crisis. The key measures to curtail speculation on the NTD exchange rate are listed as follows[1]:

(1) The establishing of a large-amount foreign exchange transactions reporting system;
(2) The examination of the final destination of foreign inward remittances with their original declarations;
(3) The prohibition of foreign portfolio investors from making NTD time deposits;
(4) The raising of the required reserve ratio of foreigners' NTD demand deposits exceeding their 2010 balances from 25 to 90%;
(5) Requiring foreigners' cash collateral of securities borrowing and futures margins in foreign currencies;
(6) Lowering the cap of the combined position of non-deliverable NTD forwards and NTD exchange-rate options to one-fifth of the total foreign exchange position held by authorised banks; and
(7) Constraining the total amount that foreigners can invest in government bonds, corporate bonds, financial debentures, money market instruments and money market mutual funds to less than 30% of their net inward remittance.

Policy measures cited above effectively reduce volatilities of the NTD exchange rate, which fulfils one of the CBC's operational objectives, *i.e.* maintaining the stability of the internal and external value of the currency, as shown in Table 5.1.

[1]Detailed foreign exchange regulations of the CBC can be accessed at https://www.cbc.gov.tw/ct.asp?xItem=857&CtNode=481&mp=2.

Table 5.1 Volatilities of selected exchange rates

	Nominal effective exchange rates				(%)
	NTD	KRW	SGD	JPY	EUR
2008–2012	3.27	8.17	1.87	9.10	4.95
2013–2017	2.39	4.95	1.78	7.63	4.14
	Exchange rates against USD				(%)
	NTD	KRW	SGD	JPY	EUR
2008–2012	5.70	14.81	7.46	10.53	12.88
2013–2017	4.16	8.25	5.00	9.44	7.81

Volatilities here are average annualised monthly standard deviations of exchange rates movements.
Source Bloomberg

The stability of the NTD exchange rate is highly praised by international rating agencies, for example, Moody's, S&P, Fitch, etc. In addition, empirical studies, for example, Lin et al. (2012), prove that the NTD exchange rate shows anti-inflationary and counter-cyclical characteristics.

5.4 The CBC's Policy: Dynamic Stability of the NTD Exchange Rate

As financial liberalisation and de-regulation continue unabated, mostly occurring in the advanced economies, financial transactions have essentially determined exchange rates and the 2008 global financial crisis worsened this situation. During this global financial crisis, the advanced economies introduced unconventional monetary policies, for example, quantitative easing and their spillover effects caused massive capital inflows to flood the emerging market economies. Figure 5.6 shows that the daily average ratio of world trade value to foreign exchange turnover has consistently declined to a recent level of 3.3%.

After the 1998 Asian financial crisis, the emerging market economies, including Taiwan, have learned to increase their reserve holdings as a major buffer against

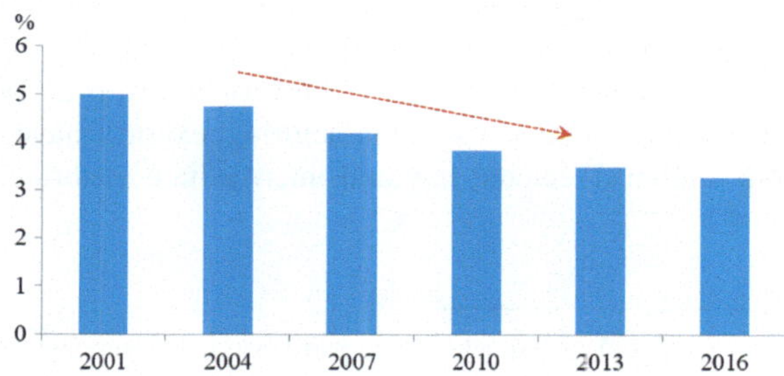

Fig. 5.6 Ratio of world trade value to foreign exchange turnover (daily average).
Source BIS, WTO

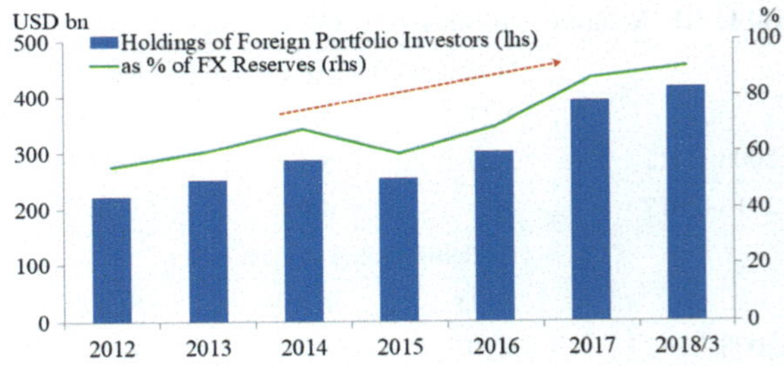

Fig. 5.7 Holdings of foreign portfolio investors. *Source* Central Bank of the Republic of China (Taiwan)

Fig. 5.8 Taiwan's saving rate and investment rate. *Source* Directorate General of Budget, Accounting and Statistics (Taiwan)

external shocks, particularly short-term capital flows. Even though Taiwan's reserves amounted to 452 billion USD at the end of 2017, the ratio of foreigners' portfolio investments to Taiwan's foreign exchange reserves has moved to a record high level of 91%, as depicted in Fig. 5.7. Moreover, Taiwan heavily relies on imported energy, lacks IMF membership and reserve currency status, and holds a great degree of openness, all of which make Taiwan maintain a high level of reserves. As a result, conventional measures of reserve adequacy, for example, import coverage, are not adequate in the current environment.

After the 2008 global financial crisis, the rising current account surplus in Taiwan sent a worrying signal to the Taiwanese authorities, as shown in Fig. 5.8. It is because this higher current account surplus is attributed to the excess savings of domestic firms, *i.e.* more savings and less investment. The government is striving to address this issue by channelling domestic funds towards infrastructure investment in order to help to improve the internal and external balances, which cannot simply be solved by the exchange rate. Furthermore, Fig. 5.9 shows that Taiwan's global value chain (GVC) participation ratio[2] is as high as 67.6%, with foreign value-added (VA) content accounting for 43.6% of its exports. With high global value chain participation, Taiwan's manufacturing exports have significant demand for the importation of related raw and intermediate materials. A weak NTD would drive

[2]Explanation of global value chain participation measurement can be found at: https://www.wto.org/english/res_e/statis_e/miwi_e/countryprofiles_e.htm.

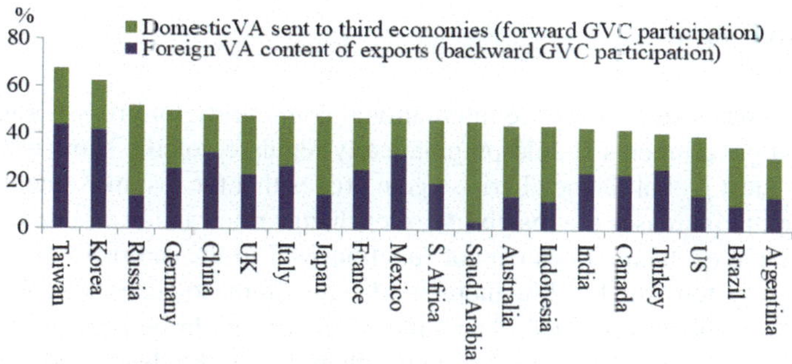

Fig. 5.9 Global value chain participation ratio.
Source OECD-WTO TiVA database

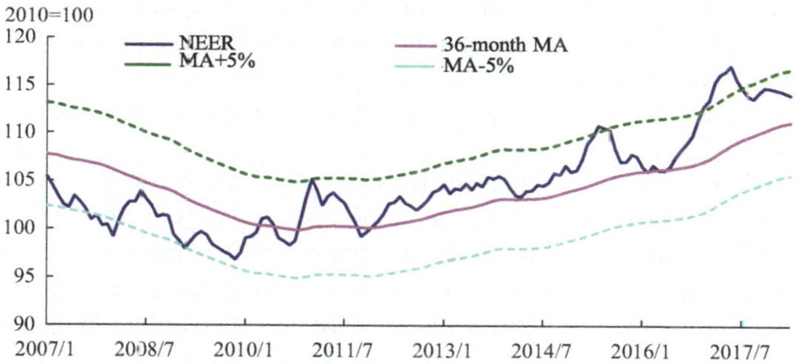

Fig. 5.10 Nominal effective exchange rate of the NT dollar.
Source BIS

the prices of Taiwan's imported intermediate goods up, which would not benefit its exports. Thus, the CBC makes no attempt to depreciate the NTD exchange rate.

For small open economies such as Taiwan, the exchange rate is one of the most important channels through which economic activities are affected. The CBC adopts a leaning-against-the-wind[3] policy to smooth out excess volatility in the NTD without any attempt to turn the market around. The CBC has been consistent in its exchange-rate policy, which is to ensure the dynamic stability of the NTD exchange rate, not to gain an unfair trade advantage. For years, the nominal effective exchange rate (NEER) of the NTD has broadly stayed within the range of a plus/minus 5% change in its 36-month moving average, demonstrating dynamic stability (Fig. 5.10).

[3]In economic terms, "leaning-against-the-wind" refers to a counter-cyclical policy where monetary authorities take action to reduce excess price movements.

5.5 Conclusion

The current consensus among the international community for cross-border capital flows is that governments should pragmatically regulate volatile short-term capital flows. The latest global financial crisis again proves that the fast movement of international capital increases the instability of exchange rates and even throws them in disorder. When exchange rates cannot function well in the international monetary and financial system, the local financial market and domestic economy of emerging markets will be badly impacted. This kind of impact could be persistent for quite a long time, and would generally be greater than that in the developed economies. Due to the harmful side effects of cross-border capital flows, international organisations suggest that governments should properly manage their financial accounts in order to reduce currency fluctuations. The 2011 Trade and Development Report of UNCTAD even supported government intervention in currency markets as one of the policy options available to prevent exchange-rate misalignment. Moreover, two IMF policy papers published in 2012 and 2013 proposed a policy framework for capital-flow management to assist governments in coping with unstable cross-border capital flows.

Because of the 2008 global financial crisis, the central banks of the major advanced economies have pursued unconventional monetary policies, one after the other, such as quantitative easing, and zero or even negative policy rates to stimulate their domestic economies. These policies have, on the other hand, created mass international capital flows to the emerging markets. To prevent overheating in local credit markets and future capital flight brought about by the international capital inflows, many of these emerging market economies were forced to accumulate their foreign exchange reserves as a buffer. Moreover, for better capital-flow management, a spectrum of measures is provided by international organisations, including, but not limited to, the reserve requirement for local currency deposits held by non-residents, limits on the net open foreign currency positions of banks, limits on the ratio of banks' foreign currency loans and securities to foreign currency borrowing, capital requirements for foreign currency loans and bank derivatives, levies on banks' non-deposit foreign liabilities, etc.

It is found that non-residential capital flows can strongly influence the local financial market in Taiwan, and that the authorities have taken the advice of international organisations by implementing the appropriate macro-prudential policies to lessen the negative impact of volatile capital flows. The outcome shows that the spillover effect from the major developed economies' unconventional monetary policies is successfully limited in the local financial market and domestic economy of Taiwan. The effectiveness of the policies has been recognised by the international community. For example, the United Nations Economic and Social Commission for Asia and the Pacific, in its official document, has praised the policies designed to manage capital flows since 2009 in Taiwan, and Rodrik (2010) described this as a notable achievement.

Rey (2017) pointed out that the spillover effect from the monetary policies adopted by large economies results in global financial cycles, so that even a floating exchange-rate regime cannot guarantee monetary policy independence. As financial transactions have become a dominant factor for exchange-rate determination, it is more difficult to resolve domestic structural issues via the exchange-rate channel. The CBC applies the rule of "leaning-against-the-wind" to reduce the volatility of the NTD exchange rate, and the technique of big data to enhance capital-flow management. By following the rule of "leaning-against-the-wind", proposed in Grauwe and Grimaldi (2006), the CBC smoothes the trend path of the NTD exchange rate to maintain its dynamic stability. By employing the technique of big data, the CBC is able to analyse high-frequency data, which generates extra information on short-term capital flows. The CBC has been observing cross-border capital flows closely, and principally lets the NTD exchange rate be determined by the market. However, if irregular factors (such as massive inflows or outflows of short-term capital), as well as seasonal ones, lead to excess volatility and disorderly movements in the NT dollar exchange rate, with adverse implications for economic and financial stability, the CBC will, in accordance with its mandate, step into maintain an orderly foreign exchange market.

References

Bluedorn, J., et al. (2013). *Capital flows are fickle: anytime, anywhere* (IMF Working Paper).

Chen, Q., et al. (2015). *Financial crisis, us unconventional monetary policy and international spillovers* (IMF Working Paper).

Dadush, U., & Stancil, B. (2011). The capital flow conundrum. *VoxEU*.

Grauwe, D., & Grimaldi, M. (2006). *The exchange rate in a behavioral finance framework*. Princeton, NJ: Princeton University Press.

International Monetary Fund. (2012, November 14). Policy paper: The liberalization and management of capital flows—An institutional view.

International Monetary Fund. (2013, April 25). Policy paper: Guidance note for the liberalization and management of capital flows

Lin, Y., Zhang, Z., Chen P. (2012). Empirical study on reaction function of new Taiwan dollar and its comparison with other Asian Currencies. *Central Bank of the Republic of China Quarterly Bulletin*. Spring

Rey, H. (2015) *Dilemma not Trilemma: The global financial cycle and monetary policy independence* (NBER Working Paper).

Rey, H. (2017, June 25). The global financial system, the real rate of interest and a long history of boom-bust cycles. BIS Andrew Crockett Memorial Lecture.

Rodrik, D. (2010, March 11). The end of an era in finance. *Project Syndicate*.

United Nations Conference on Trade and Development. (2011, September 6). Trade and Development Report.

United Nations Conference on Trade and Development. (2013, September 12). Trade and Development Report.

United Nations Development Programme. (2009, November). The global financial crisis and the Asia-Pacific region.

United Nations Economic and Social Commission for Asia and the Pacific. (2011, May 5). Economic and social survey of Asia and the Pacific.

Chapter 6
Monetary Policy Implementation in Singapore

Hwee Kwan Chow and Fot Chyi Wong

Abstract Singapore's monetary policy is centred on the management of the Singapore dollar exchange rate against a trade-weighted basket of currencies of its major trading partners. The Monetary Authority of Singapore (MAS) manages the Singapore dollar exchange rate within an undisclosed band by intervening in the foreign exchange market as necessary through the purchase and sale of the Singapore dollar against the US dollar. In the context of a small open economy, the choice of the exchange rate as an instrument of monetary policy implies that the domestic interest rate is endogenous. As such, MAS' money-market operations are aimed at ensuring adequate liquidity in the banking system to meet the demand of banks for reserves both for the statutory reserve requirement as well as for the settlement of interbank transactions. Given Singapore's status as an international financial centre and the attendant high degree of capital mobility, monetary policy operations in Singapore—involving foreign exchange interventions and money-market operations—are not without their challenges. This chapter discusses the key features in the market mechanisms and operating procedures that enhance the effective implementation of monetary policy operations in Singapore.

6.1 Implementing an Exchange Rate-Centred Monetary Policy

Singapore's monetary policy is centred on the management of the Singapore dollar exchange rate. The Monetary Authority of Singapore (MAS) uses the exchange rate instead of the interest rate as its policy-operating tool because the former is deemed

---

H. K. Chow (✉) · F. C. Wong
Singapore Management University, Singapore, Singapore
e-mail: hkchow@smu.edu.sg

F. C. Wong
e-mail: fcwong@smu.edu.sg

F. Rövekamp et al. (eds.), *Monetary Policy Implementation in East Asia*, Financial and Monetary Policy Studies 51,
https://doi.org/10.1007/978-3-030-50298-0_6

to be more effective than the latter for stabilising inflation.[1] Adopting the exchange rate instead of the benchmark interest rate as an intermediate monetary policy target reflects the trade-dependent nature of the Singapore economy, which is susceptible to imported inflation. In any case, Singapore has a high degree of capital mobility due to its role as an international financial centre, thereby limiting its control on the domestic interest rate. Wilson (2015) provides a discussion on the rationale of Singapore's unusual exchange rate-centred monetary policy.

Monetary policy operations are carried out by managing the Singapore dollar under a basket–band–crawl system (Khor et al. 2004). Under this system, the MAS monitors the value of the domestic currency in terms of a currency basket (S$NEER: Singapore dollar nominal effective exchange rate) which is a trade-weighted average of the currencies of Singapore's major trading partners and competitors. The constituent currencies represent the various sources of imported inflation and competition in the export markets, while the basket weights are periodically updated to reflect their degree of importance. In the light of Singapore's diversified trade pattern, targeting a currency basket, instead of a single foreign currency, results in a more stable effective exchange rate, and also helps to mitigate volatility in international foreign exchange markets.

As part of its monetary policy operations, the MAS intervenes in the foreign exchange market through the purchase and sale of the Singapore dollar against the US dollar (USD). The MAS monitors the S$NEER closely, even though it "refrains from intervening unnecessarily and allows market forces to determine the level of the Singapore dollar within the policy band" (MAS 2013). The S$NEER is allowed to float within a prescribed policy band, and the MAS avoids intervening within the band except to smooth out unwarranted short-term volatility which could impair confidence in the currency. However, when the S$NEER approaches or exceeds the boundaries of the policy band, the MAS may carry out interventions to "lean against the wind" to prevent the band limits from being breached.[2]

Using a band not only provides flexibility in managing the exchange rate but also allows for short-term fluctuations in foreign exchange markets. The band itself is adjustable and allowed to "crawl" to reflect underlying fundamentals and prevent the misalignment of the Singapore dollar. Indeed, market participants tend to keep within the band, as they are mostly convinced of the MAS' commitment to enforce it, which, in turn, reduces the need for frequent intervention operations. This is mainly

[1]Chow (2005) shows through a monetary VAR model that the exchange rate plays a much bigger role than the interest rate as a source of macroeconomic fluctuations in Singapore. Furthermore, Chow et al. (2014) uses a DSGE-VAR model to show the exchange rate system has a comparative advantage over Taylor rule in terms of lowering inflation volatility as export price shocks are a major source of Singapore's output volatility.

[2]Neither the constituent currencies nor their assigned weights in the basket are publicly disclosed, in order to avoid destabilising speculation. Having some constructive ambiguity would ensure that currency speculators do not have a one-way bet on the Singapore dollar as it approaches the upper or lower band limits. This is particularly important, as speculative pressures tend to build up quickly near the band limits, thereby hampering the effectiveness in foreign exchange interventions (see Chiu 2003; Fernholz 2015, among others).

due to the institutional framework in Singapore which supports the monetary policy. In particular, the ethos of fiscal prudence and rectitude of the Singapore government, as seen by the persistent government budget surpluses over the years, has not only freed the MAS from the "pressures" of the need to finance the government but has also complemented monetary policy in countering inflation (Asher et al. 2015). Moreover, Singapore holds a large pool of foreign reserves ready for use to defend the domestic currency. The high level of reserves standing at 285.3 billion USD at the end of 2018 helps to reinforce the effectiveness and credibility of Singapore's exchange-rate policy.

The three policy levels accorded by the basket–band–crawl system are adjustments to the policy band in terms of its slope, level and width. The three types of adjustments are shown in Figs. 6.1a to c respectively. The S$NEER Index is computed in terms

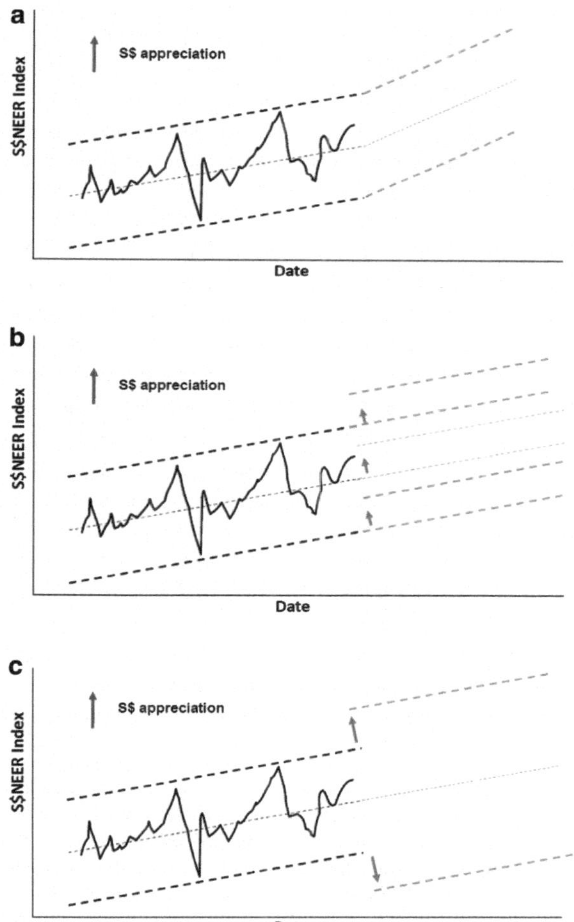

Fig. 6.1 **a** Tightening monetary policy by steepening the slope of policy band. **b** Tightening monetary policy by shifting the level of policy band upwards. **c** Allowing more flexibility by increasing the width of policy band

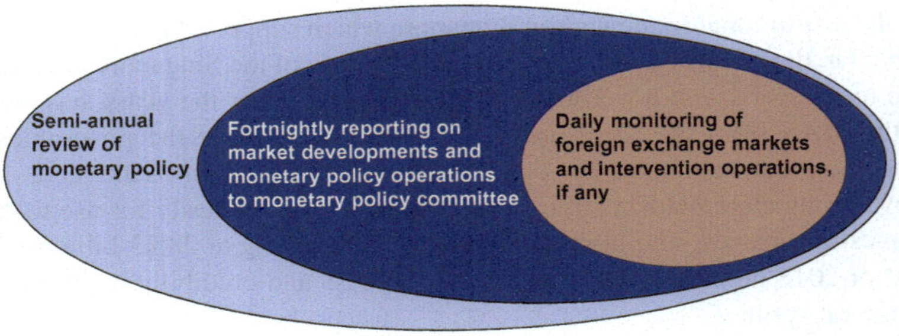

Fig. 6.2 Implementation cycle of monetary policy

of the various foreign currencies *per* Singapore dollar so that an increase in its value corresponds to an appreciation of the home currency. Consequently, a steepening of the slope reflects a tightening of monetary policy, while a flattening of the slope reflects a loosening of monetary policy. The slope of the band is normally adjusted when the MAS assesses that the trajectory of economic activity in the medium term is changing gradually. In comparison, adjustments are usually made to the level when developments cause an abrupt shift in the path of economic activity. Meanwhile, changes to the width of the band are called for when developments cause a short-term increase in S$NEER volatility. While the first two types of adjustments to the slope and level of the policy band tend to be undertaken only during the MAS semi-annual monetary policy formulation cycle, changes to the bandwidth are sometimes made off-cycle such as at the onset of a financial crisis.

Figure 6.2 depicts the implementation cycle of Singapore's monetary policy. The MAS monitors the S$NEER daily, carrying out foreign exchange interventions as and when necessary. A report on these and money-market operations, as well as an update on domestic and regional market developments, is provided to the monetary policy committee, which normally meets once a fortnight. The central bank reviews its monetary-policy stance twice a year. An adjustment or a combination of adjustments to the slope, level and width of the policy band may be made when they are deemed appropriate after an economic assessment of the Singapore economy and its outlook.

While the actual level, slope and width of the policy band are not publicly disclosed, a monetary policy statement (MPS) is issued specifying the changes made. For instance, we consider the excerpts of two of the MAS' monetary policy statements. First, the April 2009 statement illustrates the loosening of the monetary-policy stance following the onset of the global financial crisis:

> Amidst the global downturn and continuing stresses in world financial markets, external and domestic inflationary pressures are dissipating. Meanwhile, the domestic economy is likely to remain below potential till a decisive recovery is seen in Singapore's export markets. In our assessment, the current level of the S$NEER is appropriate for maintaining domestic price stability over the medium term, taking into account the prospects for growth in the Singapore economy. MAS will therefore re-centre the exchange rate policy band to the prevailing level of the S$NEER, while keeping the zero percent appreciation path. The width of the band will remain unchanged. The Singapore economy continues to be anchored by sound fundamentals

and a resilient financial system. There is therefore no reason for any undue weakening of the Singapore dollar. (MAS 2009)

Second, the April 2010 statement illustrates the tightening of monetary policy in response to the sharp economic rebound in 2010:

The Singapore economy has rebounded from the downturn and is expected to continue on its firm recovery path given the more favourable global economic outlook. At the same time, inflationary pressures are likely to pick up, driven by rising global commodity prices as well as some domestic cost factors. MAS will therefore re-centre the exchange rate policy band at the prevailing level of the S$NEER. Further, we will shift the policy band from that of a zero percent appreciation to one of modest and gradual appreciation. There will be no change to the width of the policy band. MAS will continue to be vigilant over developments in the external environment and their impact on the domestic economy, and stands ready to curb excessive volatility in the S$NEER. (MAS 2010)

To increase public and market participants' understanding on why a particular monetary stance is adopted, the monetary policy statement is accompanied by the publication of the *Macroeconomic Review*, which is the flagship publication of the MAS, that details the prevailing economic and market conditions and their outlook. Other transparency measures include the publication of the *Survey of Professional Forecasters*, which provides the private sector forecasts of the economy which the MAS collates every quarter as well as the annual *Financial Stability Review*. Enhancing the public and market participants' understanding of its assessment of the economy and the stability of the financial system no doubt influences market expectations on future monetary stance. In addition, the MAS publishes monographs that explain the monetary policy framework and its *modus operandi* in monetary policy operations.

6.2 Assessing Banks' Demands for Reserves

In the context of a small open economy, the use of the exchange rate as an instrument of monetary policy implies that the domestic interest rate is endogenous. This follows from the open economy trilemma which says that, at most, two of the three policy goals of monetary independence, to wit, exchange-rate stability and capital account openness, can be fully achieved at the same time (Obsfeld et al. 2004). Singapore's domestic interest rate is thus determined by foreign interest rates and investor expectation about the future value of the Singapore dollar. Hence, unlike most other countries, money-market operations in Singapore are not aimed at targeting the level of domestic interest rates, but at ensuring the appropriate amount of liquidity in the banking system. Sufficient liquidity is required in the money market for banks and financial institutions to meet their demand for reserves, such as to comply with statutory reserve requirement, as well as to settle inter-bank transactions.

As bank reserves levels fall to nearly 3% of their liabilities base, which is the required reserve ratio known as the minimum cash balance (MCB), their demand for reserves will naturally become interest-rate insensitive, in which case, a small error

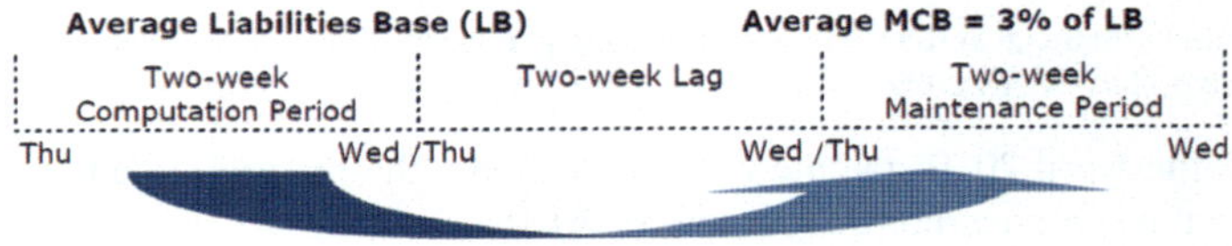

Fig. 6.3 Computation and maintenance of minimum cash balance

in the actual supply of reserves to the banking system can result in wide swings in interest rates and market uncertainty. It is thus pertinent for the MAS to have a reasonably accurate estimate of the demand for funds in the banking system. Several design elements of the minimum cash balance help to mitigate such interest-rate volatility. For instance, average provisions for reserve requirements and a lagged maintenance period (as opposed to a contemporaneous maintenance period) for computation of required reserves are used; see Fig. 6.3.

As illustrated in Fig. 6.3, a bank's minimum cash balance is computed as 3% of its 2-week lagged qualifying liabilities average over the previous 2 weeks. In this way, there is less uncertainty regarding the demand for the reserves required by banks. Further, a bank's cash balance ratio at the end of the day is allowed to fluctuate between 2% to 4% of the qualifying liabilities over the 2-week maintenance period. This helps to reduce interest-rate volatility by increasing the price elasticity of bank demand for reserves. In fact, it has been observed that banks tend to hold higher levels of cash balances at the beginning of the maintenance period so as to avert being short of cash at the end of the period. Moreover, to alleviate intraday liquidity pressures, the full amount of the cash balance is also allowed to settle intraday payments.

Apart from knowing the bank base demand for required reserves, the MAS needs to assess the overall level of the bank reserves held with the central bank. This, in turn, is determined by the net impact of the five main processes affecting the level of bank reserves held with the MAS. They are (i) currency issuance; (ii) foreign exchange intervention and maturity of past money-market operations; (iii) net issuance and redemption of Singapore Government Securities (SGS), MAS Bills and Singapore Savings Bonds; (iv) government fund transfers; and (v) Central Provident Fund (CPF) board contributions and withdrawals. Interest-rate volatility can be mitigated by the MAS having full knowledge of these major factors affecting bank reserves and, hence, money-market liquidity. For instance, currency issuance and redemption are part of the operations carried out by the Currency Department which is within the MAS. Every morning, the gross amounts of currency to be issued to and returned by the banks that day, and thereby its net effect on bank reserve balances, are taken into account as an autonomous money-market factor in MAS' money-market operations.[3]

[3]Each Singapore dollar currency note in circulation must be at least 100% backed by foreign assets under the Currency Act. When the stock of Singapore currency notes in MAS' currency holding is above (below) the desired level, the MAS will remove (add) currency notes from (into) circulation and simultaneously transfer an equivalent amount of foreign currency at prevailing exchange rates from (to) the Currency Fund.

Meanwhile, direct intervention operations are undertaken by the MAS' Monetary Management Department. When the MAS sells the Singapore dollar in the foreign exchange market to loosen the monetary stance, this results in a net increase in the reserves of those banks with which it transacts the foreign exchange. Conversely, there will be a decrease in the bank reserves when the MAS buys the Singapore dollar to tighten monetary policy. The net effect of the foreign exchange intervention on bank reserves, together with the maturity of past money-market operations, form part of the MAS' consideration of all the money-market factors affecting the overall level of bank reserves.

As the fiscal agent of the government, the MAS manages the issuance of SGS T-bills and bonds on behalf of the government, according to an advance calendar of issuance.[4] The fiscal role was extended, from 2015, to include the issuance of Singapore Savings Bonds, which are a special type of SGS, designed to make them accessible and suitable to individual investors. Both SGS and Singapore Savings Bonds are issued on behalf of the government and, hence, are the liabilities of the government. Since July 2010, the MAS has started issuing short-term bills of its own. These are the MAS' liabilities to augment its arsenal of the three money-market instruments (described in the next section) for monetary management. The effect on bank reserves arising from the net issuance and redemption of SGS, Singapore Savings Bonds and MAS Bills is also taken into account when MAS conducts its money-market operations.

The other two key determinants affecting the level of bank reserves held with the MAS are related to public sector operations. The Account-General Department, acting as the government's accountant, would normally transfer funds between its accounts with commercial banks and its deposit account with the MAS. Meanwhile, the CPF is a government-administered compulsory savings scheme[5] that transfers its net proceeds from its accounts with the banks to the MAS for the subscription of non-marketable Singapore Government Securities issued specifically for the CPF. Importantly, the MAS builds close working relations and communications with these two external agencies. Both the Accountant-General and the CPF Board inform the MAS in advance of fund transfers between their accounts both with the banks and with the MAS.[6]

---

[4]Despite its persistent budget surpluses, the Singapore government issues SGS bills and bonds to meet banks' demand for a safe and liquid asset. Moreover, the SGS serve the important purpose of establishing a viable and liquid benchmark yield curve for the pricing of corporate bonds.

[5]Both employees and employers are required to contribute a certain percentage of the employees' income to the CPF. Funds are disbursed to members by the CPF Board under various withdrawal schemes.

[6]The budget surpluses and positive net contribution to CPF (contributions net of withdrawals) in the past and present exert contractionary effect on the liquidity in the economy which, if not countered, would put upward pressure of the Singapore dollar (Chow 2017). These have therefore necessitated MAS to "lean against the wind" by intervening in the foreign exchange market to moderate the appreciation of the Singapore dollar.

With a good assessment of the net impact of the key factors on bank reserves, the MAS is thus better able to determine the amount of its money-market operations, thereby mitigating any interest-rate volatility.

6.3 Conducting Money-Market Operations

As its counterparties for foreign exchange intervention and money-market operations, the MAS appoints and works with a dozen or so local and foreign banks, called the primary dealers. These include the three major local banks: *DBS Bank Ltd.*, *Oversea-Chinese Banking Corporation Ltd.* and *United Overseas Bank Ltd.*, as well as the following foreign banks: *Australia and New Zealand Banking Group Limited*; the *Bank of America National Association*; *Barclays Bank Plc*; *BNP Paribas*; *Citibank N.A.*; *Credit Suisse AG*; *Deutsche Bank AG*; *Malayan Banking Bhd*; *Standard Chartered Bank*; and *The Hongkong and Shanghai Banking Corporation Limited*. The primary dealers have the obligation to underwrite SGS auctions and make two-way prices for SGS in order to develop a more active SGS market. As a *quid pro quo*, they enjoy exclusive dealing with the MAS in its foreign exchange and money-market operations.

Over the years, the longest maturity of the SGS market has progressively been extended from 10 years, first to 15 years, then to 20 and now to 30 years. Measures taken to enhance the SGS market include having greater transparency with the publication of an advanced calendar of SGS issuance for the year ahead (MAS 2012). For instance, Fig. 6.4 is the SGS bonds issuance calendar for 2018. In this way, market participants know in advance the amount of SGS that will come on stream and can plan accordingly. In 2003, in line with the government bond auction format in the US and other developed countries, the auction format for the issuance of SGS was changed from multiple price to uniform-price auctions. This encourages greater participation in SGS auctions by relatively less informed investors, both retail and institutional, such as insurance companies. With less risk of the winner's curse and hence less bid-shading, the cost of SGS issuance can be expected to be lower.

The MAS conducts its daily money-market operations with the dozen or so SGS primary dealers. To provide greater certainty to the primary dealers, a broadcast is made to them at a fixed known time in the morning daily. The broadcast provides information on the details of the MAS' money-market operations for that day. These include the size of the operation; the direction on whether it is injecting or withdrawing liquidity from the banking system; the tenure, such as overnight, 1 week, 1 month and so on; and the money-market instrument that the MAS intends to use that day. Following the broadcast, the primary dealers will respond with their interest-rate quotations upon a fairly competitive basis.

The four main money-market instruments that the MAS uses in its money-market operations are direct borrowing or lending, foreign exchange swaps, SGS re-purchase agreements (repos) and MAS bills. We first consider the case where the MAS is withdrawing Singapore dollar liquidity from the banking system. This can be carried

Announcement Date	Auction Date	Issuance Date	Term	New/ Re-opening	Issue Code/ ISIN Code	Maturity Date
22 Jan 2018	29 Jan 2018	1 Feb 2018	5-yr	New	N518100E/TBA	1 Feb 2023
19 Feb 2018	26 Feb 2018	1Mar 2018	30-yr	Reopen	NA16100H/SG31A7000004	1 Mar 2046
20 Mar 2018	27 Mar 2018	2 Apr 2018	2-yr	Reopen	N15100S/SG31A7000000	1 Apr 2020
19 Apr 2018	26 Apr 2018	2 May 2018	10-yr	New	NX18100A/TBA	1 May 2028
21 May 2018	28 May 2018	1 Jun 2018	5-yr	Reopen	NX13100H/SG3260987684	1 Jun 2023
20 Jun 2018	27 Jun 2018	2 jul 2018	20-yr	Reopen	NZ16100X/SG31A90000002	1 Jul 2036
20 Jul 2018	27 Jul 2018	1 Aug 2018	7-yr	Reopen	NX16100F/SG31A8000003	1 Aug 2026
21 Aug 2018	29 Aug 2018	3 Sep 2018	2-yr	Reopen	NY05100N/SG792892054	1 Sep 2020
19 Sep 2018	26 Sep 2018	1 Oct 2018	15-yr	Reopen	NZ11100V/SG3261987691	1 Sep 2033

Fig. 6.4 2018 SGS bonds issuance calendar

out in one or a combination of the following ways. First, direct borrowing which refers to the MAS borrowing Singapore dollars from banks upon an uncollateralised and interest-paying basis. Second, the MAS enters a foreign exchange swap contract, in which it buys Singapore dollars in the first leg and simultaneously sells the Singapore dollars on the date of maturity. Third, MAS borrows Singapore dollars using SGS as collateral, which it will receive upon maturity when it returns the Singapore dollars upon an interest-paying basis. Fourth, the MAS can issue more MAS bills than maturing ones. Conversely, to inject liquidity into the banking system, the MAS can conduct the aforementioned operations in the reverse direction.

In addition to the daily money-market operations used for the broad liquidity management of the banking system, the MAS provides a re-financing (deposit) facility to supply (absorb) funds. This is to fine-tune liquidity in the banking system and to minimise the intraday volatility in overnight interest rates. Eligible financial institutions that participate in the MAS' *Real-Time Gross Settlement* system have access to MAS' *Intraday Liquidity Facilities*. This facility allows financial institutions to obtain Singapore dollar funds upon an intraday basis through repo transactions involving SGS and MAS Bills, with appropriate haircuts. Similarly, the MAS' *Standing Facility*, which is a two-sided discount window, allows participants to deposit Singapore dollar funds with, or borrow Singapore dollar funds against, eligible collateral from the MAS upon an overnight basis. Besides mitigating interest-rate volatility, this facility strengthens market confidence by providing the assurance that financial institutions can meet their liquidity needs during periods of market stress. Over the years, the pool of eligible collateral has been expanded to enhance the MAS liquidity-provisioning framework.

6.4 Summary

In summary, Singapore's monetary policy implementation framework comprises exchange-rate management and liquidity management. While the former is executed through foreign exchange intervention, the MAS conducts money-market operations and provides liquidity facilities for the latter. Over time, the MAS has enhanced market mechanisms and operating procedures to increase the effectiveness of its monetary operations in Singapore. These include the introduction of transparency measures as well as close communications with primary dealers and key players determining fund flows in the banking system. Further, interest-rate volatility in the money market is mitigated through various design features for bank maintenance of minimum cash balance and the provision of several liquidity facilities. Finally, the development of the SGS market and Singapore's institutional framework also helps support monetary-policy operations. In particular, Singapore has maintained a conservative fiscal policy as well as a commitment to low inflation and a strong Singapore dollar over the years that contributes to the building of the MAS' credibility.

References

Asher, M. G., Bali, A. S., & Kwan, Y. K. (2015). Public financial management in Singapore: Key characteristics and prospects. *Singapore Economic Review, 60*(3), 1550032 (18 pages).

Chiu, P. (2003). Transparency versus constructive ambiguity in foreign exchange intervention. *BIS Working Papers* No. 144, Bank for International Settlements.

Chow, H. K. (2005). A VAR analysis of singapore's monetary transmission mechanism. In T. H. Winston Koh & R. S. Mariano (Eds.), *The Economic Prospects of Singapore* (pp. 274–298). Singapore: Addison Wesley.

Chow, H. K., Lim, G. C., & McNelis, P. (2014). Monetary regime choice in Singapore: Would a Tayor rule outperform exchange-rate management? *Journal of Asian Economics, 30*(1), 63–81.

Chow, H. K. (2017). Domestic liquidity conditions and monetary policy in Singapore. In F. Rovekamp, M. Balzand, & H. G. Hilpert (Eds.),*Cash in East Asia* (pp. 65–76). Springer: Cham.

Fernholz, R. T. (2015). Exchange rate manipulation and constructive ambiguity. *International Economic Review, 56*(4), 1323–1348.

Khor H. E., Robinson, E. & Lee, J. (2004). Managed floating and intermediate exchange rate systems: The Singapore experience. *MAS Staff Paper* No. 37.

Monetary Authority of Singapore. (2009). Monetary policy statement on 14 April 2009. *Macroeconomic Review*, Volume VIII, Issue 1, April.

Monetary Authority of Singapore. (2010). Monetary policy statement on 14 April 2010. *Macroeconomic Review*, Volume IX, Issue 1, April.

Monetary Authority of Singapore. (2012). Singapore's bond market guide. *MAS Monograph.*

Monetary Authority of Singapore. (2013). Monetary policy operations in Singapore. *MAS Monograph.*

Obstfeld, M., Shambaugh, J. C., & Taylor, A. M. (2004). *The Trilemma in History: Tradeoffs among Exchange Rates, Monetary Policies, and Capital Mobility*. Mimeo: University of California, Berkeley, Dartmouth College, March.

Wilson, P. (2015). Monetary policy and financial sector development. *Singapore Economic Review, 60* (3), 1550031 (25 pages).

Part III
Dimensions of Monetary Policy Implementation

Chapter 7
The Asset Purchase Programmes of the ESCB in the Courts

Helmut Siekmann

Abstract The planned and the realised asset purchase programmes of the European System of Central Banks (ESCB) have spurred highly controversial debates. Not least, legal concerns have been expressed, mainly in Germany. A score of decisions of the German Federal Constitutional Court and two judgments of the Court of Justice of the European Union have so far been the result. A novelty here was the reference to the European court for a preliminary ruling by the highest German Court in 2014. A second referral took place in 2017. The final judgment of the German Federal Constitutional Court (GFCC) on the purchases in the framework of the Public Sector Purchase Programme (PSPP) of 5 May 2020 could not be considered any more; for a first evaluation see Siekmann, Europäische Zeitschrift für Wirtschaftsrecht, p. 491–500.

7.1 Introduction

In the course of the crisis, originating in 2007, the European System of Central Banks (ESCB) has acted several times to support the EU Member States and the banking systems in financial distress, mainly by purchasing debt instruments and granting loans at extraordinarily favourable conditions: Covered Bond Purchase Programmes (CBPP), Securities Market Programmes (SMP), Long-Term Refinancing Operations (LTRO), and Targeted Longer-Term Refinancing Operations (TLTRO). The outright acquisition and holding on the balance sheets were (later) subsumed under the term "asset purchase programmes". These measures were accompanied by a substantial

H. Siekmann (✉)
Institute for Monetary and Financial Stability (IMFS), Goethe University Frankfurt, Frankfurt am Main, Germany
e-mail: siekmann@jur.uni-frankfurt.de

F. Rövekamp et al. (eds.), *Monetary Policy Implementation in East Asia*, Financial and Monetary Policy Studies 51,
https://doi.org/10.1007/978-3-030-50298-0_7

lowering of the quality standards[1] for the (outright) purchase of securities or for accepting them as collateral,[2] and by allowing national central banks to provide liquidity to basically insolvent banks in their home countries through the granting of "Emergency Liquidity Assistance" (ELA).[3] Within this context, the Agreement on Net Financial Assets (ANFA), which was kept confidential for quite some time, has to be mentioned. The agreement was concluded between the national central banks (NCBs) of the euro area and the European Central Bank (ECB), which together form the Eurosystem. The agreement sets rules and limitations for the holdings of financial assets which are related to national tasks of the NCBs. Although, in applying these measures, already a substantial amount of sovereign debt from selected Member States found its way eventually onto the balance sheets of the Eurosystem and a major part of the banking system was protected from bankruptcy; the public outcry was relatively mild and the judiciary did not object in substance, as will explicated in detail in Sect. 7.4.

This changed in 2012 with the announcement of a new, more comprehensive programme for purchasing sovereign debt instruments of Member States whose currency is the euro, the Outright Monetary Transactions (OMT), addressed in Sect. 7.5. This programme was heavily criticised both from the economic and the legal side. Although it was never executed, the announcement, as such, spurred discernible effects. Lastly, in 2015, there followed both the announcement and the implementation of another instrument, the Extended Asset Purchase Programmes ((E)APP)[4]—colloquially labelled as Quantitative Easing (QE).[5] Functionally, the Quantitative Easing of the ESCB has been in place since the initiation of the CBP

---

[1]For example, Regulation (EC) No. 1053/2008 of the ECB of 23 October 2008 (ECB/2008/11), O.J. 2008/L 282/17; Decision of the ECB of 14 November 2008 on the implementation of regulation EZB/2008/11 (ECB/2008/15); Guideline of the ECB of 21 November 2008 (ECB/2008/18), O.J. 2008/L 314/14; Guideline of the ECB of 10 December 2009 (ECB/2009/24), O.J. 2009/L 330/95; Decision of the ECB on temporary measures relating to the eligibility of marketable debt instruments issued or guaranteed by the Greek Government (ECB/2010/3), O.J. 2010/L 117/102; Decision of the ECB on temporary measures relating to the eligibility of marketable debt instruments issued or guaranteed by the Irish Government (ECB/2011/4), O.J. 2011/L 94/33; Decision of the ECB on temporary measures relating to the eligibility of marketable debt instruments issued or guaranteed by the Portuguese Government (ECB/2011/10), O.J. 2011/L 182/31; Decision of the ECB of 14 December 2011 (ECB/2011/25), O.J. 2011/L 341/65; Decision of the ECB of 5 March 2012 (ECB/2012/3), O.J. 2012/L 77/19. For more details, see Hoffmann (2015, pp. 63–156).

[2]Re-purchase agreements (repos) are used as collateral with the effect that the underlying debt stays in place. Like any other lien, it yields the creditor two debtors, whereas in an outright (final) purchase the same debtor remains by himself and only the creditor is finally replaced.

[3]See, for details, Hoffmann (2015, pp. 179–235).

[4]Sometimes simply labelled as Asset Purchase Programme (APP). For a comprehensive overview of the measures and their rationale as seen from the ECB, see Hammermann et al. (2019).

[5]*Sachverständigenrat* [German Council of Economic Experts] (2015), at no. 278; Jędrzejowska-Schiffauer and Schiffauer (2016, p. 203), Ludwigs (2017, p. 3564), Ruffert (2019, p. 181). The term "quantitative easing"—and perhaps the policy itself—was probably coined by the Bank of Japan as early as in 2001, see Shirakawa (2002).

in 2009, but only received its label from the APP in 2014. It is still in place—with a short interruption at the end of 2018.[6]

Specifically, its Public Sector Purchase Programme (PSPP) raised severe objections and lead to another court case which was finally decided by the Court of Justice of the European Union (CJEU) at the end of 2018,[7] and is now pending in the German Federal Constitutional Court (GFCC) for a final decision.

The multitude of these measures is part of the "unconventional" policy of the central banks. The list of these "non-standard" measures, as the European Central Bank calls them, includes the following measures: fixed-rate, full-allotment liquidity provision, expansion of list of assets eligible as collateral, longer-term liquidity provision, liquidity provision in foreign currencies, changes in the required reserve ratio, and outright purchases of specific debt securities.[8]

7.2 The Programmes

The following chapter provides a brief description of the facts about the various programmes.

7.2.1 *Covered Bond Purchase Programmes (CBPP)*

Covered bonds are issued by commercial institutions backed by specific secured debt. In principle, these debts serve to finance investments in real estate, but also extend to government entities, ships and aircraft. They are secured by specific types of lien. Although the collateral securing the underlying loans is now almost never a mortgage—in the legal sense of the word—any more, they are often called "mortgage-backed securities". Despite some similarities, they do not have to meet the (relatively) strict pre-requisites of a German *Pfandbrief*; the wide variety of deviation depends, however, on the national statutory rules.

On 7 May 2009, the Governing Council of the ECB decided to initiate the first programme to purchase covered bonds with the aim of promoting the ongoing decline in money market term rates, to ease the funding conditions of banks and enterprises, to encourage credit institutions to maintain and expand their lending to clients, and

[6]For details, see, below, Sect. 7.6.

[7]CJEU judgment of 11 December 2018, Case C-493/17 [Heinrich Weiss and Others], ECLI:EU:C:2018:1000, Press Release No. 192/18, http://curia.europa.eu/juris/document/document.jsf?docid=208741&mode=req&pageIndex=1&dir=&occ=first&part=1&text=&doclang=EN&cid=7557213.

[8]See Giannone et al. (2011), Philippine Cour-Thimann and Bernhard Winkler (2012), eidem, (2013), International Monetary Fund (2013), Helmut Siekmann (2013a, p. 145 et seq.), Jäger and Grigoriadis (2017), Varghese and Zhang (2018).

to improve liquidity in the segment of the market they are used for (CBPP1).[9] It was started in July 2009 and ended after one year, when the nominal amount of €60 billion had—as planned—been attained, on 30 June 2010. The Eurosystem intends to hold the assets bought under this programme until maturity.[10]

More than one year later, in November 2011, a second Covered Bond Purchase Programme (CBPP2) was initiated.[11] This programme ended—as planned—on 31 October 2012, when it reached a nominal amount of €16.4 billion. Again, the Eurosystem intends to hold the purchased assets until maturity.[12]

A third Covered Bond Purchase Programme (CBPP3) was set up in October 2014, with a planned duration of two years.[13] The objective of this programme was the restoration of the transmission mechanism of monetary policy and to bring the inflation rate closer to the intended 2%.[14] The ECB considered the transfer of the (conventional) monetary policy measures into the financial markets to be impaired. Contrary to the original plans, CBPP3 was "extended until the end of December 2017, or beyond, if necessary",[15] and was kept in force; as part of the (Expanded) Asset Purchase Programme ((E)APP).

The legality of these Covered Bond Programmes was rarely questioned even though they contained a (small) fraction of loans to government entities—mainly municipalities—and their agencies. At the beginning of the programme, the money provided in this way by the central banks was sterilised in its effects on monetary policy, i.e. it was not to contribute to the growth of money volume.

7.2.2 Securities Market Programme (SMP)

On 10 May 2010, the central banks of the Eurosystem started purchasing securities in the context of the Securities Markets Programme (SMP) "with regard to addressing

[9]Decision of the European Central Bank of 2 July 2009 on the implementation of the covered bond purchase programme, ECB/2009/16, Official Journal 2009/L 175/18 recital 2.

[10]ECB press release of 30 June 2010.

[11]Decision of the European Central Bank of 3 November 2011 on the implementation of the second covered bond purchase programme, ECB/2011/17, Official Journal 2011/L 297/70.

[12]ECB: https://www.ecb.europa.eu/mopo/implement/omt/html/index.en.html.

[13]Decision of the European Central Bank of 15 October 2014 on the implementation of the third covered bond purchase programme, ECB/2014/40, Official Journal 2014/L 335/22.

[14]Ibid., recital 2.

[15]Decision (EU) 2017/101 of the European Central Bank of 11 January 2014 amending Decision ECB/2014/40 on the implementation of the third covered bond purchase programme (ECB/2017/2), Official Journal 2017/L 53/53, recital 4; amended by Decision (EU) 2017/1360 of the European Central Bank of 18 May 2017 amending Decision ECB/2014/40 on the implementation of the third covered bond purchase programme (ECB/2017/14), Official Journal 2017/L 190/22.

the severe tensions in certain market segments" which had been hampering the monetary policy transmission mechanism, according to the view of the ECB.[16] The official decision of the Governing Council ensued a few days later.[17]

According to Article 1 of the decision, debt instruments issued by central governments or the public entities of Member States whose currency is the euro, or debt issued by private entities incorporated in the euro area, were eligible to be purchased. In fact, only securities from a small group of states, mainly from Southern Europe, were bought. In this way, the interest rates in these states were lowered in a highly selective manner. This procedure spurred legal concerns because of its nature as a selective subsidy for some state budgets.

Following a Governing Council decision on 6 September 2012 to initiate outright monetary transactions, the SMP was terminated. The Eurosystem intends to hold the purchased securities to maturity.[18]

7.2.3 Long-Term Refinancing Operations (LTRO)

The first two longer-term refinancing operations (LTRO) provided about one trillion euro to commercial banks at favourable interest rates for three years.[19] As they were aimed at improving bank lending to the euro area non-financial private sector and do not comprise the purchase of assets, they are not considered further in this context.

A similar programme was resumed in 2014 as the Targeted Longer-Term Refinancing Operations. A first series of was announced on 5 June 2014 (TLTRO I)[20] and a second series on 10 March 2016 (TLTRO II).[21] Due to the apparent slowdown of growth, the Governing Council decided, on 7 March 2019, to launch another

---

[16]ECB: https://www.ecb.europa.eu/mopo/implement/omt/html/index.en.html.

[17]Decision of the European Central Bank of 14 May 2010 establishing a securities markets programme (ECB/2010/5), Official Journal 2010/L 124/8.

[18]ECB: https://www.ecb.europa.eu/mopo/implement/omt/html/index.en.html.

[19]ECB press release of 8 December 2011: https://www.ecb.europa.eu/press/pr/date/2011/html/pr111208_1.en.html.

[20]ECB press release of 5 June 2014; Targeted Longer-Term Refinancing Operations, Updated modalities; Decision (EU) 2014/34 of the European Central Bank of 29 July 2014 on measures relating to targeted longer-term refinancing operations; Decision (EU) 2015/299 of the European Central Bank of 10 February 2015 amending Decision ECB/2014/34 on measures relating to targeted longer-term refinancing operations (ECB/2015/5): https://www.ecb.europa.eu/ecb/legal/1002/1014/html/index-tabs.en.html; Decision (EU) 2016/811 of the European Central Bank of 28 April 2016 amending Decision ECB/2014/34 on measures relating to targeted longer-term refinancing operations (ECB/2016/11), Official Journal 2016/L 132/129.

[21]ECB press release of 10 March 2016: https://www.ecb.europa.eu/press/pr/date/2016/html/pr160310_1.en.html; Decision (EU) 2016/810 of the European Central Bank of 28 April 2016 on a second series of targeted longer-term refinancing operations (ECB/2016/10), Official Journal 2016/L 132/107; Decision (EU) 2016/1974 of the European Central Bank of 31 October 2016 amending Decision (EU) 2016/810 on a second series of targeted longer-term refinancing operations (ECB/2016/30), at: https://www.ecb.europa.eu//ecb/legal/1002/1014/html/index-tabs.en.html.

programme directed at financing investments in the private sector (TLTRO III).[22] It consisted of seven targeted longer-term refinancing operations, each with a maturity of three years, starting in September 2019. Borrowing conditions in these operations can be as low as the interest rate on the deposit facility.[23] The ECB describes them as

> Eurosystem operations that provide financing to credit institutions for periods of up to four years.[24] They offer long-term funding at attractive conditions to banks in order to further ease private sector credit conditions and stimulate bank lending to the real economy.[25]

They endeavour to enhance monetary policy transmission into the "real" economy, but contain elements of a central planning of economic activities. Since they do not encompass the purchase of assets, they can be dismissed here as well.

7.2.4 Outright Monetary Transactions (OMT)

In the summer of 2012, the ECB designed a programme for the outright purchase of sovereign bonds. It was aligned to replace the Securities Markets Programme and to integrate the ongoing Covered Bonds Programme (CBPP3). One of its main traits was again the narrow limitation of the bonds that could be purchased. Under certain pre-requisites, bonds from selected Member States in need were to be eligible. The purchase was to be performed by the ESCB.

On 6 September 2012, the Governing Council of the ECB took decisions on a number of technical features regarding the Eurosystem's outright transactions in these secondary sovereign bond markets (OMT). These technical features were publicised on the same day, but the programme has never been activated to date.

The purchases were to be conducted in a specific framework which required adherence to a European support programme ("conditionality"), with no *ex-ante* quantitative limits ("coverage"), accepting same creditor treatment with private creditors ("creditor treatment"), and promising full "sterilisation" of the created liquidity, i.e. suppressing the growth of the money volume by the purchases, and enhanced "transparency".[26]

This announcement spawned a lively debate on its economic suitability, political feasibility and—particularly—on its legality. From the legal concerns, several

[22] ECB press release of 7 March 2019; Decision (EU) 2019/1311 of the European Central Bank of 22 July 2019 on a third series of targeted longer-term refinancing operations (ECB/2019/21), Official Journal 2019/L 204/100; Decision (EU) 2019/1558 of the European Central Bank of 12 September 2019 amending Decision (EU) 2019/1311 on a third series of targeted longer-term refinancing operations (ECB/2019/28), Official Journal 2019/L 238/2.

[23] https://www.ecb.europa.eu/mopo/implement/omo/tltro/html/index.en.html.

[24] For the first series two years, ECB press release of 5 June 2014.

[25] https://www.ecb.europa.eu/mopo/implement/omo/tltro/html/index.en.html.

[26] Press release of 6 September 2012; ECB Monthly Bulletin September 2012, p. 8; Siekmann (2015, p. 103, 119–121).

lawsuits were brought against the programme before the German Federal Constitutional Court (*Bundesverfassungsgericht*), with petitioners also asking the court to issue temporary injunctions with the goal of halting the ratification process.[27]

7.2.5 Expanded Assets Purchase Programme (EAPP)

On 19 November 2014, the Governing Council of the ECB took the decision to implement the Asset-Backed Securities Programme (ABSPP),[28] and, on 15 October 2014, to continue with the purchase of covered bonds, CBPP3.[29] The difference is marked by the type of collateral for the underlying claim, as has been outlined above in Sect. 7.2.1. Whereas covered bonds are in general backed by highly specific claims which are collateralised by a selected number of liens (originally mortgages), asset-backed securities can be backed by any kind of asset. The ESCB has, however, restricted them by specified quality requirements for them to be eligible for a purchase. The Programme is also open for the purchase of securities issued by private corporations.

These programmes were already to be seen as part of a comprehensive bond buying programme[30] in the manner of the quantitative easing carried out by the Bank of Japan, the Bank of England, the Swiss National Bank, and the Federal Reserve System. The focus of APP was, however, directed on the outright purchase of sovereign debt from all Member States whose currency is the euro and not only from one sovereign entity as in the other countries. On 4 March 2015, the Governing Council of the ECB adopted a decision on a secondary markets Public Sector Asset Purchase Programme (PSPP).[31] It was complemented by the Decisions of the European Central Bank of 1 June 2016[32] on the implementation of the Corporate Sector Purchase Programme (CSPP).

The main objective of the programmes was to lower interest rates on a large scale and to bring inflation closer to the planned target. They were not designed to support

---

[27] Siekmann and Wieland (2013), eidem (2014a, b), Siekmann (2015, p. 103 et seq.) with references.

[28] Decision (EU) 2015/5 of the European Central Bank of 19 November 2014 on the implementation of the asset-backed securities purchase programme (ECB/2014/45), Official Journal 2015/L 1/4, as amended by the decision of the European Central Bank of 10 September 2015 (Decision [EU] 2015/1613).

[29] See notes 13 and 15 above.

[30] Decision of the Governing Council of the ECB of 22 January 2015 on an Expanded Asset Purchase Programme (ECB/2015/10), press release of 22 January 2015. The decision itself was not publicised.

[31] Decision [EU] 2015/774, Official Journal 2015/L 121/20; amended by the Decision of the European Central Bank of 5 November 2015 (Decision [EU] 2015/2101), Official Journal 2015/L 301/106, the Decision of the European Central Bank, (Decision [EU] 2015/2464), Official Journal 2015/L 344/1, the Decision of the European Central Bank of 18 April 2016 (Decision [EU] 2016/702), Official Journal 2016/L 121/24, and the Decision (EU) of the European Central Bank of 11 January 2017, Official Journal 2017/L 16/51.

[32] Decision [EU] 2016/948, Official Journal 2016/L 157/28.

selected Member States with interest rates deemed to be exaggerated, as was the case of the SMP, which had been terminated. The Covered Bond Purchase Programme was re-started as CBPP3 and integrated in the new strategy.

The Expanded Asset Purchase Programme (EAPP) (or Asset Purchase Programme (APP)) is thus a framework containing four elements:[33]

- Third Covered Bond Purchase Programme (CBPP3);
- Asset-Backed Securities Purchase Programme (ABSPP);
- Public Sector Purchase Programme (PSPP);
- Corporate Sector Purchase Programme (CSPP).

After four recalibrations, the Governing Council of the ECB decided on 13 December 2018 to end the net purchases under the APP in December 2018, and announced that it "intends to continue reinvesting, in full, the principal payments from maturing securities purchased under the APP for an extended period of time past the date when it starts raising the key ECB interest rates, and in any case for as long as necessary to maintain favourable liquidity conditions and an ample degree of monetary accommodation".[34] In fact, the net purchases were halted at the end of 2018.

On 12 September 2019, the ECB Governing Council decided that "net purchases will be restarted under the Governing Council's asset purchase programme (APP) at a monthly pace of €20 billion as from 1 November 2019". No limitation for its duration was given. Instead, the Governing Council expressed its expectation that they would be continued "as long as necessary to reinforce the accommodative impact of its policy rates, and to end shortly before it starts raising the key ECB interest rates".[35]

7.3 Economic Facts

For a sound evaluation of the purchase programmes of the ESCB, it is useful to build on the evolving economic facts.

[33] Details of the attribution according to the capital key (excluding Greece and Estonia) and the technical implementation of the purchases (bilateral trading, auctions, bids wanted in competition) are discribed by Hammermann et al. (2019, pp. 6–11); for details of the chronology, see the statement of the facts within the judgment of the GFCC of 18 July 2017, cases: 2 BvR 859/15, 2 BvR 1651/15, 2 BvR 2006/15, 2 BvR 980/16 [PSPP-referral], BVerfGE [Reports of Judgments of the Federal Constitutional Court] 146, 216 (223–240); English version available at: https://www.bundesverfassungsgericht.de/SharedDocs/Entscheidungen/EN/2017/07/rs20170718_2bvr085915en.html, margin nos. 4–23.

[34] https://www.ecb.europa.eu/mopo/implement/omt/html/index.en.html; for the recalibrations and other policy measures during that time, see Hammermann et al. (2019, p. 6).

[35] https://www.ecb.europa.eu/mopo/implement/omt/html/index.en.html.

Table 7.1 Composition and Outstanding Amounts (21 February 2013)

Issuer country	Outstanding amounts		Average remaining maturity (in years)
	Nominal amount (EUR billions)	Book value[a] (EUR billions)	
Ireland	14.2	13.6	4.6
Greece	33.9	30.8	3.6
Spain	44.3	43.7	4.1
Italy	102.8	99.0	4.5
Portugal	22.8	21.6	3.9
Total	**218.0**	**208.7**	**4.3**

Source ECB: http://www.ecb.europa.eu/press/pr/date/2013/html/pr130221_1.en.html
[a]The SMP holdings are classified as held-to-maturity and consequently valued at amortised cost

7.3.1 *Terminated Programmes*

7.3.1.1 Securities Markets Programmes

The last operation of the Securities Markets Programme took place on 10 June 2014. The present holdings are as follows:

SMP holdings[a]	
EUR	47,908 millions
Date	31 January 2020

[a]At amortised cost; see https://www.ecb.europa.eu/mopo/implement/omo/html/index.en.html

In view of the selectivity of the programme, which is of major legal concern, the composition of the holdings according to the country of origin of the debt is especially interesting. The numbers are from a time near the end of the programme (Table 7.1).

7.3.1.2 Covered Bond Purchase Programme 1

As of 31 January 2020, the holdings of the first Covered Bond Purchase Programme amount to EUR 1.58 bn.

7.3.1.3 Covered Bond Purchase Programme 2

The purchases of the second Covered Bond Purchase Programme took place both on the primary and the secondary market. The present holdings amount to EUR 2,911 bn.

Market	Primary	Secondary
EUR mil.[a]	**6,015**	10,375
Share[a]	36.70%	63.30%
Date	31 October 2012	

[a] At amortised cost; see https://www.ecb.europa.eu/mopo/implement/omo/html/index.en.html

7.3.2 *Asset Purchase Programme (APP)*

7.3.2.1 Volumes and Composition of Purchases

The net monthly purchases, i.e. total purchases minus redemption after maturity were—initially—terminated in December 2018. Their development is specified in the following compilation provided by the ECB:[36]

- €60 billion from March 2015 until March 2016;
- €80 billion from April 2016 until March 2017;
- €60 billion from April 2017 to December 2017;
- €30 billion from January 2018 to September 2018;
- €15 billion from October 2018 to December 2018;
- €20 billion from November 2019 on.

As can be derived from Fig. 7.1, the lion's share of all purchases has been acquired as part of the PSPP, hence it is debt stemming from the public sector. It was mainly this part of the programme which led to the legal concerns and court cases.

The PSPP has spurred serious legal concerns, despite the fact that, in contrast to SMP and OMT, not only the bonds of selected Member States are bought, but also assets issued by the public sector of all Member States whose currency is the euro—with the exception of Greece. This means that, in principle, the whole currency area is targeted, in proportion to the national central bank's share of the capital of the ECB. Another striking difference is the risk distribution: 80% of the purchased assets remain on the balance sheet of the national central bank of the country in which they have been issued. Only 20% of the additional purchases were to be subject of a risk-sharing regime.[37]

[36] https://www.ecb.europa.eu/mopo/implement/omt/html/index.en.html; for an in-depth analysis of the APP as seen from the ECB, see Hammermann et al. (2019), Sect. 7.4; for its effect on the market liquidity see: ibid., p. 10: "detrimental effects… at most transitory"; Jurkšas et al. (2018). Since the purchases were executed with counterparties from a country different from the country of the acting national central bank, they affected the distribution of Target 2 balances.

[37] ECB press release of 22 January 2015; *Sachverständigenrat* [German Council of Economic Experts] (2015), at no 308: 12% issued by European institutions, 8% bought be the ECB itself, later changed to 10% and 10%. Moreover, not more than 33% of a bond in circulation should be bought. For a description of the details, see *Deutsche Bundesbank* (2018, pp. 17–20).

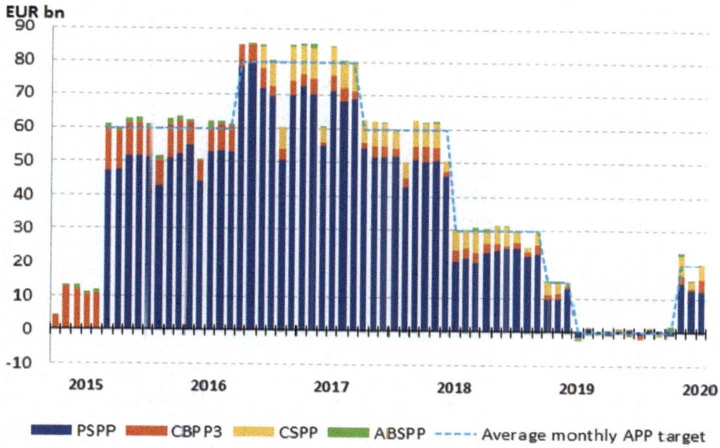

Fig. 7.1 Net monthly purchases.
Source ECB, https://www.ecb.europa.eu/mopo/implement/omt/html/index.en.html

7.3.2.2 Redemption and Re-Investment

Although at the time when the net purchases were reduced to zero at the end of 2018, no time limit for the "re-investment" of the redeemed debt was in sight. The demand for these securities by the central banks would have continued—so far indefinitely—and influence interest rates even when the net purchases were zero. Whether it can be pursued following the original distribution is not, however, out of question.

Table 7.2 shows the anticipated amounts which will be "re-invested" during the 12 months following January 2020.

7.3.3 Consolidated Volume and Asset Structure

The size and the composition of the consolidated balance sheet of the Eurosystem can be derived from Figs. 7.2 and 7.3. Until the (temporary) halt at the end of 2018, the purchases had accumulated €2.6 trillion on the consolidated balance sheet of the Eurosystem. The composition of the holdings mirrors the predominance of purchases of debt originating from the public sector. They have a share of approximately 81.84% of all holdings under the Asset Purchase Programme. What is also noteworthy here is the development over time.

Both the size and the structure of the balance sheet of a central bank reflect all the policy decisions that have been taken in the past. For a long time, these balance sheets attracted little interest, especially from academic research. This changed dramatically from the moment that the measures of the central banks to fight the crisis of 2007 and to mitigate its effects came to the public interest. Now, it is a keenly debated

Table 7.2 Expected monthly redemption amounts for the APP over a rolling 12-month horizon (in EUR millions)

Month	ABSPP	CBPP3	CSPP	PSPP	APP
Jan 20[a]	**1,034**	**3,660**	**2,503**	**24,761**	**31,958**
Feb 20	451	1,184	565	4,596	6,796
Mar 20	614	2,546	2,467	13,151	18,778
Apr 20	937	1,722	1,115	30,368	34,142
May 20	384	371	2,153	12,511	15,419
Jun 20	667	2,916	1,312	13,082	17,977
Jul 20	703	3,588	1,156	28,681	34,128
Aug 20	357	1,621	74	423	2,475
Sep 20	528	3,427	961	18,930	23,846
Oct 20	798	6,496	850	23,629	31,773
Nov 20	583	5,183	2,431	22,509	30,706
Dec 20	494	302	696	8,871	10,363
Jan 21	1,265	4,968	2,253	15,064	23,550

[a]Actual redemption, based upon month-end data
ECB estimates in italics. Figures may not add up due to rounding. Figures are preliminary and may be subject to revision
Note Realised redemptions may differ from estimated redemptions
Source ECB, https://www.ecb.europa.eu/mopo/implement/omt/html/index.en.html

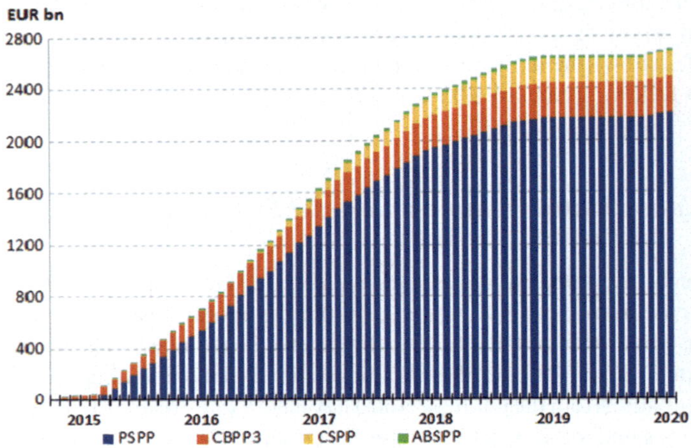

Fig. 7.2 Holdings.
Source ECB, https://www.ecb.europa.eu/mopo/implement/omt/html/index.en.html

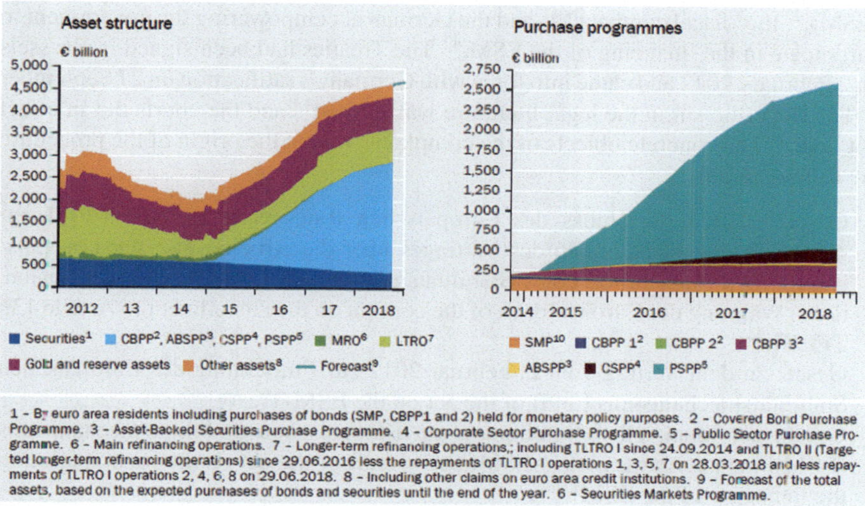

Fig. 7.3 Asset structure and purchases of the Eurosystem.
Source Sachverständigenrat [German Council of Economic Experts] (2018), Chart 48

question whether the balance sheet—in the first place, its size—is a policy tool, and/or whether it should be used as one. With its growing size, the political pressure increases to use it for the host of "grand" objectives outside of monetary policy, such as financing a "green" revolution, fighting climate change, or a cut in government debt, thus potentially endangering central bank independence, as, for example, can be seen in the U.S., Italy, and Turkey.

7.4 Challenging the Legality of the Securities Market Programme (SMP)

In Germany, the legality of the Securities Market Programme (SMP) was challenged[38] in the course of the legal fight against the insertion of paragraph 3 in Article 136 TFEU,[39] the treaty establishing a permanent European Stability Mechanism

---

[38]Constitutional complaints (*Verfassungsbeschwerden*) on the part of several German citizens and some members of the (elected chamber of the) German federal parliament (*Deutscher Bundestag*). The parliamentary fraction of the party *Die Linke* lodged proceedings as an *Organstreit*. This is a special type of action in the GFCC, which is open basically only to high level organs of the German governmental system to resolve disputes between them on constitutional questions.

[39]European Council Decision of 25 March 2011 amending Article 136 of the Treaty on the Functioning of the European Union with regard to a stability mechanism for Member States whose currency is the euro (2011/199/EU), Official Journal 2011/L 91/1; entering into force only on 1

(ESM),[40] the "fiscal compact",[41] and the German act empowering the government to participate in the financing of the ESM.[42] The Treaties had been signed in Brussels on 2 February 2012 and came into force with Germany's ratification on 27 September 2012. The criticism in the legal literature was limited[43] and the courts did in effect not object. The concrete objects of the complaint were at the origin of the procedure the following bills:

- Gesetz zu dem Beschluss des Europäischen Rates vom 25. März 2011 zur Änderung des Artikels 136 des Vertrages über die Arbeitsweise der Europäischen Union hinsichtlich eines Stabilitätsmechanismus für die Mitgliedstaaten, deren Währung der Euro ist [draft of the consent on the amendment to Article 136 TFEU];[44]
- Gesetz zu dem Vertrag vom 2. Februar 2012 zur Einrichtung des Europäischen Stabilitätsmechanismus [draft of the act on the ESM-Treaty];[45]
- Gesetz zur finanziellen Beteiligung am Europäischen Stabilitätsmechanismus (ESM-Finanzierungsgesetz—ESMFinG) [draft of the act on the participation in the financing of the ESM];[46]
- Gesetz zu dem Vertrag vom 2. März 2012 über Stabilität, Koordinierung und Steuerung in der Wirtschafts- und Währungsunion [draft of the act on the "fiscal compact"].[47]

May 2013 due to the lengthy ratification procedure following Article 49 para. 6 TEU; see Richter (2015, margin no. 7), and Häde (2016 margin no. 9).

[40]Treaty establishing the European Stability Mechanism between the Kingdom of Belgium, the Federal Republic of Germany, the Republic of Estonia, the Republic of Ireland, the Hellenic Republic, the Kingdom of Spain, the French Republic, the Italian Republic, the Republic of Cyprus, the Grand Duchy of Luxembourg, Malta, the Kingdom of The Netherlands, the Republic of Austria, the Portuguese Republic, the Republic of Slovenia, the Slovak Republic, and the Republic of Finland, replacing the temporary European Financial Stability Facility (ESFS) and the European Financial Stabilisation Mechanism (EFSM), BGBl II of 18 September 2012, 981 (German consenting act), 983 (treaty proper).

[41]Treaty on Stability, Co-ordination and Governance in the Economic and Monetary Union between the Kingdom of Belgium, the Republic of Bulgaria, the Kingdom of Denmark, the Federal Republic of Germany, the Republic of Estonia, the Republic of Ireland, the Hellenic Republic, the Kingdom of Spain, the French Republic, the Italian Republic, the Republic of Cyprus, the Republic of Latvia, the Republic of Lithuania, the Grand Duchy of Luxembourg, Hungary, Malta, the Kingdom of The Netherlands, the Republic of Austria, the Republic of Poland, the Portuguese Republic, Romania, the Republic of Slovenia, the Slovak Republic, the Republic of Finland and the Kingdom of Sweden of 2 March 2012, BGBl II, 1006 (German consenting act), 1008 (treaty).

[42]Gesetz zur finanziellen Beteiligung am Europäischen Stabilitätsmechanismus (ESM-Finanzierungsgesetz—ESMFinG) of 13 September 2012, BGBl I, 1918.

[43]Supporting, or at least not questioning, the "unconventional" measures: Herrmann (2010a), idem (2010b), critical: Martin Seidel (2010), idem (2011), Frenz and Ehlenz (2010, p. 334), Siekmann (2013a, pp. 144–149).

[44]BTDrucks 17/9047.

[45]BTDrucks 17/9045.

[46]BTDrucks 17/9048.

[47]BTDrucks 17/9046.

A previous direct complaint had been dismissed by the General Court of the EU (GCEU). The ensuing appeal was rejected by the Court of Justice of the EU (CJEU) in 2012.[48]

7.4.1 Temporary Injunction

The petitioners asked the German Federal Constitutional Court (GFCC) to issue a temporary injunction prohibiting the German President from signing the statutes and thereby consenting and transforming the treaties into German Law. On 10 July 2012, the Court heard oral arguments, which is quite unusual for a petition to issue a temporary injunction.

In its judgment of 12 September 2012, it dismissed the petition but imposed several conditions for ratification.[49] It emphasised, however, already even in this temporary procedure, that Article 123 TFEU, which explicitly prohibits only the "direct" purchase of government debt instruments, would also prohibit its circumvention by purchases on the secondary market. The Court also expressed substantial concerns about the financing of the ESM, but left the final assessment to the principal proceedings.[50]

The ratification procedure was also not halted at European level, although a case was already pending before the CJEU, which had been referred to it by the High Court of the Republic of Ireland (*Pringle*) which called into question the legality of establishing the ESM as well.[51]

7.4.2 Procedural Separation and Referral to the CJEU by the GFCC

In the course of the proceedings, the interest shifted increasingly to the OMT decision of the ECB,[52] which had not been part of the original petitions but was subsequently

[48]GCEU of 16 December 2011, Case T-532/11—*Städter* v *ECB*; CJEU of 15 November 2012, Case C-102/12 P.

[49]GFCC judgment of 12 September 2012, cases: 2 BvR 1390/12, 2 BvR 1421/12, 2 BvR 1438/12, 2 BvR 1439/12, 2 BvR 1440/12, 2 BvE 6/12, BVerfGE [Reports of Judgments of the Federal Constitutional Court] 132, 195 et seq.

[50]Ibid., at 274 (margin no. 189); ibid., at 268 (margin no. 174): "For an acquisition of government bonds on the secondary market by the European Central Bank aiming at financing the Members' budgets independently of the capital markets is prohibited as well, as it would circumvent the prohibition of monetary financing (…)."

[51]*Pringle* v *Government of Ireland* [2012] IEHC 296, court record number: 2012 3772 P, judgment of 17 July, specifically at para. 35.

[52]See Sect. 7.2.4 above.

treated extensively by the petitioners. Eventually, on 7 February 2014, the German Federal Constitutional Court announced the following:

- The charges concerning the OMT decision of the ECB of 6 September 2012 are separated from the other matters subject to adjudication: the amendment of Article 136 TFEU, the creation of a permanent support mechanism (ESM), and the "fiscal compact".[53]
- The proceedings with regard to the OMT decision are suspended and a list of questions with regard to its compatibility with EU law is referred to the CJEU for a preliminary ruling pursuant to Article 19 (3) letter b TEU, Article 267 (1) letters a and b TFEU.[54]
- A final decision on the part of the case which is not suspended will be pronounced on Tuesday, 18 March 2014.

7.4.3 GFCC Final Judgment I

As a result, the final judgment of the GFCC, delivered on 18 March 2014, dismissed the remaining complaints as mainly inadmissible and the rest as unfounded.[55] Only some minor reservations concerning primarily the prerogatives of the *Bundestag* to participate in crucial questions regarding the new support mechanism in plenary session were made, which could be resolved if the statutory rules were interpreted in a specific way which respected German constitutional law.[56]

Prior to this decision, the CJEU had already accepted, in its *Pringle* decision, the compatibility of the amendment of Article 136 TFEU, the Treaty establishing the ESM, and the "Fiscal Compact" with the EU law. For this, the Court advocated a narrow demarcation of monetary policy,[57] so that the measures under scrutiny as instruments, following the law of nations, would not infringe the exclusive competences of the EU in view of monetary policy. To the assessment of the CJEU, they belong to the domain of economic policy reserved almost completely to the Member States, pursuant to Article 119 TFEU.[58]

---

[53]GFCC judgment of 17 December 2013, cases: 2 BvR 1390/12, 2 BvR 1421/12, 2 BvR 1438/12, 2 BvR 1439/12, 2 BvR 1440/12, 2 BvR 1824/12, 2 BvE 6/12 [ESM separation order], BVerfGE [Reports of Judgments of the Federal Constitutional Court] 134, 357.

[54]GFCC, judgment of 14 January 2014, cases: 2 BvR 2728/13, 2 BvR 2729/13, 2 BvR 2730/13, 2 BvR 2731/13, 2 BvE 13/13, English version available at: http://www.bundesverfassungsgericht.de/SharedDocs/Entscheidungen/EN/2014/01/rs20140114_2bvr272813en.html?nn¼5403310, [OMT-referral], BVerfGE [Reports of Judgments of the Federal Constitutional Court], 134, 366; pronounced on 7 February 2014.

[55]GFCC judgment of 18 March 2014, cases: 2 BvR 1390, 1421, 1438, 1439, 1440, 1824/12, 2 BvE 6/12, BVerfGE [Reports of Judgments of the Federal Constitutional Court], 135, 317 et seq.

[56]Ibid., margin nos. 176, 223–242.

[57]Judgment of 27 November 2012, Case C-370/12, Pringle, collection of Cases 2012, S. I-0000, ECLI:EU:2012:756, margin nos. 53–57.

[58]Ibid., margin no. 60.

7.5 The Battle Over the Outright Monetary Transactions (OMT)[59]

5,216 citizens of the EU filed complaints against the OMT announced by the ECB in 2012. The General Court of the EU (GCEU) denied admissibility and held that the applicants were not directly concerned, in the sense of the fourth paragraph of Article 263 TFEU, since OMT needed additional legal instruments and decisions subject to the discretion of the ECB in order to become operative. The appeal against this decision had no success.[60]

7.5.1 The First Referral of the German Federal Constitutional Court

In its seminal decision of 14 January 2014, the GFCC referred the case concerning the OMT decision of the ECB to the CJEU with questions concerning EU law.[61] This petition for a preliminary ruling was based upon Article 19(3)(b) TEU and Article 267(1)(a) TFEU, and was the first in the history of the GFCC.

In contrast to its (final) judgment on the complaints spawned by the Securities Markets Programme, delivered two months later, the German Federal Constitutional Court expressed serious doubts about the compatibility of the ECB's decision on the OMT with EU law, and consequently with German constitutional law. In this (referral) decision, the Securities Markets Programme was (again) not considered, although it was still active. The consistency of this approach has to be questioned, since the SMP contains some of the same legally critical traits as the OMT; foremost, the selectivity of the purchased assets, which implies the risk of arbitrarily subsidising the interest which a government has to pay for its debt, and thus seriously distorting market reactions for an unsound fiscal policy. As a result, market forces, which secure fiscal discipline, are likely to be impaired.

7.5.1.1 Admissibility

The Court admitted the complaints and petitions even though actual purchases had not been executed (1) and the control of the acts of an organ of the EU is, in principle, not the task of the GFCC (2).[62] As a justification for its handling of the complaints,

[59]Parts of this section are adopted from Siekmann (2015)

[60]Order of the General Court of 10 December 2013, Case T 492/12—*Sven A. von Storch and Others* v *ECB*, ECLI:EU:T:2013:702, Official Journal 2014/C 45/32; CJEU, Order of the Court in Case C-64/14P of 30 April 2015, Press release of 30 April 2015, available at: https://curia.europa.eu/jcms/upload/docs/application/pdf/2015-04/cp150048en.pdf.

[61]GFCC OMT-referral (note 54 above).

[62]Siekmann (2015, p. 105), with further references.

the Court resorted to its judicature on a reserved *ultra vires* (transgression of competences) control and the defence of the "constitutional identity" (*Verfassungsidentität*) of Germany (2). In the end, however, the court referred the case to the CJEU for preliminary rulings on several questions of EU law.[63]

1. *Preventive Legal Protection*

In effect, the GFCC granted in this (extraordinary) case a preventive legal protection.[64] The Court underlined that "the case-law of the Federal Constitutional Court recognises that preventive legal protection can [...] be warranted in constitutional complaint proceedings in order to avoid consequences that cannot be corrected [references]".[65] In its opinion, the admissibility "does not depend on whether the OMT Decision can already be understood as an act with an external dimension within the meaning of Art. 288 s. 4 TFEU, or only as the announcement of such an act". Instead, it held that "the requirements for granting preventive legal protection are met".[66] The complainants had satisfactorily stated "that the execution of the OMT Decision could lead to such consequences that could not be corrected" even if "further implementing measures" were required. The OMT decision of the ECB was to the assessment of the Court sufficiently specified. It could be executed "at any time and within a very short timeframe".[67] Somewhat surprisingly, it did not refer to the real effects which might be caused, in fact, by the simple announcement of the measure.

2. *Ultra vires Act and Constitutional Identity*

The Court affirmed and elaborated its demarcation of competences between the CJEU and the GFCC, which had been outlined in a series of prior decisions. This demarcation of competences is, in theory, clear: the CJEU is to ensure that, in the interpretation and application of the Treaties, the EU law is observed, whereas the German Court is installed as the "guardian" of the German Federal Constitution (*Grundgesetz*), the "Basic Law". The domain of the CJEU is the enforcement of EU law; that of the GFCC, the compliance with the German Basic Law. In particular, the GFCC has the power to control whether a statute is in accordance with the constitution. Although no formal hierarchy has been established between the CJEU and the national courts, the described distribution of competences—in conjunction with the primacy of Union law in application (*Anwendungsvorrang*),—would give the word of the European Court precedence. As a consequence, OMT and all other actions of the ECB would not fall within the jurisdiction of the German Court.[68]

In a series of decisions, however, the Court has held that the acts of the institutions, agencies, and organs of the European Union are binding in the Federal Republic of

[63] GFCC OMT-referral (note 54 above).

[64] GFCC OMT-referral (note 54 above), margin no. 9; see, also, Sect. 7.2.4 above.

[65] GFCC OMT-referral (note 54 above), margin no. 34.

[66] Ibid.

[67] Ibid., at margin no. 35.

[68] See, for details, Siekmann (2015, p. 105 et seq.), with references; critical, see Gärditz (2014).

Germany only under the condition that they do not transgress their competences in a "manifest" way and do not lead to a "structurally significant shift in the allocation of Powers to the detriment of Member States". In addition, it assumed the "last word" in controlling compliance with this requirement (*ultra vires control*) despite the review power of the CJEU, pursuant to Article 263 TFEU. The required "structurally significant" transgressions would have to be inferred "if they cover areas that are part of the constitutional identity of the Federal Republic of Germany (*Verfassungsidentität*), which is protected by Art. 79 s. 3 Basic Law or if they particularly affect the democratic discourse in the Member States".[69] What is noteworthy here is that the Court does not strictly differentiate here between the *ultra vires* control and the protection of the *Verfassungsidentität* as in other (ensuing) decisions.[70]

Ultimately, the Court held that a manifest and structurally significant transgression of powers would have to be assumed if the European Central Bank acted beyond its monetary policy "mandate" or if the prohibition of the monetary financing of the budget was violated by the OMT programme. In addition, it reserved the right to determine whether the OMT—even after an interpretation by the CJEU has taken the concerns of the German Court into account—would infringe the "inviolable core content of the constitutional identity".[71] This constitutional identity would be jeopardised by touching the parliamentary budget autonomy which the Court considers to be an essential trait of it.[72]

7.5.1.2 Merits of the Case

In substance, the German Court assessed OMT as an act of economic policy beyond the competences of the ECB. Furthermore, it judged OMT as a monetary financing of sovereign debt prohibited by EU primary law, and found that these infractions could not be justified. Finally, the Court presented a way for a compromise by an interpretation of OMT which was in conformity with EU law.

With regard to the transgression of competences, it points out that the "mandate of the ECB" is limited to monetary policy, while economic policies in general are reserved to Member States relying on Articles 119 and 127 TFEU, and Articles 17 et seq., ESCB/ECB Statute.[73] According to its assessment, the OMT Decision—not to mention its implementation—already interferes with Member State competences in economic policy.[74] The reasons for this assessment are as follows:

---

[69]GFCC OMT-referral (note 54 above), at margin no. 21, 37, with references.The stated requirements were initially introduced by GFCC judgment of 6 July 2010, 2 BvR 2661/06 [Honeywell], BVerfGE [Reports of Judgments of the Federal Constitutional Court], 126, 286 (303–307).

[70]Sect. 7.6.1 below.

[71]GFCC, OMT-referral (note 54 above), at margin no. 27: "… it is for the Federal Constitutional Court to determine the inviolable core content of the constitutional identity, and to review whether the act (in the interpretation determined by the Court of Justice) interferes with the core."

[72]GFCC OMT-referral (note 54 above), at margin no. 28, 42.

[73]Ibid., at margin no. 56.

[74]Ibid., at margin nos. 56–83.

- with OMT, the ECB aims to neutralise the risk premiums on the debt of certain sovereigns which are market results;[75]
- an approach that differentiates between Member States does not fit in with the monetary decision-making framework for a monetary union;[76]
- the linkage to the conditionality of an ESM programme of the Member States indicates that OMT reaches into the realm of the economic policies reserved to the Member States;[77]
- the purchase of government debt, as outlined in the OMT decision of the ECB Council, exceeds the support of the general economic policies in the European Union that the European System of Central Banks is allowed to pursue.[78]

In view of a violation of the prohibition of the monetary financing of Member State budgets, the GFCC assumes a wide understanding. It resumes its argumentation from the temporary injunction proceedings[79] and holds that the (explicit) interdiction of direct purchase of government debt on the primary market also applies to functionally equivalent measures that are simply intended to circumvent this prohibition.[80] Article 123 TFEU is considered as "an expression of a broader prohibition of monetary financing of the budget".[81] To specify, it lists aspects that "indicate the OMT Decision aims at a circumvention of Art. 123 TFEU and 214 violates the prohibition of monetary financing of the budget"; in particular, the willingness to waive claims, to participate in a debt-cut, the increased risk of such a cut, the option of keeping the purchased bonds until maturity, the interference with the price formation on the markets, and the encouragement of market participants to purchase government bonds.[82] In essence, it judges the OMT Decision as "likely to violate" the prohibition of monetary financing of the budget as "enshrined in Art. 123 TFEU".[83]

With regard to a justification of the possible violations of EU law, the Court judges the objective used by the ECB to justify its decision—"to correct a disruption of the monetary policy transmission mechanism"—as irrelevant,[84] an unusually blunt judgment. The main argument is that it would amount to granting *carte blanche* to the European Central Bank to remedy any deterioration of the credit rating of any euro area Member State. Furthermore, it also "seems irrelevant" to the Court that the ECB only intends to assume a disruption to the monetary policy transmission mechanism if the interest rate charged from a Member State of the euro-currency area were "irrational". In its view, it would be an almost "arbitrary interference with market

[75]Ibid., at margin no. 70.

[76]Ibid., at margin no. 73.

[77]Ibid., at margin no. 74.

[78]Ibid., at margin no. 80.

[79]See GFCC judgment of 12 September 2012 (note 49 above).

[80]GFCC OMT-referral (note 54 above), at margin no. 86.

[81]GFCC OMT-referral (note 54 above), at margin no. 85.

[82]GFCC OMT-referral (note 54 above), at margin no. 87, with details at margin nos. 88–90.

[83]GFCC OMT-referral (note 54 above), at margin no. 84.

[84]GFCC OMT-referral (note 54 above), at margin no. 95.

activity" to single out individual causes as irrational. Thus, the distinction between "rational and irrational" ultimately appears to be "meaningless in this context".[85]

Finally, the Court explored an alternative interpretation of the OMT programme in order to achieve its conformity with EU law. This could be secured if OMT did not subvert the conditionality of the rescue programmes set up by the European Financial Stability Facility (EFSF) and the European Stability Mechanism (ESM), and if it had only had the nature of a "contribution" to the "smooth conduct of policies pursued by the competent authorities". The Court saw its concerns mitigated if the following conditions were met: exclusion of a debt-cut, no unlimited purchases of selected Member States' debt, and the avoidance of interference with price formation on the financial market. Within this context, the Court appears to concur with the ECB, since its representative emphasised at the hearing the limited volume of a possible purchase, the absence of a participation in a debt-cut, the observance of certain time-lags between the emission of a government bond and its purchase, and the intention of not holding the bonds to maturity.[86] This would lead the Court to the conclusion that its alternative interpretation would "most likely be consistent with the meaning and purpose of the OMT Decision".[87]

7.5.1.3 Critique

Although the wide interpretation of the prohibited monetary financing of Member States' budgets has followers in legal literature,[88] both the procedure and the findings of this judgment were harshly criticised not only by many economists,[89] but also by the majority of legal scholars.[90] This criticism is, by and large, convincing, in view of the admissibility of the complaints. It is also questionable whether the referral to the CJEU was indicated.[91] The arguments of the Court are, however, conclusive in

[85] GFCC OMT-referral (note 54 above), at margin no. 98.

[86] GFCC OMT-referral (note 54 above), at margin no. 100.

[87] Ibid.

[88] Schmidt (2015); Keller (2013) Article 18 ECB/ESCB Statute at margin no. 120 et seq; Borger (2013) 14, pp. 113–140, at 119, 134; Alberto de Gregorio Merino, (2012), p. 1613, 1625, note 36, p. 1627); Koen Lenaerts and Piet Van Nuffel (2011), n. 11–037.

[89] Winkler (2014), imputing that the Court has decided on a financial theory.

[90] Thym (2013), at 264; Thiele (2013) at 320; idem, (2014a) at 244, 246–250; idem, (2014b), stating serious technical flaws (p. 694), disagreeing with the demarcation between monetary policy and general economic policy, and stipulating, in essence, an almost free discretion of the ECB (pp. 694–697); Heun (2014), questioning the admissibility of the original complaints (p. 331), also questioning the admissibility of the referring order (p. 332), and distinctively criticising the qualification of OMT as *ultra vires* (p. 333); Jędrzejowska-Schiffauer and Schiffauer (2016) at 201 and 204, in specific disagreeing with the Court's "parallelism", albeit with some reservations: "a measure of this kind needs to be carefully balanced and monitored as to avoid that its implementation is in breach of the EMU's Maastricht macroeconomic constitution"; see, also, Ukrow (2014) at 120: "not continuously convincing".

[91] Siekmann (2015, pp. 113–116), with further references for the various arguments.

view of the transgression of competences by the ECB, and—to a somewhat lesser extent—with regard to the monetary financing of sovereign debt.[92]

In addition, the facts, as outlined in Sect. 7.2 above, especially the Public Sector Purchase Programme, also reveal that only part of the alleged concord existed in reality, especially with regard to the holding until maturity and the pre-determined volume.

7.5.2 *The Judgment of the Court of Justice of the European Union*

More than a year later, the CJEU delivered its judgment[93] on the referral of the German Constitutional Court from the beginning of 2014.[94] In sum, the CJEU decided that Article 119 TFEU, Article 123(1) TFEU, Article 127(1) and (2) TFEU, and Articles 17 to 24 ESCB/ECB Statute must be interpreted as permitting the European System of Central Banks to adopt a programme for the purchase of government debt on the secondary market, such as the OMT.[95]

7.5.2.1 Admissibility

Although a considerable number of Member States' governments, the European Parliament, the European Commission, and the ECB had challenged the admissibility of the request for a preliminary ruling, the Court decided in favour of admissibility[96] and affirmed its obligation to reply to the referring German court.[97] In this context, it underlined that the decisions of the CJEU are binding for courts requesting a preliminary ruling.

7.5.2.2 Competences

However, in substance, it—to a large extent—rejected the legal concerns of the German Federal Constitutional Court. Despite being subject to judicial review by

[92] Ashoka Mody (2014, p. 6 et seq), discussing the tasks the CJEU now has to fulfil (p. 17 et seq); see, for a detailed discussion of both the transgression of competences and the circumvention of the prohibition of monetary financing of Member States' budgets, Siekmann (2015, pp. 116–118), with further references for the various arguments.

[93] CJEU, judgment of 16 June 2015, Case C-62/14, *Gauweiler*, ECLI:EU:14:C:2015:400, available at: *Europäische Zeitschrift für Wirtschaftsrecht* (EuZW) 2015, 599.

[94] GFCC OMT-referral (note 54 above).

[95] CJEU *Gauweiler* (note 93 above), at margin no. 128.

[96] CJEU *Gauweiler* (note 93 above), at margin nos. 18–31.

[97] CJEU *Gauweiler* (note 93 above), at margin no. 17.

the Court,[98] the Governing Council of the ECB was to command a wide margin of discretion in interpreting the clauses delineating its competences and in designing the content of its monetary policy.[99]

In de-limiting the competence of the ESCB for monetary policy, the European Court built—principally—upon the objectives of the measure in question, but conceded that the instruments used to "attain those objectives" were also "relevant".[100] It reflected briefly on the *Pringle* decision in which it had advocated a narrow delineation of monetary policy,[101] but did not see a contradiction because of the difference between the objectives of the ESM and those of the ESCB, which were to be judged as "decisive".[102] In its opinion, the purchase of government bonds "on the secondary market subject to a macroeconomic adjustment programme could be regarded as falling within economic policy" when "undertaken by the ESM", whereas this did not mean that the same purchase should be treated equally in cases in which "that instrument is used by the ESCB".[103]

Solely relying on the ESCB's price stability objective in order to consider such a purchase as monetary policy[104] is too simplistic, especially when taking the selectivity of OMT into account.[105] However, the CJEU dismissed this aspect without closer scrutiny. In its opinion, "a bond buying programme may prove necessary in order to rectify... the disruption" that the ESCB wants to mitigate.[106]

7.5.2.3 Monetary Financing of Budgets

In view of bond buying operations, the CJEU states that Article 123(1) TFEU does not preclude, in general, the possibility of such purchases pointing to the existence of the Article 18.1 ESCB/ECB Statute.[107] This, however, was not questioned. In the next step, however, it follows the complainants and the GFCC in so far as it concedes that the ESCB, nevertheless, "does not have authority to purchase government bonds on secondary markets under conditions which would, in practice, mean that its action has an effect equivalent to that of a direct purchase ... from public authorities ..., thereby undermining the effectiveness of the prohibition in Article 123(1) TFEU",[108]

[98]CJEU *Gauweiler* (note 93 above), at margin no. 153.

[99]CJEU *Gauweiler* (note 93 above), at margin nos. 48 and 68: "a broad discretion".

[100]CJEU *Gauweiler* (note 93 above), at margin no. 46, referring to *Pringle* (note 57 above) at margin nos. 53 and 55.

[101]See note 58 above.

[102]CJEU *Gauweiler* (note 93 above), at margin nos. 53, 55, 64.

[103]CJEU *Gauweiler* (note 93 above), at margin no. 63.

[104]Ibid.

[105]See Sect. 7.5.1 above.

[106]CJEU *Gauweiler* (note 93 above), at margin no. 89.

[107]CJEU *Gauweiler* (note 93 above), at margin no. 95.

[108]CJEU *Gauweiler* (note 93 above), at margin no. 97.

a stance the GFCC had repeatedly underscored before.[109] Furthermore, the CJEU concedes that the "ESCB's intervention could, in practice, have an effect equivalent to that of a direct purchase of government bonds…".[110] This would—at the very least—prohibit the use of open market operations at the discretion of the ECB.[111]

In applying these findings, it follows, however, again the explanations provided by the ECB in the course of the proceeding[112] with the result that (i) "the Member States cannot, in determining their budgetary policy, rely on the certainty that the ESCB will at a future point purchase their government bonds" and that (ii) the programme cannot be implemented in a way which would bring about a harmonization of the interest rates applied to the government bonds … regardless of the differences arising from their macroeconomic or budgetary situation".[113] In essence, a programme like OMT "would not lessen the impetus for the Member States concerned to follow a sound budgetary policy".[114]

7.5.3 GFCC Final Judgment II

In its final decision, pronounced 21 June 2016,[115] the German Federal Constitutional Court dismissed the constitutional complaints and the applications for *Organstreit* proceedings with only some minor reservations. It did not activate the (stipulated) right to deviate from a decision of the European Court in cases of manifest and structurally significant transgression of competences (*ultra vires*) or of endangering the "constitutional identity" (*Verfassungsidentität*) of Germany, which it had reserved in several previous decisions.[116] As a result, the complaints and applications were finally rejected.[117] But this was not the end of the quarrels between the German Court and the CJEU (see Sect. 7.6.1). An open conflict between the courts was, however, avoided, which would have jeopardised the reputation of both.

---

[109]GFCC judgment of 12 September 2012 (note 49 above) at margin no. 175; GFCC OMT-referral (note 54 above), at margin no. 86 with concretisation of the likely circumvention by the OMT Programme at margin nos. 87–93.

[110]CJEU *Gauweiler* (note 93 above), at margin no. 104.

[111]Disagreeing, see Petch (2013, p. 15), erroneously deriving from the systematic position of Article 18 Statute in Chapter IV headed "Monetary Functions and Operations", that the legality of OMT may per se not be questioned.

[112]CJEU *Gauweiler* (note 93 above), at margin nos. 105–121.

[113]CJEU *Gauweiler* (note 93 above), at margin no. 113.

[114]CJEU *Gauweiler* (note 93 above), at margin no. 121.

[115]GFCC, judgment of 21 June 2016, cases: 2 BvR 2728/13, 2 BvR 2729/13, 2 BvR 2730/13, 2 BvR 2731/13, 2 BvE 13/13, [OMT-final], BVerfGE [Reports of Judgments of the Federal Constitutional Court], 142, 123. Another oral hearing had taken place on 16 February 2016; see margin no. 70.

[116]GFCC OMT-referral (note 54 above), at margin no. 27.

[117]GFCC OMT-final (note 115 above) at margin nos. 76 and 114.

7.5.3.1 Admissibility and Range of Control

The GFCC judged the constitutional complaints—as in the prior decisions—as admissible to "the extent that they challenge the fact that the Federal Government did not take steps to challenge the policy decision of the Governing Council of the European Central Bank regarding the OMT Programme…". The rest were declared inadmissible. The application for *Organstreit* proceedings was judged "to the extent that it seeks a declaration to the effect that the German *Bundestag* is obliged to take steps towards having the policy decision of 6 September 2012 regarding the OMT Programme rescinded". The rest was again declared inadmissible.[118] What is noteworthy is the fact that the Court underscored that the programme under scrutiny "has not been rendered obsolete by more recent purchase programmes". "The ongoing possibility that it may be implemented" was "the true reason for the effect the policy decision of 6 September 2012 … still has on the financial markets".[119]

In addition, the Court took the opportunity to clarify that "neither the SMP nor the OMT Programme as such are proper objects of a constitutional complaint", but only the "inaction on the parts of the German constitutional organs".[120] It also reiterated its reservation in view of the review of the constitutional identity of Germany (*Identitätskontrolle*) and of structurally significant infractions of the competence order (*Ultra-vires-Kontrolle*) conceding, however, again an interpretation that was open to European integration (*europafreundlich*).[121] A transfer of competences to decide on its own competence to the European Union (*Kompetenz-Kompetenz*) and blanket empowerments would nevertheless still be incompatible with German constitutional law.[122] A slight shift in concretising the identity review and the *ultra vires* review is visible, since the Court carefully outlined that the two instruments "are independent of one another", deviating from its former reasoning in treating the infraction of the constitutional identity as a specific and most severe case of acting *ultra vires*.[123] Both would constitute an "independent instrument of review".[124] In addition, it focused their application on the omissions of the "constitutional organs … to counter acts, institutions, bodies, offices, and agencies of the European Union that constitute a violation of identity as well as *ultra vires* acts".[125] Apart from this, it resumed and explicated its former judicature.[126]

---

[118] GFCC OMT-final (note 115 above) at margin no. 76.

[119] GFCC OMT-final (note 115 above) at margin no. 91.

[120] GFCC OMT-final (note 115 above) at margin no. 100; see note 69.

[121] GFCC OMT-final (note 115 above) at margin nos. 121, 142 and 144 et seq.

[122] GFCC OMT-final (note 115 above) at margin no. 130.

[123] GFCC OMT-referral (note 54 above), at margin nos. 21 and 37, with references.

[124] GFCC OMT-final (note 115 above) at margin no. 153 et seq.

[125] GFCC OMT-final (note 115 above) at margin no. 163 et seq.

[126] GFCC OMT-final (note 115 above) at margin nos. 155–162.

7.5.3.2 Substance

In substance, the GFCC rejected the constitutional complaints and the application in the *Organstreit* proceedings. The decision of the ECB of 6 September 2012 was neither a violation of the complainants' rights under Article 38(1)(1), Article 20(1)(2) in conjunction with Article 79(3) Basic Law, nor of the budgetary rights of the *Bundestag* as long as the conditions formulated by the Court of Justice of the European Union in its ruling of 16 June 2015 were met. The policy decisions of the Governing Council of the European Central Bank of 6 September 2012 and its possible implementation (OMT Programme) neither constituted a qualified exceeding of its competences nor a violation of the prohibition of monetary financing.[127]

The Court expressed, however, some "serious objections" in respect of the establishment of the facts of the case, the principle of conferral, and the judicial review of acts of the ECB. It criticised the fact that the CJEU had accepted the assertion of the ECB that the OMT Programme pursues monetary policy objectives "without questioning or at least discussing and individually reviewing the soundness of the underlying factual assumptions, and without testing these assumptions against indications that evidently argue against a character of monetary policy—particularly the selectivity of the purchases…".[128] Furthermore, even if a "wide margin of assessment to bodies of the European Union" and a resulting considerable decrease of the "judicial review" was acceptable, the principle of conferral was to have "an effect on the methodical review of whether it is respected". The asserted "discretion" must not lead to the result that the judicial review "simply accepts the asserted positions of organs of the European Union without verification".[129] Finally, it re-states that, as a consequence of the independence granted to the ESCB, entailing a "limitation on the democratic legitimation" "by way of compensation, the principles of democracy and the sovereignty of the people require that the monetary policy mandate" of the ECB be "interpreted restrictively", and that "its observance be subject to strict judicial review in order to at least limit the decrease in the level of democratic legitimation".[130]

Despite these well-founded concerns, in the end, the GFCC—hesitantly—did not object to the policy decision on the OMT Programme as unconstitutional since it would—in the interpretation of the CJEU—not (yet) "manifestly" exceed the competences of the European Central Bank, thus not fulfilling the requirements for an *ultra*

---

[127] GFCC OMT-final (note 115 above) at margin nos. 174 et seq.

[128] GFCC OMT-final (note 115 above) at margin no. 182, referring to GFCC OMT-referral (note 54 above), at margin no. 73. The factual contention of the ECB is also not challenged by Jędrzejowska-Schiffauer and Schiffauer (2016), p. 199, stating that it is "broadly recognised in the specialist literature" but providing only one (peripheric) reference: Beukers and Reestman (2015, p. 231).

[129] GFCC OMT-final (note 115 above) at margin nos. 184 and 186.

[130] GFCC OMT-final (note 115 above) at margin nos. 187 and 189: "…the principles of democracy and the sovereignty of the people require that the monetary policy mandate of the European Central Bank be interpreted restrictively and that its observance be subject to strict judicial review in order to at least limit the decrease in the level of democratic legitimation of the Bank's actions to what is absolutely necessary…"

vires act as defined by the judicature of the GFCC.[131] The limitations stated in *Gauweiler* would ensure that the potential of the policy decision of the ECB which reach far into economic policy, i.e. far beyond its competences, "is limited". The OMT Programme would only be allowed to secure price stability, but not to "stabilise the euro area". Moreover, it would have to be limited to alleviate "disruptions of the monetary policy transmission mechanism or the uniformity of monetary policy". It would have to be terminated as soon as they were achieved. These limitations could "at least be reviewed ex post".[132] In addition, the Court demanded that "the volume of future purchases must be mandatorily fixed from the outset and may not exceed the amount necessary for restoring the transmission mechanism".[133]

The policy decision would also not "manifestly" violate the prohibition of monetary financing[134] if it fulfilled certain requirements set up by the GFCC:

- Purchases may not be announced;
- The volume of the purchases must be limited;
- There must be a minimum period between the issue of government bonds and their purchases by the ESCB that is defined from the outset and prevents the issuing conditions from being distorted;
- The ESCB may purchase only government bonds of Member States that have bond market access enabling the funding of such bonds;
- Purchased bonds may only in exceptional cases be held until maturity;
- Purchases must be restricted or ceased and purchased bonds must be remarketed should continuing the intervention or further holding of the bonds become unnecessary for achieving the monetary income policy aims.[135]

The Court tries to secure the enforcement of these rules by declaring a failure to fulfil them as "a sufficiently qualified exceeding of competences within the meaning of the *ultra vires* review" and assessing their observance as a mandatory pre-requisite for the German *Bundesbank* to participate in the bond buying programme.[136]

With regard to the budgetary responsibility of the *Bundestag*, the Court does not at the moment see an apparent threat, but, looking forward, it points out that the "overall budgetary responsibility" was "part of the constitutional identity of the Basic Law".[137] It warns that "the purchases of government bonds by the Eurosystem may lead to losses of revenue that are relevant for the budget.[138] In excess to forfeited losses in revenue (*Bundesbank* profits), it reflects on a special liability (*Anstaltslast*)

[131] GFCC OMT-final (note 115 above) at margin no. 190, under the assumption that the reservations of the Gauweiler decision are treated as binding.

[132] GFCC OMT-final (note 115 above) at margin no.194, referring to CJEU *Gauweiler* (note 94 above), at margin nos. 62, 64 and 112.

[133] GFCC OMT-final (note 115 above) at margin no. 195.

[134] GFCC OMT-final (note 115 above) at margin nos. 197 and 201.

[135] GFCC OMT-final (note 115 above) at margin nos. 199 and 206.

[136] GFCC OMT-final (note 115 above) at margin no. 207.

[137] GFCC OMT-final (note 115 above) at margin no. 210.

[138] GFCC OMT-final (note 115 above) at margin no. 215.

of the Federal Republic of Germany for the functioning of the *Bundesbank*, which might even lead to an obligation to inject additional capital.[139]

7.5.4 Critique

7.5.4.1 The European Court

Some of the pre-requisites that the GFCC has demanded for an interpretation of OMT as compatible with EU law[140] appear to have been met: the CJEU acknowledges that the ECB will (i) ensure that a "minimum period is observed between the issue of a security on the primary market and its purchase on the secondary market"; and (ii) the ECB will "refrain from making any prior announcements concerning either its decision to carry out such purchases or the volume of purchases envisaged".[141]

Regarding a transgression of competences, the CJEU used the *Pringle* delimitation of monetary policy as a starting-point and essentially built on the objectives of the measure under scrutiny but conceded that the instruments which the measure employs in order to attain these objectives "are also relevant".[142] In the opinion of the CJEU, the requirement is met that the "implementation" of OMT "will not, in practice, have an effect equivalent to that of a direct purchase of government bonds", which is explicitly prohibited. Specifically, it did not follow the concerns of the GFCC that, by the "neutralisation of interest spreads", the waiving of "securitised claims against individual Member States", "the increased risk of failure or even a debt-cut", and the holding of "government bonds to maturity" will be an indication for a circumvention of the prohibition of monetary financing, and a negation of an infringement of the "principle of proportionality".[143]

The argumentation of the CJEU lacks—to quite a considerable extent—a critical analysis of the assertions of the ECB. Especially in the demarcation of the competences, it follows quite indiscriminately the contentions of the ECB. An individual, in-depth assessment of its own would have been appropriate, as the GFCC rightly demands. The question was, whether a bond buying programme was indeed "necessary". The Court takes intentions of the ECB as a given fact. Solely relying on the objectives of a measure for assessing its legal nature comes close to a circular reasoning, especially when addressing the concept and purpose of the ESM—created by secondary law of the EU—on the same level as the tasks, goals and objectives of the ESCB, carefully designed after long discussions by the primary law.

---

[139]GFCC OMT-final (note 115 above) at margin no. 217; see, disagreeing, Siekmann (2017, p. 1164 et seq).

[140]GFCC OMT-referral (note 54 above), at margin no. 100.

[141]CJEU *Gauweiler* (note 93 above), at margin no. 106.

[142]CJEU *Gauweiler* (note 93 above), at margin no. 46.

[143]GFCC OMT-referral (note 54 above), at margin nos. 87–91.

Similarly, the CJEU uncritically asserts that the "conduct of monetary policy will always entail an impact on interest rates and bank refinancing conditions" which would necessarily have "consequences on the financing conditions of the public debt of the Member States".[144] The same holds for the supposition that the OMT Programme "provides for the purchase of government bonds only in so far as is necessary for safeguarding the monetary policy transmission mechanism and the singleness of monetary policy".[145] This would have to be scrutinised closer. The Court's further assumption that the "purchases will cease as soon as those objectives are achieved" may be doubted considering the factual development more than three and a half years later.[146]

Particularly critical is the Court's opinion on risk-taking by the ESCB,[147] following—so far without discussion—the final plea of the Advocate General at the European Court of Justice, Pedro Cruz Villalón. He had elaborated that all monetary policy implies risk-taking by the monetary authorities.[148] In this way, the Court opens the door for a—very hard to limit—transfer of risks from the private or public sector to the central bank. The wishes for a presumably "easy" path to alleviate debt burdens are already getting louder. At the very least, a more comprehensive and in-depth reasoning would have been suitable. This opinion on the tasks and powers of a central bank is far from self-evident, and is not a long-lasting, generally accepted practice.

The reasoning of the Advocate General, not rescinded by the CJEU, is particularly dangerous, as he stipulated that the Member States had agreed to the risk transfer from private or sovereign bond issuers to the ESCB by creating the ECB.[149] This is highly questionable and lacks any underpinning by facts.

---

[144] CJEU *Gauweiler* (note 93 above), at margin no. 110.

[145] CJEU *Gauweiler* (note 93 above), at margin no. 112.

[146] Very outspoken *Sachverständigenrat* [German Council of Economic Experts] (2018), at no. 342: "The ECB is postponing interest rate increases and the reduction of its bond holdings for too long."

[147] CJEU *Gauweiler* (note 93 above), at margin no. 125: "a central bank, such as the ECB, is obliged to take decisions which, like open market operations, inevitably expose it to a risk of losses …"

[148] Final plea of Advocate General Cruz Villalón, delivered on 14 January 2015, at no. 194 et seq. In effect, he rejected all concerns regarding: i) waiver of rights and *pari passu* status, ii) default risk; iii) holding the bonds until maturity; iv) time of purchase; and v) encouragement to purchase newly issued bonds (nos. 232–261). In his test of proportionality, *stricto* sensu the (potential) costs of the programme do not outweigh the benefits (at margin nos. 185 et seq) referring repeatedly to "common wisdom" or "common knowledge" instead of providing concrete references.

[149] Final plea (note 149 above) at no. 194: "It is common knowledge that the central banks intervene in the sovereign debt market, since purchases of government bonds, or repurchase agreements in respect of those bonds, are among the monetary policy instruments which are a means of controlling the monetary base. When they intervene in that market, the central banks always assume a degree of risk, a risk which was also assumed by the Member States when they decided to create the ECB."

7.5.4.2 The German Court

It can clearly be seen that the GFCC tries to expurgate, or at least rescind, the discretion of the institutions of the EU to define their competences. Following this line, it is consistent when the OMT Programme is judged to be a transgression of the monetary policy competences of the ESCB. Its backdoor for avoiding an open conflict with the CJEU is to declare them as not being "manifest", in the sense of the *ultra vires* review, but a clear signal is sent that, in the next case, this might not be open any more—and it came with PSPP. The pre-requisites that it sets up for bond buying programmes to secure the observance of the prohibition of monetary financing of Member States' budgets and its threatening with *ultra vires* control and an infraction of the "constitutional identity" of Germany are well intended, but it remains to be seen whether they will succeed in producing the aspired results.

The lurking discord on whether possible debt-cut conflicts with the prohibition of monetary financing may only be postponed when accepting the CJEU's assertion that "only government bonds of such Member States that have bond market access may be purchased" as sufficient safeguard against a circumvention of the prohibition of monetary financing of Member States' budgets by the ESCB.[150] This assertion may later be interpreted as a requirement at the time of purchase but does not interdict a participation in such a cut or waiving of claims.

7.6 Public Sector Purchase Programme (PSPP)

Again, some members of the *Bundestag* and a large group of citizens—by individual complaint—questioned the legality of the Public Sector Purchase Programme (PSPP), which had been initiated in spring 2015.[151] On 18 July 2017, the German Federal Constitutional Court decided once more to refer the case to the Court of Justice of the EU for a preliminary ruling in accordance with Articles 19(3)(b) and 267(1)(a) TFEU on several questions of EU law.[152] A petition for issuing a temporary injunction interdicting the *Deutsche Bundesbank* to execute the purchases was denied, however, by the Court in a judgment of 10 October 2017.[153] The case was

[150]GFCC OMT-final (note 115 above) at margin no. 204; CJEU *Gauweiler* (note 93 above), at margin no. 86.

[151]See Sect. 7.2.5 above.

[152]GFCC, judgment of 18 July 2017, cases: 2 BvR 859/15, 2 BvR 1651/15, 2 BvR 2006/15, 2 BvR 980/16, English version available at: https://www.bundesverfassungsgericht.de/SharedDocs/Entscheidungen/EN/2017/07/rs20170718_2bvr085915en.html [PSPP-referral], BVerfGE [Reports of Judgments of the Federal Constitutional Court] 146, 216.

[153]GFCC, judgment of 10 October 2017, cases: 2 BvR 859/15, 2 BvR 1651/15, 2 BvR 2006/15, 2 BvR 980/16 [PSPP-temporary], BVerfGE [Reports of Judgments of the Federal Constitutional Court] 147, 39.

decided by Court of Justice of the EU on 11 December 2018.[154] The final decision of the German Federal Constitutional Court is still open.

7.6.1 *The Second Referral of the German Federal Constitutional Court*

In the first place, the GFCC questioned the compatibility of the decision of the ECB to introduce the PSPP and the manner and method of its implementation with Article 123(1) TFEU.[155] But here again, it also questioned whether the ECB might have violated Article 119 and Article 127(1) and (2) TFEU as well as Articles 17 to 24 ESCB/ECB Statute by exceeding its monetary policy "mandate"[156] and thus "encroaching upon the competences of the Member States".[157] In the final part of its reasons, the Court elaborated the (possible) negative impact on the "overall budgetary responsibility of the *Bundestag*".[158]

7.6.1.1 Relevance of the Referred Questions

Following the procedural requirements that the CJEU had set up for the preliminary rulings, the German Court explicated the relevance of the referred questions for deciding the case brought up to its adjudication. It held that, in the event that the PSPP Decision did constitute, "in a sufficiently qualified manner, an exceeding of the mandate of the ECB and encroached upon the economic policy competences of the Member States and/or a violation [of] the prohibition of monetary financing of Member State budgets", the proceedings would be successful. In this case, the PSPP Decision would have to be "qualified as an *ultra vires* act under German constitutional law" and the "inaction on the part of the Federal Government and the *Bundestag* would amount to a violation of the complainants' constitutional rights".[159]

The Court followed its judicature on *ultra vires* and confirmed that an act of the European Union constitutes a "sufficiently qualified violation" if it "manifestly"

---

[154] CJEU *Heinrich Weiss* (note 7 above). For details, see Sect. 7.6.3 below.

[155] GFCC PSPP-referral (note 152 above) at margin nos. 77–99.

[156] The term was originally propagated by economists including the president of the ECB, journalists and politicians although it is not a legal category of the relevant primary law of the Union and cannot be found there. Goals, objectives, competences, and powers are the (defined) legal categories used by the primary law.

[157] GFCC PSPP-referral (note 152 above) at margin nos. 100–123.

[158] Ibid., at margin nos. 124–134.

[159] Ibid., at margin no. 62.

exceeds "EU competences, resulting in a structurally significant shift in the distribution of competences to the detriment of Member States".[160] If "the ECB acted outside its monetary mandate" or "if the PSPP violated the prohibition of monetary financing of Member States budgets" it would "constitute" such a "significant exceeding of competences".[161]

Ultra vires acts would also give rise to duties on the part of "German state organs to take or refrain from action". These duties are held to be "justiciable before the Federal Constitutional Court"[162] since the German *Bundestag* and the Federal Government "may not simply tolerate *ultra vires* acts of institutions, bodies, offices and agencies of the European Union".[163]

7.6.1.2 Prohibition of Monetary Financing

In its interpretation of European Union law, the Court expresses serious doubts as to whether the PSPP Decision is compatible with the prohibition of monetary financing of government budgets according to Article 123 TFEU. Building on the cornerstones of the *Gauweiler* ruling of the CJEU,[164] it again takes up from its referral decision in OMT proceedings[165] that Article 18.1 ESCB/ECB Statute permits the ESCB "in order to achieve its objectives and to carry out its tasks" [not: mandate!] "to operate in the financial markets, *inter alia*, by buying and selling outright marketable instruments, which include government bonds",[166] but again emphasising that "the ESCB does not have authority to purchase government bonds on secondary markets under conditions which would, in practice, mean that its action had an effect equivalent to that of a direct purchase of government bonds from the public bodies and institutions of the Member States, thereby undermining the effectiveness of the prohibition in Article 123(1) TFEU".[167] Thus far, it explicitly follows the opinion of the CJEU[168] and its own prior judicature.[169] Furthermore, it stipulates again—taking up verbatim the CJEU—that any programme "relating to the purchase of government bonds on the

[160] Ibid., at margin no. 63, citing BVerfGE [Reports of Judgments of the Federal Constitutional Court] 126, 286 (304 et seq., 209); 142, 123 (200 et seq., margin nos. 147 et seq.).

[161] GFCC PSPP-referral (note 152 above) at margin no. 64.

[162] Ibid., at margin no. 69.

[163] Ibid., at margin no. 71.

[164] CJEU *Gauweiler* (note 93 above), at margin nos. 94–97.

[165] GFCC PSPP-referral (note 152 above) at margin no. 90; see, also, GFCC OMT-final (note 115 above) at margin no. 199.

[166] Ibid., at margin no. 78 in its first part.

[167] Ibid., at margin no. 78, citing literally CJEU *Gauweiler* (note 93 above), at margin no. 97.

[168] CJEU *Gauweiler* (note 93 above), at margin no. 97.

[169] GFCC judgment of 12 September 2012 (note 49 above) at margin no. 175; GFCC OMT-referral (note 54 above), at margin no. 86 with concretisation of the likely circumvention by the OMT Programme at margin nos. 87–93.

secondary market must provide sufficient guarantees to effectively ensure observance of the prohibition of monetary financing".[170]

The Court sees—in accordance with the CJEU[171]—the objective of Article 123 TFEU as to "encourage the Member States to follow a sound budgetary policy" and refrain from "excessively high levels of debt or excessive Member States deficits".[172] Purchases on the secondary market may not be used "to circumvent" this objective.[173] Such a circumvention would be precluded if the following conditions were met,[174] which are partially taken from *Gauweiler* and its own OMT final decision from June 2016:[175]

- Market operators must not know for certain that the ESCB is going to purchase those bonds within a certain period and under conditions allowing them to act, de facto, as intermediaries for the ESCB when investing in those bonds;[176]
- Member States "may not, in determining their budgetary policy, be afforded certainty that the ESCB will at a future point purchase their government bonds on secondary markets";[177]
- A "minimum period must be observed between the issue of a security on the primary market and its purchase on the secondary market. Any prior announcement concerning either the ESCB's decision to carry out such purchases or the volume of the envisaged purchases must be ruled out";[178]
- "Purchased bonds may only in exceptional cases be held until maturity";[179]
- "Purchases must be limited or suspended, and purchased bonds must be remarketed, should continuing intervention or further holding the bonds no longer be necessary for achieving the monetary policy objectives".[180]

---

[170] GFCC PSPP-referral (note 152 above) at margin no. 78, citing CJEU *Gauweiler* (note 93 above), at margin no. 102 et seq.

[171] CJEU *Gauweiler* (note 93 above), at margin no. 100.

[172] GFCC PSPP-referral (note 152 above) at margin no. 78.

[173] GFCC PSPP-referral (note 152 above) at margin no. 78, referring to CJEU *Gauweiler* (note 93 above), at margin no. 101.

[174] GFCC PSPP-referral (note 152 above) at margin no. 78.

[175] GFCC OMT-final (note 115 above) at margin nos. 199 and 201.

[176] CJEU *Gauweiler* (note 93 above), at margin no. 92.

[177] GFCC PSPP-referral (note 152 above) at margin no. 78, citing CJEU *Gauweiler* (note 93 above), at margin no.113.

[178] GFCC PSPP-referral (note 152 above) at margin no. 78, citing CJEU *Gauweiler* (note 93 above), at margin no. 106.

[179] GFCC PSPP-referral (note 152 above) at margin no. 78, citing CJEU *Gauweiler* (note 93 above), at margin nos. 117 and 118.

[180] GFCC PSPP-referral (note 152 above) at margin no. 78, citing CJEU *Gauweiler* (note 93 above), at margin nos. 112 et seq., and 117 et seq.

Again, the Court tried to lend bite to these requirements by re-stating that it considers them to be "legally binding criteria" and that a non-compliance with them would be considered "an exceeding of competences".[181]

Applying the criteria on PSPP, the Court sees a violation of Article 123 TFEU, namely, because of four reasons which are elaborated in detail:

(1) The details of the purchases were "announced in a manner that could create de facto certainty on the markets that issued government bonds will, indeed, be purchased by the Eurosystem".[182]
(2) It would not be "possible to verify compliance with certain minimum periods between the issuance of the securities on the primary market and their purchase on the secondary market".[183]
(3) All "purchased bonds were—without exception—held until maturity".[184]
(4) Purchases "include bonds that, from the outset, return a negative yield".[185]

7.6.1.3 Transgresion of Competences

The GFCC starts with underlining that the competences of the ESCB in general and the ECB in particular are limited to monetary policy.[186] Beyond this, the ESCB is only authorised to support the general economic policy of the European Union, Articles 119(2), 127(1) second sentence, 282(2) third sentence TFEU.[187] Based upon these principles, the Court expresses doubts as to whether the PSP Decision falls within the "mandate" of the ECB, "given the volume and its implementation … and the effects resulting therefrom".[188] The power to support the general economic policy of the Member States at the level of the European Union, according to Article 127(1) second sentence TFEU, would "not justify a steering influence of the Eurosystem over economic matters".[189]

In its argumentation, the Court again emphasises the crucial role of the "principle of conferral", following Article 5(1) and (2) TEU, which also holds for the functions and powers of the ESCB. To satisfy democratic requirements, the "mandate" has to be "narrowly restricted" and is subject to *full judicial review*. Referring to its case law, the Court re-iterates that the encroachment on the democratic principle by granting

---

[181] GFCC PSPP-referral (note 152 above) at margin no. 79, affirming GFCC OMT-final (note 116 above) at margin no. 192.

[182] GFCC PSPP-referral (note 152 above) at margin nos. 80 and 81–92.

[183] GFCC PSPP-referral (note 152 above) at margin nos. 80 and 93–95.

[184] GFCC PSPP-referral (note 152 above) at margin nos. 80 and 96–98.

[185] GFCC PSPP-referral (note 152 above) at margin nos. 80 and 99.

[186] GFCC PSPP-referral (note 152 above) at margin no. 100, referring to its Maastricht decision, BVerfGE [Reports of Judgments of the Federal Constitutional Court] 89, 155 (208 et seq).

[187] CJEU *Gauweiler* (note 93 above), at margin no. 59; GFCC PSPP-referral (note 152 above) at margin nos. 100 and 113.

[188] GFCC PSPP-referral (note 152 above) at margin nos. 100 and 114.

[189] GFCC PSPP-referral (note 152 above) at margin no. 113.

independence to central banks is only justified by the empirically supported "particularity of monetary policy" in guaranteeing monetary stability. This "endorsement" hinges on a restrictive interpretation of monetary policy; "it cannot be extended to other areas of policy".[190]

In drawing the line, the Court again follows the CJEU in employing, in the first place, the aim (objective) pursued with the measure—determined "objectively"—but also the means (instruments) chosen with a view to achieving this aim. The "decisive factor" for delineating competences is to be whether a measure pursues economic policy objectives "directly". Granting financial assistance to a Member State "clearly" does not fall within monetary policy.[191] From this, the Court derives "that if and to the extent that the ESCB grants financial assistance, it engages in economic policy in a manner that the European Union is prohibited from doing".[192]

The GFCC deviates, however, from the CJEU, which discards indirect effects almost completely. The CJEU had held that simply because a programme could, to a certain degree, have further economic policy objectives would not mean that it must be treated as an economic policy measure.[193] Instead, the GFCC intends to use an "overall assessment".[194] In particular, it rejects the assertion that the competent EU institutions and bodies command "wide margins of assessment" thereby "decreasing "the intensity of judicial review". Conceding the autonomy to delineate competences for the institutions, bodies, offices and agencies of the European Union would "not sufficiently give consideration to the principle of conferral and the necessity of interpreting the ECB's mandate in a restrictive manner. Rather it is necessary to conduct an overall assessment and evaluation, also take into account factors contradicting the proclaimed objective".[195]

This overall assessment leads to the result that the PSPP Decision does not fall within the ECB "mandate", considering its volume and duration. In the opinion of the GFCC, it could no longer be qualified as a monetary policy measure, but, instead, constitutes a "measure that is primarily of an economic policy nature".[196] Its justification is mainly based upon the sheer volume of the purchases, which leads to considerable economic policy effects with steering effects on the economy, as an inevitable consequence. It would "affect balance sheet structures in the commercial banking sector by transferring large quantities of Member State bonds, including

---

[190] BVerfGE [Reports of Judgments of the Federal Constitutional Court] 89, 155 (208 et seq.), 97, 350 (368 et seq.), 142, 123 (220 et seq., margin nos. 188 et seq).

[191] CJEU *Gauweiler* (note 93 above), at margin no. 57.

[192] GFCC PSPP-referral (note 152 above) at margin no. 109.

[193] CJEU Pringle (note 57 above), at margin nos. 56 and 97; affirmed by CJEU *Gauweiler* (note 93 above), at margin nos. 58 et seq.

[194] GFCC PSPP-referral (note 152 above) at margin nos. 114 and 119: "It might be untenable, however, to still consider economic policy effects as 'indirect' in nature if the economic policy effects of a measure are intended or deliberately accepted, and these effects are at least comparable in weight to the monetary policy objective pursued."

[195] GFCC PSPP-referral (note 152 above) at margin no. 119, referring to GFCC OMT-final (note 115 above) at margin nos. 183 et seq.

[196] GFCC PSPP-referral (note 152 above) at margin no. 114.

high-risk ones, from the balance sheets of the Member States [banks] to the balance sheets of the ECB and national central banks". This would lead to a significant improvement of their economic situation and their credit ratings.[197] In addition, the PSPP improves the refinancing conditions for the Member States. Beyond the effects of "normal" open market operations, allowed by Article 18.1 ESCB/ECB Statute, on the economy, the "particularly large volume" of the purchases might have "deliberately accepted consequences" of such a weight that they might be seen as superseding the monetary policy objectives. Thus, it could be concluded that the economic policy effects of the PSPP were not mere "indirect effects" of a monetary policy, "but rather constituted and at least equally weighty aim pursued by the programmes".[198]

Regarding the development of inflation, and given the fact that the euro area Member States can deliberately use low-yield government bonds as a means of budgetary policy, and that the activities of commercial banks are "factually subsidised", the GFCC questions that the means chosen are still proportionate to achieving the proclaimed monetary policy objective.[199]

7.6.1.4 Budgetary Responsibility

The GFCC also sees dangers for the overall budgetary responsibility of the German *Bundestag* and repeats its opinion, stated in the final decision on OMT, in which it had not seen an apparent threat "at the moment".[200] It re-states that "the purchases of government bonds by the Eurosystem may lead to expenditures or losses of revenue that are relevant for the budget".[201] In excess to forfeited losses in revenue (*Bundesbank* profits), it reflects again (above sect. 7.5.3.2) on a special liability (*Anstaltslast*) of the Federal Republic of Germany for the functioning of the *Bundesbank*, which might even lead to an obligation to inject additional capital.[202]

Closer scrutiny, however, reveals that the risk-sharing regime established by PSPP differs considerably from the design of OMT. The risk of defaults is, in fact, largely attributed to the various national central banks and only to a small fraction it is "communitised" at the ECB.[203] Some German economist recently tried to construe a liability in view of TARGET2 and Emergency Liquidity Assistance (ELA) even without the exit of a Member State whose currency is the euro. In their view, this liability would also be relevant for write-downs stemming from a (partial) default of

[197] Ibid., at margin no. 120.

[198] Ibid., at margin no. 121.

[199] Ibid., at margin no. 122.

[200] GFCC OMT-final (note 115 above) at margin no. 210.

[201] GFCC OMT-final (note 115 above) at margin no. 215.

[202] GFCC PSPP-referral (note 152 above) at margin no. 126, referring to GFCC OMT-final (note 115 above) at margin no. 217; see, disagreeing, Siekmann (2017, p. 1164 et seq).

[203] GFCC PSPP-referral (note 153 above) at margin no. 127.

bonds purchased in the context of PSPP.[204] However, this view suffers from non-negligible flaws both in facts and in legal assessment. Specifically, the asserted liability is highly questionable. However, despite the lack of evidence that PSPP could or would, at the moment, result in losses ultimately infringing on the overall budgetary responsibility of the *Bundestag*,[205] the Court points out that the rules of risk distribution in the context of PSPP could be changed fairly easily, to the detriment of Member States.[206] At the moment, it is highly questionable that in effect they would have to bear such a burden. In addition, the GFCC deliberates that Article 32.4 ESCB/ECB Statute might allow a redemption of the losses of a national central bank and, in this way change the appropriation of incurring financial losses from the asset(s) purchased.[207]

Looking forward, the Court again points out that the "overall budgetary responsibility" was "part of the constitutional identity of the Basic Law".[208]

7.6.2 Denial of Temporary Injunctions

In autumn 2018, the German Federal Constitutional Court[209] rejected petitions to issue temporary injunctions:

- releasing the *Deutsche Bundesbank* from its obligation to purchase assets in executing the Public Sector Purchase Programme (PSPP) and the Corporate Sector Purchase Programme (CSPP) of the ESCB and interdicting further purchases within the framework of PSPP;
- ordering the German Federal Government to file lawsuits against those programmes in the appropriate Court of the EU and to secure that—in the meantime until a final judgment is handed down—the effects of the programmes in Germany remain as much as possible limited;
- interdicting the Federal Government of Germany, and, in particular, the Federal Minister of Finance, to aid the European Central Bank in conducting the PSPP, specifically by public statements, until the German Federal Constitutional Court had adjudicated on the main proceedings.

The Court dismissed the petitions as inadmissible.[210] Its main reason was that they would result in a pre-emption of the decision of the main proceeding, which is, in principle, prohibited. The Court argued that the objective of PSPP would, in

---

[204] Fuest and Sinn (2018).

[205] GFCC PSPP-referral (note 152 above) at margin no. 128.

[206] GFCC PSPP-referral (note 152 above) at margin nos. 130 and 133.

[207] GFCC PSPP-referral (note 152 above) at margin no. 132.

[208] GFCC PSPP-referral (note 152 above) at margin nos. 129 and 131, referring to the GFCC OMT-final (note 115 above) at margin no. 210.

[209] GFCC PSPP-temporary (note 153 above).

[210] GFCC PSPP-temporary (note 153 above) at margin no. 10.

effect, be impaired if the petition would be granted.[211] Reasons for an exception, such as serious, non-mendable damages to the petitioners, were not visible.[212] Another petition for issuing a temporary injunction was denied by a chamber-decision in 2019.[213]

7.6.3 The Judgment of the Court of Justice of the EU

Following the final plea of Advocate General, Melchior Wathelet, proposing that the PSPP does not infringe the prohibition of monetary financing and does not exceed the powers of the ECB, the CJEU decided on 11 December 2018 that the ESCB's PSPP does not exceed the ECB's mandate and does not contravene the prohibition of monetary financing.[214]

7.6.3.1 Exceeding Competences

In its judgment, the Court finds that the consideration of the questions referred by the Federal Constitutional Court has disclosed no factor of such a kind as to affect the validity of the PSPP. The Court found, first, that the PSPP does not exceed the ECB's mandate. The programme falls within the area of monetary policy, in respect of which the EU has exclusive competence for the Member States whose currency is the euro, and observes the principle of proportionality.[215]

It reduced, however, its judicial review of the acts of the ESCB to the control of a "manifest error of assessment" which—foreseeably—it did not find.[216] In this context, it emphasised "that Article 127(1) TFEU provides, *inter alia*, that (i) without prejudice to its primary objective of maintaining price stability, the ESCB is to support the general economic policies in the Union and that (ii) the ESCB must act in accordance with the principles laid down in Article119 TFEU". The Court also contended that, "within the institutional balance established by the provisions of Title VIII of the FEU Treaty … the authors of the Treaties did not intend to make an absolute separation between economic and monetary policies".[217] A reference for this contention was, however, not provided.

---

211 Ibid., at margin nos. 13 and 14.

212 Ibid., at margin no. 16.

213 Decision of the second chamber of the second senat of 25 April 2019—2 BvR 1728/16 https://www.bundesverfassungsgericht.de/SharedDocs/Entscheidungen/DE/2019/04/rk20190425_2bvr172816.html.

214 CJEU *Heinrich Weiss* (note 7 above).

215 CJEU *Heinrich Weiss* (note 7 above) at margin no. 100.

216 CJEU *Heinrich Weiss* (note 7 above) at margin no. 56.

217 CJEU *Heinrich Weiss* (note 7 above) at margin no. 60.

The Court did also not concur with the referring court's view that any effects of an open market operations programme that were knowingly accepted and definitely foreseeable by the ESCB when the programme was set up should not be regarded as "indirect effects" of the programme.[218]

Moreover, the Court held that the PSPP, in its underlying principle, does not manifestly go beyond what is necessary to raise inflation rates. Without scrutiny of its own, it declared it to be clear, *inter alia*, that it was not possible to counter the risk of deflation by means of the other instruments available to the ESCB. Key interest rates were at their lower bound, and the ESCB had, for several months, already been implementing a programme of large-scale purchases of private sector assets.[219]

7.6.3.2 Monetary Financing of Member States Budgets

The Court further found that the PSPP does not infringe the prohibition of monetary financing, which prevents the ESCB from granting any type of credit to a Member State. Implementation of this programme is not considered by the Court to be equivalent to a purchase of bonds on the primary markets and does "not reduce the impetus of the Member States to follow a sound budgetary policy".[220]

In the opinion of the Court, the safeguards built into the PSPP are sufficient to ensure that a private operator cannot be certain, when it purchases bonds issued by a Member State, that those bonds will actually be bought by the ESCB in the foreseeable future. The fact that the PSPP procedures make it possible to foresee, at macroeconomic level, that there will be a purchase of a significant volume of bonds issued by public authorities and bodies of the Member States does not afford a given private operator such certainty that he can act, de facto, as an intermediary of the ESCB for the direct purchase of bonds from a Member State.[221]

Furthermore, the Court held that the PSPP would not enable the Member States to determine their budgetary policy without taking account of the fact that, in the medium term, continuity in the implementation of the PSPP is in no way guaranteed and that they will thus be led, in the event of a deficit, to seek financing on the markets without being able to take advantage of the easing of financing conditions that implementation of the PSPP may entail. Moreover, the effects of the PSPP on the impetus to conduct a sound budgetary policy are considered to be limited by (i) the restriction of the total monthly volume of public sector asset purchases, (ii) the subsidiary nature of the PSPP programme, (iii) the distribution of purchases between the national central banks in accordance with the key for subscription of the ECB's capital, (iv) the purchase limits per issue and issuer (which means that only a minority of the bonds issued by a Member State can be purchased by the ESCB

---

[218] CJEU *Heinrich Weiss* (note 7 above) at margin no. 62.

[219] CJEU *Heinrich Weiss* (note 7 above) at margin nos. 86 and 100.

[220] CJEU *Heinrich Weiss* (note 7 above) at margin no. 144.

[221] CJEU *Heinrich Weiss* (note 7 above) at margin nos. 127 et seq.

under the PSPP), and (v) stringent eligibility criteria (based upon a credit quality assessment).[222]

The Court finally states that the prohibition of monetary financing does not preclude either the holding of bonds until maturity or the purchase of bonds at a negative yield to maturity.[223]

7.6.4 Critique

Some voices even contend that the implementation of PSPP against the opposition to quantitative easing in the Member States of the euro area can be viewed as "testimony to the ECB's ability to resist national pressure".[224] It does not matter whether this is a correct observation, at least the CJEU did not hesitate to grant, in effect, almost complete freedom to the Eurosystem to do what it wants to do.

7.6.4.1 Referral Decision of the German Federal Constitutional

The attempts of the German Federal Constitutional Court to define a clear demarcation between monetary policy and economic policy, and, in particular, to reject the notion of a margin of assessment or discretion in favour of the organs and institutions of the EU to delineate their competences, are fully convincing. For various reasons, the delineation of competences must not be subject to the autonomous decisions of the entities concerned, i.e. profit from its stretching. Among others, experience tells that institutions have a strong tendency to expand their sphere of power if a clear and enforceable boundary is not established. This is why the separation of powers and effective judicial review has developed into such fundamental constitutional principles. The final result that, in an overall assessment, PSPP might not be considered to be monetary policy is plausible despite the fact that the critical selectivity of OMT is avoided. The sheer volume, the assumption of various risks by the monetary authorities of the Eurosystem and the long duration in a changing economic surrounding, mainly distorting competition by keeping failing enterprises and banks alive ("Zombie firms"), and the causation of an asset price inflation are strong arguments.

Furthermore, the assessment that PSPP in effect leads to a monetary financing of government budgets can be supported, given the de facto guarantee of the purchase of questionable bonds by the Eurosystem. The described effects on the budgetary policy by the Member States, which is part of the economic policy reserved to them, are also visible as the waning efforts for structural reform due to reduced market forces.

---

[222] CJEU *Heinrich Weiss* (note 7 above) at margin nos. 133–142.

[223] CJEU *Heinrich Weiss* (note 7 above) at margin nos. 145–158.

[224] Lombardi and Moschella (2016) at 865; Müller-Graff (2019, p. 172 et seq).

The reflections on the admissibility of the petitions are still not fully convincing, although it can clearly be seen that the Court has further rescinded the admissible grounds for a petition since it judged them largely to be inadmissible.

As already pointed out in Sect. 7.6.1.4, the reflections of the Court on the liability structure within the Eurosystem, the obligation by the *Bundestag* to provide for an injection of capital in the *Bundesbank*, and the range of Article 32.4 ESCB/ECB Statute are questionable in view of the statutory rules on the liability for a corporation in general and both the ECB and the *Bundesbank* in specific.

7.6.4.2 The Ruling of the Court of Justice of the European Union

The first annotations to the judgment appreciate that the Court did not question the principle of limited conferral and did not refrain from a judicial control of the observance of the limits of the "mandate" of the ESCB despite its guaranteed independence.[225] Moreover, it was accepted that the impact of the programme on economic policy was only "indirect" and thus in conformity with Article 127(1) TFEU.[226]

In conceding a margin of discretion or assessment to the institutions and bodies of the European Union when deciding on their competences, the CJEU reduces the elaborated competence order severely to a mere guideline with little normative content. The distribution of competences between the organs and institutions of the EU and the Member States is not primarily a technical feature but an essential decision about the attribution of real powers. If the obedience to these cannot be strictly controlled by the judiciary, the balance of powers will be seriously endangered.

In accepting, furthermore, the uncontrolled allegation of the ESCB that the strong, automatic and not unwanted (indirect) effects on economic policy of a measure with monetary policy objective do not change its characteristic—perhaps over time—to a measure of economic policy leaves the door wide open for substantial circumventions. Due to the lack of strict judicial control, the monetary policy objective can easily be used as a mere pretext. The rationale of Article 123(1) TFEU can be—and is—easily thwarted by using a dummy to act in between the sovereign issuer of a debt and the ESCB purchasing it. The argumentation of the Court negating the role of actors in the financial market as mere intermediaries appears to be aloof from the reality in certain countries. This way, the norm is reduced to an absurd attempt to prevent an abuse of monetary policy instruments by governments following an irresponsible fiscal policy. In the interpretation of the CJEU, it comes close to a merely symbolic piece of legislation without any real directing power.

[225] Müller-Graff (2019, p. 172), consenting Gentzsch (2019), 298 in view of the superior expertise of the ECB and the complexity of economic problems. The narrative of the ECB was taken as a given, that APP would "provide the degree of policy accommodation necessary to deliver on the price stability mandate"; Hammermann et al. (2019, p. 6).

[226] Müller-Graff (2019, p. 172), Gentzsch (2019, p. 298).

The alleged safeguards for limiting the effects of the PSPP on the impetus to conduct a sound budgetary policy are largely counterfactual. Contrary to the allegations of the Courts, it can be seen in several Member States that the impetus for structural reforms enabling a sound fiscal policy has withered away over the years of conducting the asset purchases in conjunction with a zero-interest policy. The time which the asset purchases have bought to rehabilitate government finances and banking systems was not utilised to the needed extent.

7.7 Overall Evaluation

The CJEU has propelled European integration as well as its own stature by its longstanding judicature of a wide interpretation of the provisions on the competences and powers of the EU and its organs and institutions.[227] This has been partially deplored in the German legal literature as a softening of the principle of limited conferral.[228] In the opinion of the critics, the bond buying programmes, especially OMT, are a selective or even arbitrary subsidy of interest rates in favour of governments or banking systems in financial distress.[229] In their view, safeguarding the present composition of the euro zone is not a task conferred on the ECB.[230] Also the German National Central Bank (*Deutsche Bundesbank*) could not find any evidence for an impaired transmission of monetary policy that would need to be counteracted by such interventions.[231]

7.7.1 Monetary Policy?

7.7.1.1 Differences in Design

A final assessment of the various programmes from a distant perspective would have to come to the result that the Securities Market Programme (SMP) was the most questionable in view of a transgression of the boundaries of the competences attributed to the ESCB. It was, in effect, an arbitrary subsidy of selected Member States and their banking systems (Greece, Italy, Spain, Portugal and Ireland) having assumed almost all risks from its failing banking system). To a large extent, APP was basically a programme to recapitalise banks. This is typically an act of economic policy, as it only very distantly affects the currency and the currency area.[232]

---

[227] See Voßkuhle (2016), Section B II with details and references.

[228] See, for example, Klein (2014, p. 185); in general supportive, Voßkuhle (2016), Section B II, but emphasising the control of acts *ultra vires* of the constitution identity by the GFCC (Section B V).

[229] Murswiek (2016), Ruffert (2019, p. 181).

[230] Siekmann (2013a), Siekmann and Wieland (2013), at 3 and 7.

[231] Deutsche Bundesbank (2013).

[232] Murswiek (2015, p. 46), ibid. (2016).

The decision, which country will be supported and which not, is, in view of the criteria, intentions, and consequences, of genuine economic nature, as explicated by the CJEU in the *Pringle* case (Sects. 7.4.1, 7.5.2.2, 7.5.4.1 above). The selectivity can also be found in the OMT Programme but the decision to purchase is not designed as arbitrary as in SMP since it is tied to an EU support programme.[233] Even more, the purchases within the framework of Asset Purchase Programmes (APP) follow a predefined key, the selectivity is almost completely eliminated and PSPP could be assessed as a measure with a monetary objective—enlarging the monetary basis, amelioration of the transmission mechanism—and thus is not as critical as SMP and OMT in view of staying within the competences of the ESCB.

Deflation or a deflationary spiral was, however, realistically not in sight. From this perspective, enlarging the consolidated balance sheet of the Eurosystem was not obligatory. Recapitalising firms, especially banks, is typically a task for economic policy and not for the monetary system. Enhancing the transmission mechanism is not—as such—a measure of monetary policy.

For Germany, the rules of PSPP lead to a—probably unintended—change in the composition of the holders of the federal bonds (*Bundesanleihen*, *Bunds*) and of the structure of the balance sheet of the *Bundesbank*: The percentage of creditors from the euro area decreased from 59.8% in 2014 to 44.6% in 2017, and from Germany increased from 11.6% in 2014 to 34.4% in 2017. What is striking is the surge of the fraction of all bonds—issued by the federal government—held by the *Bundesbank* from 0% in 2014 to 23.5% in 2017. This means, that the *Bundesbank*, a federal authority, is on the way to become the biggest creditor of its bearer, the federal government of Germany. Correspondingly, at the end of June 2018, approximately €454.8 bn. of a total of €1,823.0 bn. on the balance sheet of the *Bundesbank* are bonds purchased within the framework of PSPP. €1.000 bn. of the total are claims against the ECB stemming from TARGET 2. To sum up, it can be assumed that more than 40% of all (redeemable) assets of the *Bundesbank* are claims against sovereigns from the euro area.[234] The fundamental separation of monetary policy from economic policy is becoming almost meaningless, however difficult it may be to draw the line in a specific situation, even if the ESCB were allowed to act as a "lender of last resort" and salvage illiquid but solvent debtors—public or private.

However, the transgression of competences, the prohibited monetary financing of Member States' budgetary deficits, and the necessity (proportionality) of the programmes in the present economic environment remain questionable.

7.7.1.2 No Arbitary Demarcation

The GFCC is right in emphasising that the "wording and systematic concept as well as the spirit and purpose of the Treaties" assume and demand a clear distinction

[233] Murswiek (2015, pp. 42–46 et seq): not monetary policy.

[234] *Deutsche Bundesbank* (2018, pp. 19–22).

between "matters of a monetary policy nature from economic policy matters",[235] without even mentioning the literature which denies a separability of the fields.[236] Later, the CJEU—in effect—also supported this view propagated in parts of the literature by reducing its judicial control to almost nil.[237]

The democratic principle requires a restriction of the tasks and powers conferred on an agency or authority with guaranteed independence shielding it from an effective democratic control. Specifically, it wants a narrow interpretation of the term "monetary policy" in Articles 119, 127(1) TFEU. For the same reasons, the propagated wide margin of discretion for the monetary authorities may not be acknowledged. This has been stated by the German Federal Constitutional Court with appropriate clarity.[238]

If the superior expertise of the persons framing a decision were a decisive threshold for judicial control, some of the most existential decisions would be excluded from the system of checks and balances and of democratic legitimation. This result is even more compelling in the event that the rescue operations select single institutions and countries to save from financial distress.

7.7.1.3 No Regional Selectivity of Central Bank Measures

Monetary policy at its core is characterised by its encompassing scope for the whole currency area. It alters its character when it is used to support only a part of the area.

1. *The Federal Reserve System*

Along this line, the Federal Reserve System of the USA is not allowed to support single states by buying their debt under the allegation that the interest rate the state has to accept for its debt is "irrational", or, more generally, that the "transmissions mechanism" is impaired. The Fed may not purchase any debt of these "sub-central" entities[239] in open market operations, only that of the Federal Government. It is a widely diffused misconception that the "quantitative easing" employed by the Fed is comparable to the—"installed or announced"—programmes of the ESCB. The Fed does not buy or accept as collateral debt instruments issued by any state, its agencies, or municipalities, no matter whether it be directly or on the secondary market. It does

[235] GFCC PSPP-referral (note 152 above) at margin no. 108.

[236] Thiele (2014a), at 255–264; idem (2014b), at 697 et seq; Simon (2015), at 1029; Jędrzejowska-Schiffauer and Schiffauer (2016), at 200 et seq: "methodological impossibility" assessing a "formalistic *ex-ante* legal definition" as "arbitrary and counter-productive" and defending the margin of discretion ceded to the ECB as "reasonable". Categories like "counter-productive" and "reasonable" are not really convincing arguments when exhorting the distribution of powers and competences, and, law is and has to be formalistic.

[237] GFCC PSPP-referral (note 152 above) at margin no. 132.

[238] Ibid., at margin no. 102: "Compliance with these restrictions is subject to full judicial review". For more details, see Sect. 7.5.3.2 above.

[239] Sometimes also labelled as "municipal" in the US, which has led to quite some misunderstandings in Europe.

not even provide liquidity assistance, not to mention solvency support, or subsidies for allegedly too high interest rates for sub-central entities. In the event of financial distress, they have to help themselves.

In essence, the Federal Reserve Act follows the so-called *real bill doctrine* in designing the instruments granted to the Fed. This can be demonstrated by the regulation of the discount window (12 USC § 343). It only allows to accept instruments with an underlying commercial transaction, similar to the former § 19 (1) no. 1 *Bundesbank Act* of 1957 (*gute Handelswechsel*). Notes, drafts, or bills covering merely financial operations are explicitly excluded from discount. The same holds for financial instruments of states, municipalities, or their agencies. Only obligations of the Federal Government and its agencies are exempted from this prohibition. The Dodd–Frank Act has somewhat relaxed these limitations in "unusual and exigent circumstance", but only with strict safeguards.

Even more important are the strict legal rules for open market operations. In essence, only bonds of the Federal Government and the agencies for which it has assumed liability may be purchased, provided that they are bought "in the open market". The purchase of obligations of any state, county, district, political subdivision, or municipality in the continental United States *is only allowed* if they are issued in anticipation of the collection of taxes or in anticipation of the receipt of assured revenues, and only if they have maturities not exceeding six months from the date of purchase (12 USC § 355 (1)). This is comparable to the limited power of the *Bundesbank* to grant short-term loans to public entities (*Kassenkredite*).[240] Even this very limited power of the *Bundesbank* had to be removed when establishing the European Monetary Union. What is also noteworthy is the clause requiring a purchase "only in the open market". This has to be taken literally. It requires that the instrument had been bought before by an investor. For this simple reason, manoeuvres such as the Emergency Liquidity Assistance handling in the case of Ireland and Cyprus would have been illegal in the U.S.

2. *The Bank of England*

The situation in the UK is not comparable to the US or the European Monetary Union. The Bank of England does not have to operate in a heterogeneous area of a federal type with several states. Technically, it executes its purchases by a wholly owned subsidiary, the "Bank of England Asset Purchase Facility Fund Limited" ("the Company"). Although the purchases are financed by central bank money and could be used for monetary policy purposes, the economic risk is not borne by the Bank of England. The Company is fully indemnified by the Treasury. This procedure has to be judged as an attempt to comply with Article 123 TFEU and protocol no. 15, clause 10, that provides an exemption only for the "'ways and means' facilities of the Bank of England", which are also comparable to short-term *Kassenkredite*. In effect, the Bank of England has not acquired sub-national assets and holds, as assets from the public sector, only UK government bonds ("gilts"). Loans to local authorities are

[240] § 20 (1) no. 1 Bundesbank Act 1957.

granted by the "United Kingdom Debt Management Office" and not by the Bank of England.

3. *Conclusion*

Simply because the (allegedly) not sufficient debt of a central government exists in the euro area does not justify an expansion of the range of competences; specifically, it does not allow the debt of subsets of the currency area to be selectively purchased. It would be a serious methodological flaw to conclude from the instruments provided to the ESCB, such as operations in the open market (Article 18.1, first indent, ESCB/ECB Statute), to its legality, no matter what purposes they follow, or what (regional) effect is envisaged by employing them. The provision clearly states that this instrument may only be used to achieve the objectives of the ESCB and to enable it to carry out its tasks. Not all measures involving money or having a financial objective are monetary policy.

7.7.2 Monetary Financing of Sovereign Budgets?

In essence, the support measures of the ESCB might have been judged as monetary policy but the selectivity of OMT and the upholding and resuming of APP in substantially changed economic environment makes this increasingly questionable—not to mention the prohibited (indirect) financing of budgetary deficits by the monetary authorities.

7.7.3 Necessity and Proportionality

The empirical evidence on the effectiveness of quantitative easing is not totally conclusive. Some studies see little effects beyond the secular development of long-term equilibrium in real interest rates.[241] Some acknowledge, however, a "significant impact" on both real GDP and HICP inflation.[242] At least in the short term, due to the additional demand generated by APP, the price of (eligible) securities rose, thereby augmenting the value of assets on balance sheets—namely, of banks—and, by the same token, expanding the volume of the balance sheet without injection of capital, thus enhancing the rate of equity. Another way to enhance this rate is by directly

[241] Belke et al. (2017).

[242] Weale and Wieladek (2016), Ademuyiwa et al. (2018), Dell'Ariccia et al. (2018, p. 167), Hammermann et al. (2019, p. 1), assessing the APP as an "adaptable and effective instrument *to ease monetary and financial conditions, foster economic recovery, counteract disinflationary pressures and anchor inflation expectations, thereby supporting a sustained adjustment in the path of inflation towards price stability*"; attributing some impact: Jäger and Grigoriadis (2017): "lowered the bond yield spreads" of Euro area countries; in general, also, Gambetti and Musso (2017), but conceding that the effect on GDP became "very small" by the fourth quarter of 2016 after the significant change of GDP (+0.18 percentage points) in the first quarter of 2015 and a long-term rise of the HICP; only under restrictive conditions: Cúrdia and Woodford (2011).

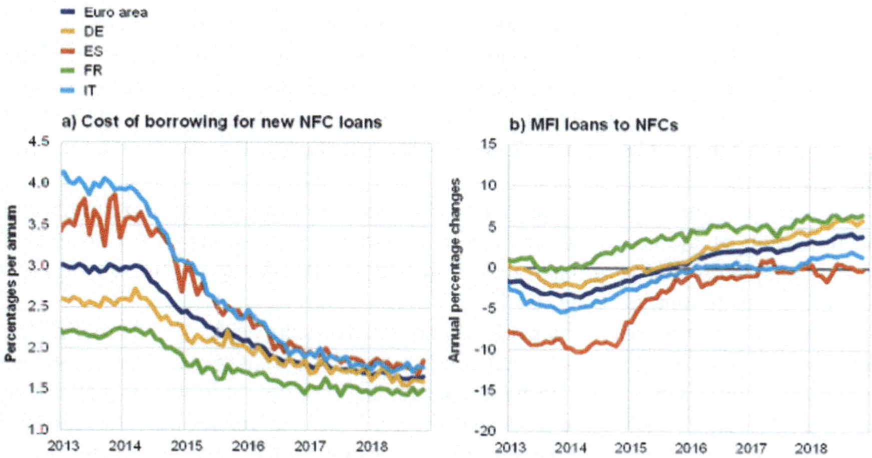

Fig. 7.4 Cost of borrowing for new NFC loans and MFI loans to NFCs. *Source* Hammermann et al. (2019, p. 19), referring to the ECB

selling assets and using the proceeds to pay back debt (deleveraging).[243] In the beginning, QE was in essence a tool to recapitalise banks.

The rising price of a bond conversely implies a decline of bond yields, which was widely diagnosed following the announcement of APP.[244] Deteriorating bond yields are likely to induce growing risk appetite in the search for yield partially supported by the augmented equity and the well-founded expectation that the central banks would continue to buy the material. The incentive to monitor debtors properly will decrease. Within the portfolio re-balancing channel, the "duration risk" borne by private investors is likely to be extracted as well, and might lead to a decrease of the "term premium component" of medium- and long-term yields, but with a diminishing degree.[245] It is contended that this would continue even after the net purchases have ceased.[246] In conjunction with the other measures, such as negative deposit rates, bank lending rates have declined and converged across euro area countries as shown in Fig. 7.4. It is, however, difficult to separate out the impact of an individual measure, such as APP.[247] In addition, the shift of risks to the central bank is not adequately comprehended.

The working of these mechanisms on the financial market is, however, no compelling evidence of a long- to medium-term effect of APP on the inflation rate

---

[243] See, among, other Murswiek (2015, p. 24), already questioning the incentive for the banks to hand out new loans instead of strengthening their equity by reducing debt (p. 25).

[244] Altavilla et al. (2015), De Santis (2016), Dell'Ariccia et al. (2018, p. 147).

[245] Belke and Gros (2019): "There is no reason to consider the impact [of the APP announcement on risk premiums] to have been permanent"; Hammermann et al. (2019, p. 17 et seq).

[246] Hammermann et al. (2019, p. 15 et seq).

[247] Even conceded by Hammermann et al. (2019, p. 19), nevertheless giving indications for an induced loan growth (p. 20), referring in addition to Altavilla et al. (2015).

for consumer prices. The self-set inflation rate, relentlessly equated with the legally prescribed "price stability",[248] appears to be missed during the whole duration of the purchases. In this respect, it is questionable whether QE does (still) work. The effect on real GDP—according to the unambiguous wording of Article 127(5) TFEU not an objective of the ESCB—is not as clear as is contended, at least not in the long run (Table 7.3).

Time has become an important factor. The sheer duration of the programmes and the transition of the economic environment also raise questions of necessity and proportionality. At the very least, their downsides and risks appear increasingly to outweigh their (potential) benefits.[249]

That the economic environment clearly has changed can be derived from Fig. 7.5. Since 2017, the output gap has turned positive indicating that production factors are over-used. In addition, the inflation rate, particularly the core inflation, is well above 1.5%, and is thus close to the goal that the ECB has set for its monetary policy. The risks and increasing downsides, which warrant an exit, are increasing. Even during that time the ESCB has halted its net purchases (January to October 2019), it nonetheless continued to "re-invest" the redeemed debt instruments. In order to return to normal, the ESCB would have to reduce these "re-investments" and reduce the size of its balance sheet, which poses a growing danger; not least for its independence. Finally, interest rates would have to be raised.

The window of opportunity for an exit might have already been closed since economic growth had slowed somewhat during Q3 and Q4 of 2018. For 2019, the German Council of Economic Experts diagnosed a clear downturn, at least in industry production, whereas services, construction and domestic consumption looked rather stable with an overall positive outlook for mid-2020.[250] Notwithstanding this, the ESCB resumed its net purchases as of 1 November 2019 at a pace of €20 billion per month and with no fixed time limit. Treating the (self-set) inflation rate as a synonym of price stability is a hermeneutic trick to enlarge almost indefinitely the competence for monetary policy. The primary law of the EU does not approve inflation targeting. Aspiring an inflation rate contradicts the primary law of the EU which does not even know the term "inflation". For good reasons it only knows price stability and sets it as (primary) objective for monetary policy.

Finally, in June 2018, the Governing Council of the ECB also came to a positive assessment of "progress towards a sustained adjustment in the path of inflation"[251] underpinned by a "stronger anchoring of longer-term inflation expectations",

[248]Objecting Murswiek (2015, p. 48), Siekmann (2018 at no. 92, 95 et seq).

[249]*Sachverständigenrat* [German Council of Economic Experts] (2015, pp. 143–145, nos. 307–309), idem (2016, p. 185, 208–213 and 223 et seq), idem (2017, pp. 179–182), idem (2018, pp. 178–190), idem (2019, nos. 71, 76 et seq., 80).

[250]For a comprehensive assessment of the need for normalisation, see *Sachverständigenrat* [German Council of Economic Experts] (2018), margin nos. 352–361; disagreeing authors from the ECB: Hammermann et al. (2019, p. 3), emphasising the aspired inflation rate and treating it as a synonymon of price stability.

[251]Press release of the meeting of the Governing Council on 14 June 2018, https://www.ecb.europa.eu/press/pr/date/2018/html/ecb.mp180614.en.html.

Table 7.3 Impact of non-standard policy measures on euro area inflation and real GDP growth

	Inflation (percentage points)						Real GDP growth (percentage points)					
	2016	2017	2018	2019	2020	Cumulative (2016–2020)	2016	2017	2018	2019	2020	Cumulative (2016–2020)
All measures taken since June 2014	0.85	0.49	0.22	0.21	0.16	1.9	0.79	0.48	0.31	0.2	0.08	1.9

Taken from Hammermann et al. (2019), Table 1
Sources Eurosystem staff calculations and NCB country-based models
Notes The table reports the estimated impact of all policy measures adopted since mid-2014. The assessment takes as reference the December 2018 BMPE information set. The estimates are derived on the basis of various modelling

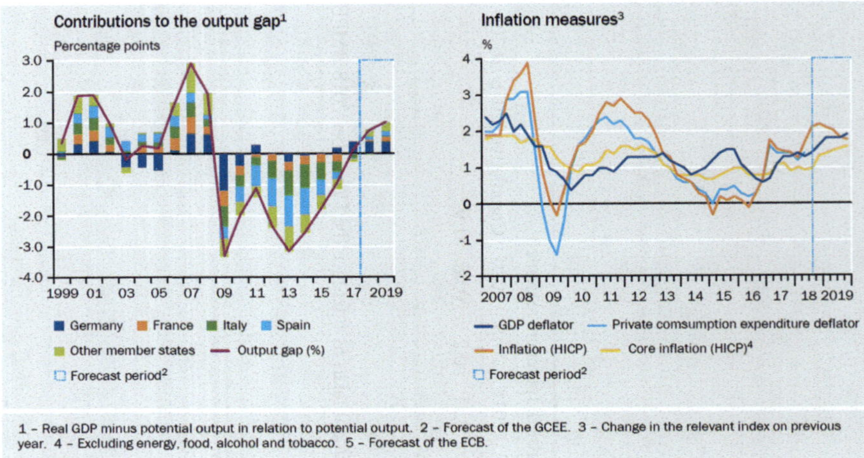

Fig. 7.5 Output gap and inflation measures.
Source Sachverständigenrat [German Council of Economic Experts] (2018), at 179, Chart 49

an "underlying strength of domestic demand", and a "continuing ample degree of monetary accommodation" which would provide "grounds for confidence that sustained convergence would continue and be maintained even after the end of net purchases".[252] This lead to the evaluation that in the medium range headline inflation had moved closer to 2% as demonstrated in Fig. 7.6 below:

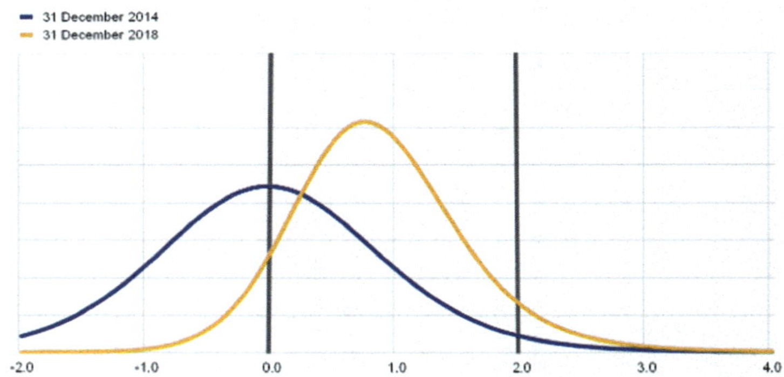

Fig. 7.6 Option-implied probability density function of euro area inflation compensation: Annual percentage changes, density.
Source Hammermann et al. (2019, p. 21), referring to the ECB

[252] Hammermann et al. (2019, p. 21).

Some doubts remain whether from this graph the alleged development can really be derived. In any case, "the path of future inflation was judged to have become more resilient over time, making it less reliant on net asset purchases".[253] Hence, net purchases were terminated at the end of 2018. A few months later, the Governing council changed its mind and net purchases were resumed in November 2019. It is difficult to see a move to the aspired inflation rate in the medium range expectation justifying the end of net asset purchases and negate this evaluation shortly afterwards without fundamentals changes in the economic situation.

The objective to enhance the transmission mechanism—granting a malfunction exists—is not per se an act of monetary policy as the ECB asserts and the necessity of APP in view of the objective of the ESCB remains questionable.[254]

7.7.4 Size of the Consolidated Balance Sheet of the Eurosystem

The sheer size of the balance sheet of a central bank represents a potential threat for its independence. It might incite demands to use it for other objectives than price stability deemed useful and desirable by both politicians and the general public. The dangers are apparent. Tampering with its independence is already visible (US, Italy, Turkey). In the euro area, another risk exists. Unlike the Federal Reserve System,[255] it has acquired to a large extent debt issued by the sub-central parts of the currency area,[256] which are basically sovereign entities. If these holdings are not reduced, they might amount to an additional monetary financing of Member States' activities and would weaken the signalling and disciplining functions for public finances of the members of the Monetary Union.[257]

The threat to the independence of the institutions, organs and acting persons (personal independence)[258] might become real, despite its comprehensive guarantees in the primary law of the Union[259] which can be amended only by unanimous consent of all Member States, pursuant to Article 48 TEU. As can be derived from the right-hand side of Fig. 7.7, a substantial part of government of some Member States, first and foremost Italy, is held by the Central Bank. The large share held by the other domestic financial institutions might also spur political pressure on the ESCB

[253] Hammermann et al. (2019, p. 22).

[254] Murswiek (2015, p. 45 et seq), Belke et al. (2017).

[255] See Sect. 7.7.1.3 above.

[256] See Fig. 7.7.

[257] *Sachverständigenrat* [German Council of Economic Experts] (2016), margin nos. 427 et seq; idem (2018), at margin no. 378.

[258] For the personal independence, see Siekmann (2013b) Article 130 TFEU at margin no. 64; idem (2018), Article 88 at margin nos. 58 et seq.

[259] Siekmann (2013b), Article 130 TFEU at margin nos. 18–23; idem (2018), Article 88 at margin nos. 51–68.

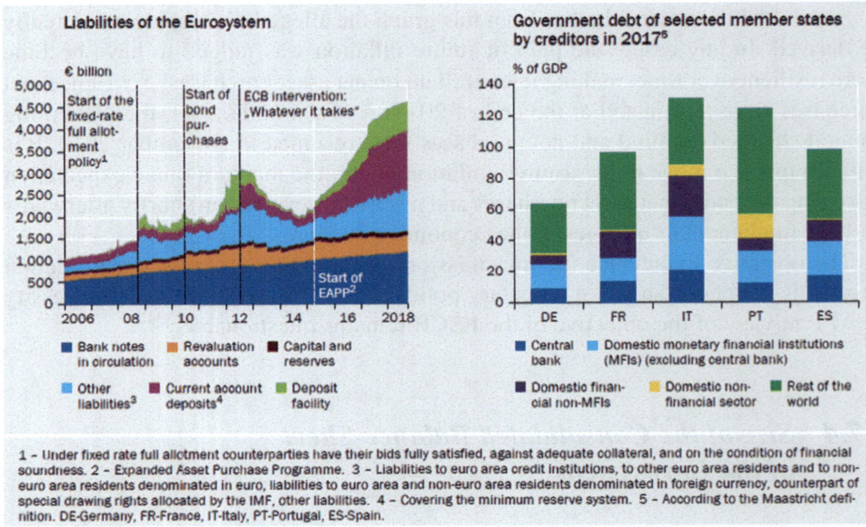

Fig. 7.7 Liabilities of the Eurosystem and government debt of selected Member States by creditors.
Source Sachverständigenrat [German Council of Economic Experts] (2018), at 190, Chart 51

with the goal of easing financing conditions irresponsibly or granting Emergency Liquidity Assistance within the frame of Article 14.4 ESCB/ECB Statute.

The distribution of losses incurring from write-downs on the purchased assets also plays a crucial role in the legal assessment of the programmes. Establishing—in effect—an equalisation system via the asset purchases of the ESCB by shifting risks of write-downs is definitely economic policy and *not* monetary policy, and hence a transgression of competences.

Moreover, QE might adversely affect the interpersonal distribution because the holders of real wealth (stock, real estate) will profit and the holders of monetary assets (typically savers) will lose, and the net effect on distribution from the savings of the government (typically the biggest debtor) is unclear, at the very least.

7.7.5 Conclusion

Initially, the support measures of the ESCB cannot be assessed as monetary policy. The selectivity of OMT and—even more—SMP in conjunction with the transfer of risks to the ESCB, speak strongly against it. In general, supporting banks or governments in parts of the currency area is not a task of monetary policy which has to be encompassing for this area. Fiscal needs of one or several states in the area is not an objective of monetary policy. The holding until maturity, the de facto guarantee for investors that the sovereign debt will be purchased by the ESCB, and the imminent threat of waiving debt or an externally imposed debt-cut, already demanded by politicians, all suggest that the asset purchase programmes have to be judged as a prohibited (indirect) financing of budgetary deficits by the monetary authorities. The substantially changed economic environment tips the balance between the benefits and the costs of the programmes increasingly to a preponderance towards the latter; thus disproving its necessity.

The Court of Justice of the EU came to a different assessment in all aspects, negating the concerns of the German Federal Constitutional Court. It remains to be seen how it will exert its reserved control of *ultra vires* acts and of the constitutional identity of the Basic Law, the German Federal Constitution. The CJEU left little space for the GFCC by granting the above-recounted wide margin of assessment to the ECB.[260]

References

Ademuyiwa, I., Siklos, P., & St. Amand, S. (2018). Central Bank Balance Sheets and Monetary Policy. VOX CEPR 08 November 2018.

Altavilla, C., Carboni, G., & Motto, R. (2015). Asset Purchase Programmes and Financial Markets: Lessons from the Euro Area. European Central Bank, Working Paper Series No. 1864, November 2015.

Bauerfeind, T. (2019). EuGH: PSPP-Anleihekaufprogramm der EZB mit EU-Recht vereinbar, GWR, 9.

Belke, A., Gros, D., & Osowski, T. (2017). The effectiveness of the Fed's quantitative easing policy. *Journal of International Money and Finance, 73,* 335–349.

Belke, A., Gros, D. (2019). QE in the Euro Area: Has PSPP Benefited Peripheral Bonds? Ruhr Economic Papers #803 (March 2019).

Borger, V. (2013). The ESM and the European court's predicament in *Pringle. German Law Journal, 14*(1), 113–127.

Cour-Thiemann, P., & Winkler, B. (2012). The ECB's non-standard monetary policy measures: The role of institutional factors and financial structure. *Oxford Review of Economic Policy, 28*(4), 765–803.

Cour-Thiemann, P., & Winkler, B. (2013). The ECB's non-standard monetary policy measures: The role of institutional factors and financial structure. European Central Bank, Working Paper Series No. 1528, April 2013.

Cúrdia, V., & Woodford. M. (2011). The central-bank balance sheet as an instrument of monetary policy. *Journal of Monetary Economics, 58,* 54–79.

Dell'Ariccia, G., Rabanal, P., & Sandri, D. (2018). Unconventional monetary policies in the Euro Area, Japan, and the United Kingdom. *Journal of Economic Perspectives, 32*(4), 147–172.

De Santis, R. (2016). Impact of the Asset Purchase Programme on Euro Area Government Bond Yields Using Market News. European Central Bank, Working Paper Series No. 1939, July 2016.

Deutsche Bundesbank. (2013). Stellungnahme gegenüber dem Bundesverfassungsgericht vom 21. Dezember 2012 in den Verfahren 2 BvR 1390/12, 2 BvR 1421/12, 2 BvR 1439/12, 2 BvR 1824/12, BvE 6/12.

Deutsche Bundesbank. (2018). Der Markt für Bundeswertpapiere: Haltestruktur und wesentliche Einflussfaktoren auf die Renditeentwicklung. *Monatsbericht Juli, 2018,* 15–39.

[260] Bauerfeind (2019).

Fuest, C., & Sinn, H.-W. (2018). Target Risks without Euro Exit. CESifo Forum 19 (4) December 2018.
Frenz, W., & Ehlenz, C. (2010). Europäische Wirtschaftspolitik nach Lissabon. *Gewerbe Archiv, 9,* 329–336.
Gentzsch, M. (2019). Gerichtliche Kontrolle geldpolitischer Entscheidungen der EZB am Beispiel des Public Sector Purchase Programme, *EuR*, 279.
Gärditz, K. F. (2014). Beyond symbolism: towards a constitutional *actio popularis* in EU affairs? a commentary on the OMT decision of the federal constitutional court. *German Law Journal, 15*(2), 183–201.
Gambetti, L., & Musso, A. (2017). The Macroeconomic Impact of the ECB's Expanded Asset Purchase Programme (APP). European Central Bank, Working Paper Series No. 2075, June 2017.
Giannone, D., Lenza, M., Pill, H., & Reichlin, L. (2011). Non-standard Monetary Policy Measures and Monetary Developments. European Central Bank, Working Paper Series No. 1290, January 2011.
Häde, U. (2016). Article 136 AEUV. In: C. Calliess and M. Ruffert (eds), *EUV/AEUV*, 5th edn., C.H. Beck, Munich.
Hammermann, F., Leonard, K., Nardelli, S., & von Landesberger, J. (2019). Taking Stock of the Eurosystem's Asset Purchase Programme after the End of Net Asset Purchases, https://www.ecb.europa.eu/pub/economic-bulletin/articles/2019/html/ecb.ebart201902_01~3049319b8d.en.html#toc1.
Herrmann, C. (2010a), *Währungshoheit, Währungsverfassung und subjektive Rechte.* Mohr Siebeck, Tübingen.
Herrmann, C. (2010b). EZB-Programm für die Kapitalmärkte verstößt nicht gegen die Verträge—Erwiderung auf Martin Seidel. *Europäische Zeitschrift für Wirtschaftsrecht, 9,* 645.
Heun, W. (2014). Eine verfassungswidrige Verfassungsgerichtsentscheidung—der Vorlagebeschluss des BVerfG vom 14.1.2014. *Juristen Zeitung, 7,* 331–337.
Hoffmann, D. (2015). Die EZB in der Krise. Pro Business, Berlin.
International Monetary Fund. (2013). Unconventional Monetary Policies—Recent Experiences and Prospects, 18 April 2013.
Jäger, J., & Grigoriadis, T. (2017). The effectiveness of the ECB's unconventional monetary policy: comparative evidence from crisis and non-crisis Euro-area countries. *Journal of International Money and Finance, 78,* 21–43.
Jędrzejowska-Schiffauer, I., & Schiffauer, P. (2016). European central Bank's OMT Decision: Still within the framework of the monetary policy? *Journal of International Studies, 9*(2), 195–206.
Jurkšas, L., Kapp, D., Nyholm, K., & Von Landsberger, J. (2018). Euro Area Sovereign Bond Market Liquidity since the Start of the PSPP. *ECB Economic Bulletin*, 2: 41–44 Boxes.
Keller, C. (2013). Article 18 ESCB/ECB Statute. In: H. Siekmann (ed.), *Kommentar zur Europäischen Währungsunion.* Mohr Siebeck, Tübingen.
Klein, H. H. (2014). Integration und Verfassung. *Archiv für öffentliches Recht (AöR), 139,* 165–195.
Lombardi, D., & Moschella, M. (2016). The government bond buying programmes of the european central bank: An analysis of their policy settings. *Journal of European Public Policy, 23*(6), 851–870.
Ludwigs, M. (2017). Die Krisenpolitik der EZB zwischen Verfassungs- und Unionsrecht. *Neue Juristische Wochenschrift (NJW), 49,* 3563–3567.
Müller-Graff, P.-C. (2019). Anmerkungen zu EuGH (Große Kammer), Urteil vom 11.12.2018—C-493/17. *Europäische Zeitschrift für Wirtschaftsrecht (EuZW), 162,* 172–173.
Murswiek, D. (2015). Das ABS-Ankaufsprogramm der EZB. Herausgeber: Stiftung Familienunternehmen.
Murswiek, D. (2016). *Die Eurokrise vor dem Bundesverfassungsgericht.* Nomos, Baden Baden.
Petch, T. (2013). The compatibility of outright monetary transactions with EU Law. *Law and Financial Markets Review*, 13–21.

Richter, C. (2015). Article 136 AEUV. In: R. Geiger, D.-E. Khan, M. Kotzur (eds.), *European Union Treaties*. C.H. Beck, Munich.
Ruffert, M. (2019). Europarecht: Anleihenkäufe der EZB. *Juristische Schulung, 2,* 181–184.
Sachverständigenrat zur Begutachtung der gesamtwirtschaftlichen Entwicklung [German Council of Economic Experts]. (2015). Zukunftsfähigkeit in den Mittelpunkt. Jahresgutachten [Annual Report] 2015/2016. Wiesbaden.
Sachverständigenrat zur Begutachtung der gesamtwirtschaftlichen Entwicklung [German Council of Economic Experts]. (2016). Zeit für Reformen. Jahresgutachten Jahresgutachten [Annual Report] 2016/2017. Wiesbaden.
Sachverständigenrat zur Begutachtung der gesamtwirtschaftlichen Entwicklung [German Council of Economic Experts]. (2017). Für eine zukunftsorientierte Wirtschaftspolitik. Jahresgutachten [Annual Report] 2017/2018. Wiesbaden.
Sachverständigenrat zur Begutachtung der gesamtwirtschaftlichen Entwicklung [German Council of Economic Experts]. (2018). Vor wichtigen wirtschaftspolitischen Weichenstellungen [Setting the Right Course for Economic Policy]. Jahresgutachten [Annual Report] 2018/19. Wiesbaden.
Sachverständigenrat zur Begutachtung der gesamtwirtschaftlichen Entwicklung [German Council of Economic Experts]. (2019). Vor wichtigen wirtschaftspolitischen Weichenstellungen [Mastering the Structural Change]. Jahresgutachten [Annual Report] 2019/20. Wiesbaden.
Schmidt, R. (2015). Die entfesselte EZB. *Juristen Zeitung, 7,* 317–327.
Seidel, M. (2010). Der Ankauf nicht markt- und börsengängiger Staatsanleihen, namentlich Griechenlands, durch die Europäische Zentralbank und durch nationale Zentralbanken—rechtlich nur fragwürdig oder Rechtsverstoß? *Europäische Zeitschrift für Wirtschaftsrecht, 14,* 521.
Seidel, M. (2011). Europarechtsverstöße und Verfassungsbruch im Doppelpack. *Europäische Zeitschrift für Wirtschaftsrecht, 7,* 241.
Shirakawa, M. (2002). One Year Under "Quantitative Easing". Discussion Paper No. 2002-E-3, Institute for Monetary and Economic Studies, Bank of Japan.
Siekmann, H. (2013a). Missachtung rechtlicher Vorgaben des AEUV durch die Mitgliedstaaten und die EZB in der Staatsschuldenkrise. In T. M. J. Möllers & F.-C. Zeitler (Eds.), *Europa als Rechtsgemeinschaft—Währungsunion und Schuldenkrise*. Tübingen: Mohr Siebeck.
Siekmann, H. (2013b). Einführung, Article 119 and 130 TFEU. In H. Siekmann (Ed.), *Kommentar zur Europäischen Währungsunion*. Tübingen: Mohr Siebeck.
Siekmann, H. (2015). The Legality of Outright Monetary Transactions (OMT) of the European System of Central Banks. In: F. Rövekamp, M. Bälz, H.G. Hilpert (eds.), *Central Banking and Financial Stability in East Asia*. Springer International, Cham et al., 101–123.
Siekmann, H. (2017). Die Einstandspflicht der Bundesrepublik Deutschland für die Deutsche Bundesbank und die Europäische Zentralbank. In H. Siekmann (Ed.), *Festschrift für Theodor Baums*. Tübingen: Mohr Siebeck.
Siekmann, H. (2018). Article 88 GG. In: M. Sachs (ed.), *Grundgesetz*, 8th edn. C.H. Beck, Munich.
Siekmann, H., & Wieland, V. (2013). The European Central Banks' Outright Monetary Transactions and the Federal Constitutional Court of Germany. IMFS Working Paper Series No. 71.
Siekmann, H., & Wieland, V. (2014a). Have Markets Misunderstood the German Court's Decision on OMT? *Vox*, 3 October 2014, 621.
Siekmann, H., & Wieland, V. (2014b). The German Constitutional Court's Decision on OMT: Have Markets Misunderstood? London: Centre for Economic Policy Research, Policy Insight 623, No. 74 (October 2014).
Simon, S. (2015). Direct cooperation has begun: Some remarks on the judgment of the CJEU on the OMT decision of the ECB in the judgment of the CJEU on the OMT decision of the ECB in response to the german federal constitutional court's first request for a preliminary ruling. *German Law Review, 16*(04), 1025–1048.
Thiele, A. (2013). *Das Mandat der EZB und die Krise des Euro*. Tübingen: Mohr Siebeck.
Thiele, A. (2014a). Friendly or Unfriendly Act? The 'Historic' Referral of the Constitutional Court to the CJEU Regarding the the ECB's OMT Program. *German Law Journal, 15*(2), 241–264.

Thiele, A. (2014b). Die EZB als fiscal- und wirtschaftspolitischer Akteur? *Europäische Zeitschrift für Wirtschaftsrecht, 18,* 694–698.

Thym, D. (2013). Anmerkung. *Juristen Zeitung, 5,* 259–264.

Ukrow, J. (2014). Von Luxemburg lernen heißt Integrationsgrenzen bestimmen. Anmerkungen zur Vorlage-Entscheidung des Bundesverfassungsgerichts vom 14. Januar 2014. *Zeitschrift für Europarechtliche Studien, 17* (2): 119–139.

Varghese, R., & Zhang, S. (2018). A New Wave of ECB Unconventional Monetary Policies: Domestic Impact and Spillovers. IMF Working Paper WP/18/11, January 2018.

Voßkuhle, A. (2016). "Integration durch Recht"—Der Beitrag des Bundesverfassungsgerichts. *Juristen Zeitung (JZ), 71*(4), 161–168.

Weale, M., & Wieladek, T. (2016). What are the macroeconomic effects of asset purchases. *Journal of Monetary Economics, 79,* 81–93.

Winkler, A. (2014). Mario Draghi und Helmut Schmidt—Retter, die gegen die Verfassung verstießen. Oder: Das Bundesverfassungsgericht entscheidet über die richtige Finanztheorie. *Credit and Capital Markets, 47*(2), 213–240.

Chapter 8
The Bank of Japan's Exchange-Traded Fund Purchases under Quantitative and Qualitative Easing with Yield Curve Control

Sayuri Shirai

Abstract This chapter highlights exchange-traded funds (ETF) purchases conducted by the Bank of Japan under Quantitative and Qualitative Monetary Easing with Yield Curve Control. The policy to purchase stocks indirectly is unprecedented in terms of both scale and duration among major central banks. The purpose of this policy is to promote portfolio re-balancing among individuals, in addition to achieving the 2% price-stability target. While stock prices have more than doubled, individuals have remained largely risk-averse, and foreign investors have increasingly dominated the stock market. Moreover, the BoJ has become one of the largest (silent) investors, with the growing impact on stock prices through the reduction of the downside risk and the possible overvaluing of some small-cap listed firms. Given that achieving 2% inflation is a distant future prospect, the BoJ may find it necessary to unwind the policy gradually by purchasing ETFs only when the stock market is under severe stress, and thereby reduce the annual pace of ETF purchases from about ¥6 trillion. This view is in line with the BoJ's adjustments announced in July 2018 on introducing flexibility and changing the composition of ETF purchases. Whether the BoJ will be able to take a clearer, more decisive step remains to be seen, however.

8.1 Introduction

In January 2013, the Bank of Japan (BoJ), led, at the time, by its previous governor, Masaaki Shirakawa, introduced its 2% price-stability target. In April 2013, under its current governor, Haruhiko Kuroda, the BoJ adopted massive and various monetary easing tools to achieve this target—the so-called Quantitative and Qualitative Monetary Easing (QQE). QQE was expanded in October 2014, supplemented with a negative interest rate in January 2016, and further with yield curve control in September

S. Shirai (✉)
Keio University, 5322 Endoh, Fujisawa, Kanagawa 252-0882, Japan
e-mail: sshirai@sfc.keio.ac.jp

F. Rövekamp et al. (eds.), *Monetary Policy Implementation in East Asia*, Financial and Monetary Policy Studies 51,
https://doi.org/10.1007/978-3-030-50298-0_8

2016—hereinafter QQE with Yield Curve Control.[1] Adopting a 2% target to raise inflation in a low inflationary or mildly deflationary environment such as Japan is a rare experiment in the world.

As part of QQE, the BoJ has been purchasing Japanese stocks—not directly, but indirectly through the purchases of Exchange-Traded Funds (ETFs). There are very few central banks in the world that have purchased stocks on this scale or for such a long time (for more than 5 years under QQE, but for nearly a total of 8 years since its introduction) as part of the conduct of monetary policy. The case of the intervention by the Hong Kong Monetary Authority (HKMA) in 2008 cannot be compared with the case of the BoJ in terms of scale and duration. So when the BoJ embarked on its course of action, it had no reference to the experiences of other central banks. Similarly, the BoJ's extremely challenging task of normalising the policy and ultimately disposing of the stocks purchased will be without precedent.

The main pillars of the BoJ's monetary-easing strategy are large-scale purchases of Japanese government bonds (JGBs), a negative interest rate, and a 10-year yield target under yield curve control. This chapter sheds light only on the BoJ's ETF purchases, as there has been very little research on this. The chapter is made up of five sections. Section 8.2 provides a brief review of the BoJ's history of stock purchases from 2002 to 2010, as well as the ETF purchases initiated by Masaaki Shirakawa, who was governor of the BoJ until March 2013. It also looks at the case of Hong Kong, where the HKMA briefly intervened in the stock market in 2008. Section 8.3 focuses on the current ETF purchasing programme being conducted under the present governor, Haruhiko Kuroda. Section 8.4 sheds light on the features of Japan's stock markets and the possible side effects. Section 8.5 concludes.

8.2 The BoJ's Purchase of Stocks and Exchange-Traded Funds Before April 2013

8.2.1 The Purchases of Stocks by the Central Bank Under the Foreign Reserve Management Strategy

Central banks across the world rarely purchase domestic stocks as a monetary-easing tool. But some central banks *do* purchase foreign stocks and ETFs as part of their foreign reserve management strategies. Such purchases should be distinguished from the practices adopted by the BoJ and the HKMA, as these two central banks focused on domestic stocks (stocks listed on the domestic stock markets). While the monetary policy meeting of a central bank determines the types and the amount of the assets to be purchased to achieve its price-stability mandate, foreign reserve management is generally conducted by professional, external (private sector), reserve managers appointed by the central bank.

---

[1] See Shirai (2018a).

These foreign reserve assets have been accumulated by the central bank typically through foreign exchange market interventions to reduce the appreciation pressure of their exchange rates and to contain excessive volatility. Foreign reserve assets are generally managed in accordance with specified objectives—including (1) providing confidence to foreign investors who provide foreign capital to the domestic government or to firms with regard to the ability to repay the foreign currency-denominated debt; and (2) supporting the exchange rate of the domestic currency at times of capital flight and depreciation pressures. Reserve managers tend to purchase stocks as a portfolio strategy by paying attention to liquidity, various risks (such as market, credit and exchange-rate risks), and reasonable returns, in line with the instructions set by the central bank.

The central banks in the emerging economies usually attempt to hold ample foreign reserve assets as compared with short-term foreign debt in preparation for volatile cross-border capital flows, especially when their exchange rates tend to face sharp depreciation pressures. Among the advanced economies, the Swiss National Bank (SNB) has intervened heavily in the foreign exchange markets since the global financial crisis (2008–2009), as the Swiss franc appreciated sharply and became overvalued due to its status as a safe-haven currency, like the Japanese yen. Given that the number of government bonds has been limited due to prudent fiscal policy in Switzerland, the SNB has found it necessary to intervene in the foreign exchange markets rather than conduct unconventional quantitative easing through government bond purchases. The SNB continues to intervene in the foreign exchange market because the Swiss franc has remained overvalued. Diversification of the resultant accumulated foreign reserve assets is sought through purchasing various foreign assets, including stocks.

Recently, the reserve managers of foreign reserve assets have increasingly invested in sovereign bonds in non-standard economies such as the emerging economies as well as in equities and other assets[2]—mostly as passive investors. This reflects their search for yields in an extremely low interest rate environment. After the global financial crisis of 2008–2009, many central banks in the advanced economies, including the United States, Europe and Japan, adopted unconventional monetary easing measures, such as large-scale purchases of government bonds and other bonds. This resulted in long-term bond yields falling to historically low levels in the advanced economies. Consequently, in their search for returns, reserve managers have had to turn to types of financial assets in which they had rarely or hardly ever invested in the past.

[2]See Jones (2018).

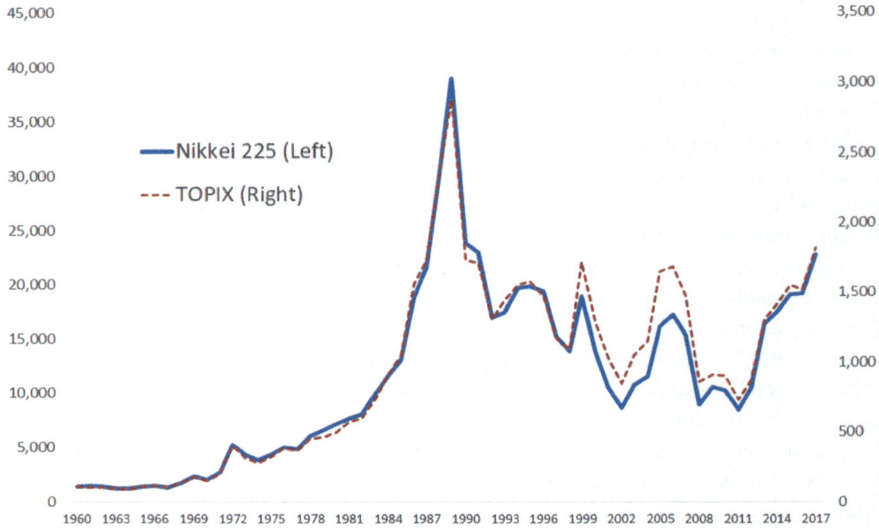

Fig. 8.1 Performance of the Nikkei 225 Stock Market Index (¥) and TOPIX Index. *Source* Bloomberg

8.2.2 The Purchases of Stocks from Banks by the BoJ in 2002–2010

Asset price bubbles in stocks and real estate had occurred in the second half of the 1980s, partly as a result of the government's economic policies and the BoJ's monetary easing to cope with the recession in the manufacturing sector, in response to a sharp appreciation of the yen after the Plaza Accord of 1985.[3] The Nikkei 225 reached ¥38,915 and the TOPIX 2,884 points in late 1989, their highest ever levels (Fig. 8.1). Generally, the Nikkei 225 and the TOPIX tend to show similar trends. The Nikkei 225—formally called the Nikkei Stock Average—is a stock price average published by the Japanese newspaper publisher Nikkei Inc., using a method of calculation similar to that of the Dow Jones Industrial Average in the United States. It has been published since 1950 and is comprised of the 225 stocks of the Tokyo Stock Exchange First Section, which are selected based upon high liquidity and by taking into account any changes in the industry structure and the balance of the sectors in terms of the number of constituents. The TOPIX, also known as the Tokyo Stock Price Index, is a capitalisation-weighted index of all companies listed on the First Section of the Tokyo Stock Exchange and calculated by the Japan Exchange Group (2,106 as of 8 August 2018), using a method of calculation similar to that of

[3]The Plaza Accord was a joint-agreement between France, West Germany, Japan, the United States, and the United Kingdom, to depreciate the US dollar in relation to the Japanese yen and the German mark by intervening in currency markets, signed at the Plaza Hotel, New York, on 22 September 1985.

the S&P 500 in the United States. The TOPIX has been calculated since July 1969 and assumes that market capitalisation, as of the base date (4 January 1968), is 100 points. Since the TOPIX is adjusted for free floats and is capitalisation-weighted, this indicator is considered superior to the Nikkei 225.

The bubbles collapsed in the early 1990s after the Ministry of Finance had tightened regulations against banks to reduce their lending concentration to the real estate sector, and the BoJ had concomitantly tightened monetary policy. The resultant bursting of the bubble-generated non-performing loans among financial institutions in Japan in the early 1990s. After this, financial conditions deteriorated and eventually caused a financial crisis which began in 1997, when several securities companies, banks and insurance firms collapsed, and there were runs on several banks. Under these circumstances, on two occasions, the BoJ bought bank stocks for *financial system stability purposes*: in the first round in 2002–2004 (when Japan suffered a domestic banking crisis), followed by the second round in 2009–2010 (during and after the global financial crisis). It purchased stocks worth about ¥2 trillion in 2002–2004, and about ¥400 billion in 2009–2010.

The First Round of the Stock Purchasing Programme (November 2002–September 2004)

In September 2002, the BoJ decided to purchase stocks directly from troubled banks to help them resolve their non-performing loan problems and to ensure the stability of the financial system. The purchase, which began in November 2002, was aimed, therefore, at *improving financial system stability, rather than conducting monetary easing*. Mounting non-performing loan problems, as a result of the bursting of the asset price bubble, led to banks disposing of more than ¥90 trillion worth of assets. Despite this, new non-performing loans emerged as a result of the aggressive restructuring efforts of the banks, low-interest margins (the gap between lending and deposit rates) and unrealised losses on the stocks held by banks. For the banking sector crisis to be resolved, it was urgently necessary for the banks to evaluate non-performing loans more properly, dispose of them as soon as possible and thus become more profitable. The BoJ viewed that the stocks held by the banks had prevented the banks from promoting these processes smoothly.

To reduce the constraint as soon as possible, the BoJ decided to purchase these stocks in order to reduce the banks' holdings of listed stocks with a credit rating of BBB and above at the market price. The BoJ set the maximum total amount of stocks that it would purchase at ¥2 trillion, and would do so until the end of September 2003 (with a possible extension until the end of September 2004 should the cumulative amount of purchased stocks not have reached ¥2 trillion by the end of September 2003). The maximum amount of stocks purchased from an individual bank would not exceed the amount of the lesser bank's Tier I capital or ¥500 billion. The maximum number of shares per issuer would be 5% of all voting rights or a specific amount in relation to the turnover, whichever was less.

In September 2003, this purchasing programme was extended for another year until the end of September 2004, and the maximum total amount of stocks to be purchased was expanded to ¥3 trillion. At the end of September 2004, the BoJ decided to discontinue its stock-purchasing programme, having purchased stocks worth ¥2,018 billion in total. The BoJ also confirmed its intention not to start selling the purchased stocks until the end of September 2007 at the earliest, as well as its plan to complete the disposal on stock exchanges by the end of September 2007. The disposal of stocks began in October 2007, according to plan.

The Second Round of the Stock Purchasing Programme (February 2009–April 2010)

The disposal of stocks held by the BoJ was subsequently suspended in October 2008 due to unfavourable developments in financial markets both at home and abroad caused by the global financial crisis. As a result, the amount of the BoJ's remaining stock holdings was ¥1,273 billion based upon a book value as of end-September 2008.

In February 2009, the BoJ resumed its stock-purchasing programme in the midst of the deepening global financial crisis and associated stock market instability both globally and domestically. While massive losses stemming from non-performing loans were largely associated with financial institutions in the United States and in Europe, Japanese financial institutions also faced massive realised and unrealised losses from their stock-holdings, even though the number of stock-holdings had been reduced in the first half of the 2000s, as stated above. Thus, the BoJ decided to purchase stocks from banks in order to reduce the market risk associated with holdings of listed stocks with a rating of BBB and above at the market price until the end of April 2010. The total amount of ¥1 trillion would be used for: (1) banks with stock holdings exceeding 50% of its Tier 1 capital; (2) banks with total stock holdings exceeding ¥500 billion; or (3) banks adhering to a capital adequacy ratio based upon international standards. The maximum amount of stocks purchased from an individual bank was not to exceed ¥250 billion. The disposal of the purchased stocks would not be resumed until the end of March 2012 (with full disposal of all the stocks to be completed by the end of September 2017).

Like the first round of stock purchases, this action was aimed at *stabilising the financial system, not at conducting monetary easing*. The purchase continued until April 2010 and the total amount of purchases amounted to ¥388 billion. In April 2016, the BoJ finally decided to begin selling the purchased stocks of about ¥3 trillion over the next 10 years at about ¥300 billion annually upon a mark-to-market value basis as of the end of November 2015. This disposal is associated with a roughly equivalent increase in ETF purchases, as part of an initiative to promote the investment of firms in R&D and human capital, as mentioned below. Hence, this disposal would roughly maintain a neutral impact on stock prices.

8.2.3 ETF Purchases as a Monetary Easing Tool Since 2010

The idea of purchasing the ETFs had been developed and announced in October 2010 under the previous governor, Shirakawa, as part of monetary easing. The ETFs trace the Nikkei 225 and the TOPIX, meaning it amounts to an indirect purchasing of stocks. The ETF purchases were *part of a monetary easing policy package* called *Comprehensive Monetary Easing* (CME)—unconventional monetary easing conducted in the face of the virtually zero lower bound. The main element of CME was to purchase various financial assets under the Asset Purchase Programme. The main assets purchased were Japanese Government Bonds (JGBs) with a remaining maturity of up to 3 years—in order to exert downward pressure on relatively longer-term interest rates. The BoJ also aimed at *reducing risk premia* through purchasing risk assets, such as the ETFs, commercial paper, corporate bonds, and Japan real estate investment trusts (J-REITs).

Lowering risk *premia* was expected to support risk asset markets and induce a portfolio re-balancing effect. And a wealth effect was envisaged, too. In particular, the BoJ hoped to generate "healthy" risk-taking behaviour among individuals, and not just among firms and financial institutions, as risk money (such as investment in stocks and real estate and foreign investment) could energise the Japanese economy and encourage individual investors to diversify their financial assets. Traditionally, individuals have held over half of their financial assets in the form of cash and deposits in Japan. They are highly risk-averse, as only 10% has been invested in stocks, compared with 36% in the United States and 18% in the eurozone, according to the BoJ (2017). Firms also hold about ¥274 trillion in the form of cash and deposits. Banks hold substantial amounts in JGBs to fill the rising gap between deposits and loans extended to the private sector. Given this background, the BoJ decided to purchase the ETFs at market price as trust property through trust banks, which were designated by the BoJ as trustees until the end of December 2011.

The BoJ had initially decided that the maximum outstanding amount for ETFs was to be about ¥450 billion. In the case of selling the purchased ETFs, the BoJ had set some basic principles, i.e., to avoid, as much as possible, incurring losses and de-stabilising the financial markets. The ETFs purchases were extended and increased thereafter. The holdings of ETFs had reached ¥1.5 trillion by the end of March 2013, before the new Quantitative and Qualitative Monetary Easing (QQE) was implemented under the newly appointed governor, Kuroda. Thus, the amount of the ETF purchases under the CME was limited.

The effectiveness of CME on macroeconomic performance and financial markets seemed limited. Yields on 1-year, 2-year and 3-year JGBs had dropped from 0.11%, 0.12% and 0.13%, respectively, at the end of September 2010, to 0.05%, 0.057% and 0.05%, respectively, by the end of March 2013. Moreover, the JGB purchases with a maturity of up to 3 years induced longer term yields as demonstrated by a drop in the 10-year yield from 0.94% at the end of September 2010, to 0.56% by end of March 2013. Nonetheless, mild deflation continued persistently and the prospect of achieving 2% inflation was considered most unlikely by economists and market participants.

The yen continued to appreciate against major currencies as a safe-haven currency. It appreciated against the US dollar from around ¥84 in September 2010 to around ¥76 immediately after the Great East Japan Earthquake and Tsunami of 11 March 2011. This led to co-ordinated intervention in the foreign exchange market on

18–19 March 2011 by the Minister of Finance of Japan with the Bank of England, the Federal Reserve, the Bank of Canada and the Swiss National Bank, with the total amount of the intervention reaching about ¥800 billion (of which Japan contributed about ¥693 billion, or 87% of the total amount). The yen again appreciated to around ¥76 on 4 August 2011, which led to another intervention in the foreign exchange market, but this time it was conducted solely by the Ministry of Finance of Japan on a massive scale of ¥4.6 trillion. However, the yen continued to move below ¥80, which led to further interventions on 31 October 2011 with an amount of ¥8.7 trillion, and on 1–4 November 2011 with an amount of around ¥1 trillion. After that, the Ministry of Finance stopped intervening in the foreign exchange market. Criticism by the public and markets against the BoJ became more vociferous because the BoJ had failed to provide sufficient monetary easing, given the over-valuation of the yen. The dollar remained at around or below ¥80 until October 2012.

Similarly, Japanese stock prices remained stagnant for most of the same period, as shown in Fig. 8.1. The Nikkei 225 rose from around ¥9,367 at the end of November 2010 to over ¥10,000 in December 2010; from March 2011, it remained mostly below ¥10,000. The Tokyo Stock Price Index (TOPIX) was at about 830 points at the end of September 2010 and remained at this level after October 2010 until it dropped to below 800 points from August 2012 to November 2012. Thus, a decline in JGB yields under CME generated an accommodative monetary environment, but this was somewhat offset by the yen's sharp and continuous appreciation, and sluggish stock prices until the end of 2012.

From late 2012, however, the financial market showed a remarkable turnaround in anticipation of the massive monetary easing to be introduced by the next BoJ governor appointed by Prime Minister Shinzō Abe. The yen began to depreciate *vis-à-vis* the US dollar to around ¥84 in December 2012 and ¥95 in March 2013 just before the introduction of QQE. The yen's nominal effective exchange rate also depreciated. Moreover, stock prices (Nikkei) began to rise from around ¥9,500, to around ¥12,400 over the same period, and the TOPIX from around 780 points to around 1,000 points.

8.2.4 Stock Purchases by the Hong Kong Monetary Authority in 1998

A well-known case of a central bank's purchase of stocks can be found in the intervention by the Hong Kong Monetary Authority (HKMA) in 1998 when it simultaneously intervened in the foreign exchange, stock and stock futures and inter-bank markets. However, in this case, the stock purchase was conducted only for a very short period (about 2 weeks). Thus, this purchase programme *should not be regarded as unconventional monetary easing*, as has been undertaken under QQE by the BoJ led by Governor Kuroda, due to the differences in the period of intervention (about 2 weeks in Hong Kong *versus* more than 5 years in Japan) and the objectives (fighting against short term-oriented speculative activities in Hong Kong *versus* achieving the 2% price-stability target in Japan).

The Government of the Hong Kong Special Administrative Region of China decided to intervene in the stock market in the face of speculative attacks over the Hong Kong dollar fixed exchange-rate policy. This policy was meant to stabilise the Hong Kong dollar against the US dollar under the Linked Exchange Rate System—the so-called currency board system where the monetary base is fully backed up with reserves denominated in the US dollar. Speculators led by foreign hedge funds adopted a "double-market play" strategy by which they pre-funded themselves with Hong Kong dollars and then used the cash to build up large short positions in the cash and future stock markets and simultaneously sold the Hong Kong dollar in large quantities to drive up inter-bank interest rates. Although the Hang Seng Index had already dropped sharply from about 16,000 in August 1997 to about 8,000 in August 1998, a further drop was anticipated by these speculative short-selling activities—even though the price-earnings ratio recorded just eight times at about 8,000, suggesting that stock prices had been substantially low. The Government of the Hong Kong Special Administrative Region of China became concerned about potential losses to shareholders in the face of a sharp fall in the stock market and weakening public and market confidence about the sustainability of the exchange-rate policy.

The Government of the Hong Kong Special Administrative Region of China considered the market conditions to be a market failure and thus intervention in the stock market could be justified. In response, the HKMA intervened in the stock market on 14 August 1998 to purchase stocks listed on the Hong Kong Stock Exchange using foreign reserves as sources of funding to counter such speculative attacks. The stock market intervention was completed very shortly before the end of August 1998 with a total of about HK$120 billion spent by the HKMA to purchase stocks. The HKMA stressed that the intervention was an extraordinary measure taken at an extraordinary time and thus would arrange to dispose of the stocks quickly. Moreover, the Government of the Hong Kong Special Administrative Region of China promised that it would not intervene in the daily operations of the listed companies concerned through its shareholdings. The scale of intervention had been adequate enough to terminate the speculative attacks by the end of August 1998, as the Hang Seng Index had risen from 6,700 just before the intervention to 7,800 points afterwards.[4]

In November 1999, the HKMA adopted an exit policy when stock prices were rising by launching the Tracker Fund, which is an open-ended exchange-traded fund, and reselling HK$33.3 billion worth of stocks to 180,000 investors (Fig. 8.2). In the subsequent 3 years, until the end of 2012, during which stock prices were more or less on a rising trend, the HKMA continued to recoup over HK$100 billion through the same mechanism. The disposal of the stocks generated a profit of nearly HK$100 billion at prevailing stock prices for the HKMA at that time because of higher stock prices (Fig. 8.2). The HKMA's successful exit from the stock purchase programme could be attributed to the short-lived nature of the purchasing intervention in the

[4]See Chan (2015).

Fig. 8.2 Performance of the Hong Kong Seng Index.
Note The Hang Seng Index is a market capitalisation-weighted stock market index in Hong Kong.
Source Bloomberg

stock market, which meant the HKMA's intervention generated little distortions to stock prices. Moreover, favourable stock market conditions enabled the HKMA to conduct a smooth exit policy and generate a profit.

The HKMA's intervention in the stock markets was extremely short-lived and its main purpose was to eliminate speculative attacks targeting the fixed exchange-rate regime and associated automatic adjustment system. Thus, the measure was significantly different from the measures taken by the BoJ both in the case of the purchases of stocks from financial institutions and the ETF purchases.

8.3 The Unprecedented Scale of the ETF Purchases Since April 2013

8.3.1 Doubling the ETF Purchases to Achieve 2% Inflation in About 2 Years

In March 2013, Haruhiko Kuroda was appointed as the new governor of the Bank of Japan and he immediately launched a massive monetary easing programme to achieve the 2% price-stability target in April 2013. The QQE was introduced as an extension of the previous CME with an increase in the scale of asset purchases and a lengthening of the maturity of JGBs to a maximum 40 years. The yearly pace of the increase in the amount of JGBs outstanding held by the BoJ was initially set at about ¥50 trillion, and then expanded to about ¥80 trillion in October 2014. The holdings of commercial papers and corporate bonds were maintained at about ¥2.2 trillion and ¥3.2 trillion by adopting re-investment strategies—mainly because of the small size of markets and the high demand for these assets. Thus, the BoJ increased the purchases of risk assets through the ETFs and the J-REITs. Given their greater market size, the ETF purchases are more important than the J-REIT purchases.

The BoJ decided that the amounts of the ETF purchases would be expanded at an annual pace—initially by ¥1 trillion in April 2013 (Fig. 8.3). To demonstrate its intention to achieve 2% inflation at the earliest possible time, with a time horizon of about 2 years, the BoJ announced that it would double the monetary base and the amounts outstanding of JGBs and ETFs in 2 years under QQE—from the prevailing level prior to QQE (end of December 2012). In the case of the ETFs, the amount of ETFs outstanding was projected to double from the end of 2012 to the end of 2014 with the expansion by about ¥1 trillion per year for 2 years. The BoJ used the number "two" a great deal—2% price-stability target, a time horizon of about 2 years, doubling the monetary base and the amounts outstanding of the JGBs and the ETFs, and doubling the average remaining maturity of JGB purchases. The BoJ did so to send a clear message about the new framework and its strong determination to achieve the 2% target as soon as possible.

As the economy began to slow, partly due to a consumption tax hike from 5 to 8% in April 2014, and inflation expectations began to decline in early 2014, the BoJ decided to expand asset purchases. To send a clear message about the boldness of QQE expansion, the BoJ intentionally used the key number "3" this time compared with the key number "2" when QQE was initially launched. For example, the BoJ emphasised the annual increase in its JGB holdings by "+30 trillion yen" (from about ¥50 trillion to about ¥80 trillion); the increase in the average remaining maturity target of JGB purchases by "+3 years" (from around 6–8 years to 7–10 years); the pace of purchases of ETFs and J-REITs "tripled" from ¥1 trillion to ¥3 trillion and from ¥30 billion to ¥90 billion, respectively.

In November 2014, the BoJ also included the ETFs that track the JPX-Nikkei Index 400 as ETFs eligible for purchase.

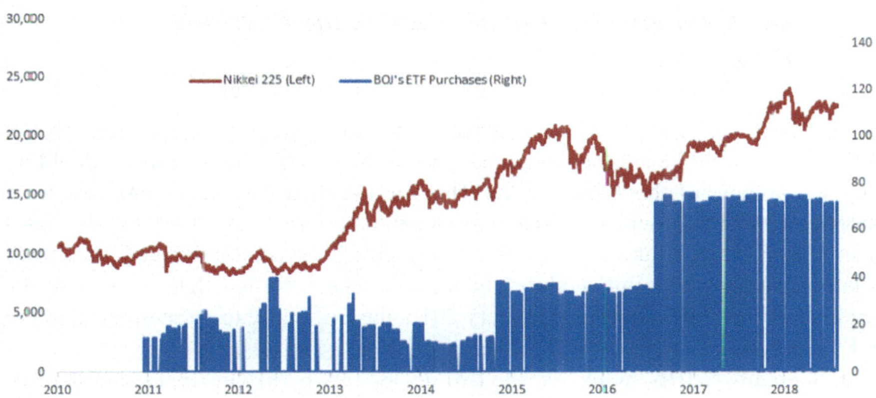

Fig. 8.3 Purchases of ETFs (billions of ¥) and Nikkei 225 (¥).
Note: BoJ's purchases are on a daily basis.
Source Bloomberg

8.3.2 Initiative to Promote the Investment of Firms in R&D and Human Capital

In December 2015, the BoJ established a new programme for purchasing ETFs, comprising stocks issued by firms that were proactively investing in physical and human capital at an annual pace of about ¥300 billion. In March 2016, the BoJ provided details. The new ETFs were to have portfolios comprising the stocks of firms whose: (1) capital expenditure or research and development (R&D) expenditure showed an upward trend (investment in physical capital); (2) expenditure on human capital showed an upward trend, as demonstrated by indicators, including the number of employees, wages, salary expenses, spending on career development, etc., (investment in human capital); and (3) investment in physical and human capital was considered to be reasonable to enhance their growth potential through effective corporate governance, from the perspective of the firms' sales, profitability, productivity, corporate value or other indicators (growth potential). This new programme started in April 2016.

It should be noted that the amount of ¥300 billion did not increase the BoJ's aggregated holdings of stocks and ETFs. This is because the BoJ decided simultaneously to sell its existing holdings of stocks purchased directly from commercial financial institutions for the above-mentioned financial stability purposes. In April 2016, the BoJ decided to begin selling the purchased stocks over the next 10 years at an amount of about ¥300 billion annually (based upon the mark-to-market value at the end of November 2015). Since the annual sales amount was roughly the same as the annual ETF purchases of around ¥300 billion, these operations offset each other.

8.3.3 Expanding the Annual Pace of the ETF Purchases and Changing the Composition of the Purchase Programme

In July 2016, the BoJ decided to increase its ETF purchases so that the amount outstanding would increase at an annual pace of about ¥6 trillion—almost doubling the previous pace of about ¥3.3 trillion. This was to enhance monetary easing against uncertainties related to the United Kingdom's referendum decision to leave the European Union (Brexit) and a slowdown in the emerging economies and associated volatile developments in the global financial markets. Rather than deepening the negative interest rate adopted in January 2016, the BoJ chose to increase the amount of ETF purchases.

In September 2016, moreover, the BoJ decided to modify the composition of its ETF purchases. This was not done to increase monetary easing, but rather to reduce the distortions created in the stock market as a result of massive purchases of ETFs that trace the Nikkei 225 Stock Average. Out of an annual increase of ETF purchases of ¥5.7 trillion—excluding ¥300 billion allocated for ETFs to support firms proactively investing in physical and human capital from ¥6 trillion—the BoJ decided to increase TOPIX-related ETFs and reduce Nikkei 225-related ETFs. Before this adjustment was made, the amount of ETF purchases for each index was roughly proportionate to the total market value of that ETF issued; thus, the amount of ¥5.7 trillion was nearly split between the TOPIX and the Nikkei 225 Stock Average, as the JPX-Nikkei 400 market is relatively small.

The modification was in reaction to the growing criticism since early 2016 from market participants that such a composition had distorted stock market prices. Specifically, the BoJ's proportionate purchase practice had tended to favour stocks included in the price-weighted Nikkei 225 Stock Average, as compared with the market value-weighted TOPIX. The TOPIX covers 2,106 firms listed in the Tokyo Stock Exchange First Section, whereas the Nikkei 225 covers only 225 listed firms. As some small-cap firms are included in the Nikkei 225 with higher weights due to relatively higher stock prices, the continuation of the BoJ's purchases tended to generate the overvaluation of such stocks. A famous example was the *Fast Retailing Co.*, owner of the well-known apparel chain *Uniqlo*, whose weight accounted for around 8% of the Nikkei 225 Stock Average while accounting for only 0.3% of the TOPIX at that time. As a result, the *Fast Retailing Co.* had benefited substantially from the BoJ's purchase of the Nikkei 225. The BoJ already owned about half of the *Fast Retailing Co.*'s free floating stocks, which were expected to rise to over 60% by the end of December 2016.

In response, the BoJ decided to reduce its ETF purchases in the Nikkei 225 Stock Average and increased ETF purchases tracking the TOPIX, instead. Out of ¥5.7 trillion, the BoJ would allocate ¥2.7 trillion annually to TOPIX ETFs, while the remaining ¥3 trillion would be spread out between TOPIX, the Nikkei 225 Stock Average and the JPX-Nikkei 400 ETFs—roughly in proportion to the total market value of each ETF issued. Consequently, the BoJ would allocate about 70% of the ¥5.7 trillion to TOPIX ETF.

8.3.4 Introduction of Flexibility in the Purchasing Programme and a Further Change in the Composition

The BoJ made two adjustments to the ETF purchases in July 2018. One was to make monthly adjustments more flexibly by purchasing more when risk premiums rose while keeping an annual purchase pace of about ¥6 trillion. This means that the BoJ would purchase ETFs more flexibly by buying more when sharp falls occurred and less when mild falls occurred. While the BoJ stressed that the annual purchase amount of about ¥6 trillion was to be maintained, this may lead to "stealth tapering", as is the case with JGBs—reducing the annual pace of JGB purchases to well below ¥80 trillion, while specifying the continuation of about ¥80 trillion in the Statement on Monetary Policy. This could be a step towards normalisation.[5]

[5] See Shirai (2018b).

Another adjustment was to change the composition of ETF purchase again. This was a good move because the continuation of Nikkei 225-related ETFs would distort stock prices more heavily than that of TOPIX-related ETFs, as pointed out above. The stock prices of a number of small-cap firms included in Nikkei 225 firms could be overpriced, as the BoJ has already become the top investor in these stocks, with fewer floating stocks available in the market. Before the adjustment, TOPIX-related ETFs, Nikkei 225-related ETFs and JPX Nikkei Index 400 based upon the purchased price (based upon the market price) had accounted for about 57 (54%), 37 (41%) and 6% (5%) of the total outstanding amount of about 21 trillion yen (about 27 trillion yen) held by the BoJ, respectively, as of August 2018. For new purchases, the BoJ would allocate ¥4.2 trillion annually to TOPIX ETFs, while the remaining ¥1.5 trillion would be spread out between TOPIX, Nikkei 225 Stock Average and JPX-Nikkei 400 ETFs—roughly in proportion to the total market value of each ETF issued. Consequently, the BoJ would allocate over 80% of the ¥5.7 trillion to TOPIX ETFs. This would enable the BoJ to continue its ETF purchases for longer.

8.4 The Effects of QQE and ETF Purchases on Stock Markets

8.4.1 Stock Market Performance During 2012–2018

Since late 2012, close to the time when Shinzō Abe became prime minister, stock prices began to rise rapidly and the yen depreciated sharply (Fig. 8.4). The Nikkei 225 (and the TOPIX) rose from around ¥9,000–9,500 (¥700–800) between June and November 2012 to above 10,000 in late December 2012, as short term-oriented foreign investors held the view that the new government led by the Liberal Democratic Party leader Abe would adopt comprehensive economic strategies including massive monetary easing to be initiated by the BoJ's incoming new governor. This massive monetary easing has clearly contributed to an improvement in stock indices and to the sentiment of the corporate sector and existing investors.

There is generally a positive correlation between the exchange rate and stock prices, and the correlation became stronger from late 2012 to 2015. This was mainly due to the yen's depreciation contributing to higher yen values of foreign profits earned by Japanese multinational firms. Given that those multinational firms tend to be listed on the stock market, the higher consolidated profits led to higher stock prices.

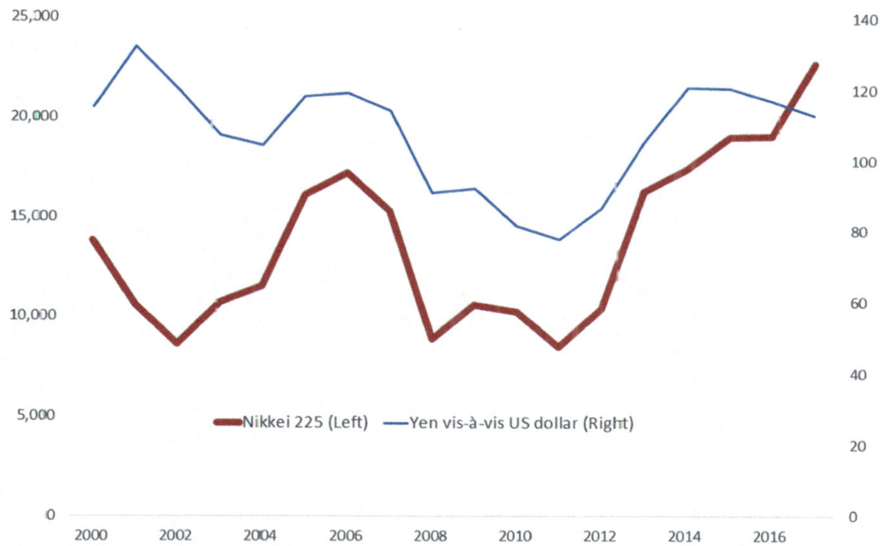

Fig. 8.4 The yen *vis-à-vis* the US dollar and the Nikkei 225 (¥).
Source Bloomberg; Bank of Japan

8.4.1.1 Fall in Stock Prices After the Negative Interest Rate and Recovery Supported by the US Presidential Election

Stock prices dropped in 2016 when the yen appreciated sharply after the adoption of a negative interest rate. Doubling the annual pace of the ETF purchases to about ¥6 trillion in July 2016 and adopting yield curve control in September 2016 neither resulted in a sharp appreciation of the yen nor a stock price plunge. This suggests that, while the negative interest rate policy adopted earlier in January 2016 had led to a sharp appreciation of the yen and a stock price plunge, expanding the ETF purchases and adopting the yield curve control did not disappoint foreign investors—even though the yield curve actually rose and steepened. At the same time, however, it did not generate strong positive momentum in the foreign exchange and stock markets, as demonstrated by the limited impact on the depreciation of the yen and the stock price hike.

Yield curve control appears to have become effective after the US presidential election of 8 November 2016 and the resultant rapid rise in stock prices and yields in the United States. Longer term yields in the US rose rapidly in the immediate aftermath of Donald Trump's surprise victory in the US presidential election; the 10-year yield, for example, rose by about 60 basis points, from around 1.8% on 7 November to around 2.4% by the end of the same month. This move reflected the anticipation of higher economic growth and inflation, mainly driven by the massive tax cuts, infrastructure investment and de-regulations promised during the election campaign. An expectation of the imposition of higher tariffs under expected new anti-global

Fig. 8.5 The performance of TOPIX and S&P 500.
Source Bloomberg

trade regimes and stricter immigration controls further added to the higher inflation outlook. The yen began to depreciate sharply—*vis-à-vis* the US dollar—from below ¥105 to over ¥117 in December 2016. This was because the US presidential election and the anticipated tighter monetary policy by the Federal Reserve, together with yield curve control, led to a rapid expansion of the interest-rate differential between the United States and Japan. Together with a depreciation of the yen, stock prices rose from around ¥17,000 to over ¥19,000 in December 2016, while the TOPIX rose from around 1,300 points to over 1,500 points over the same period.

Japanese stock prices are not only positively associated with the dollar/yen exchange rate but also closely associated with US stock prices (Fig. 8.5). After the Lehman Brothers shock, US stock prices saw strong rising trends and recorded their highest levels ever. And, after the US presidential election, stock prices strengthened again. The strong US stock price performance contributed to higher global stock prices, including Japanese stock prices, throughout 2017.

8.4.1.2 Suspension on Rising Stock Price Trends Since Early 2018

In early 2018, when the US 10-year yield rose from around 2.4% to around 3% as a result of the release of strong wage data, US stock prices stopped rising. Since then, US stock prices and global stock prices have fluctuated and have not recovered to their recent highs. While the S&P 500 managed to reach its highest level in July 2018, the Dow Industrial Average has not managed to reach its highest level—recorded in January 2018—again.

Favourable global stock market trends, including in Japan, have come to an end for several reasons. First, the normalisation of monetary policy by the Federal Reserve has led to capital outflows and the resultant sharp depreciation of the exchange rates in the emerging economies. In response, many central banks in the emerging economies have raised their policy rates. Second, the intensification of trade protectionism led by the US government and the growing trade conflicts between the United States and the People's Republic of China has increased concerns over global growth prospects. Third, the rising price of oil since late 2017 and a further hike after the US withdrawal from the nuclear deal between Iran and six countries[6] and the resultant sanctions against Iran have amplified concerns that economic growth in oil-importing economies may cool.

The Nikkei 225 achieved its recent maximum level of ¥24,124 on 23 January 2018, but, since then, has been fluctuating at around ¥22,000, and has never reached its past maximum level of ¥38,915, recorded on 29 December 1989. Similarly, the TOPIX reached its recent maximum level of 1,911 points on 23 January 2018. Since then, it, too, has fluctuated at around 1,700 points, so it has never reached its past maximum level of 2,884 points recorded on 18 December 1989, either.

8.4.2 Why Has Japan's P/E Ratio Declined Recently?

It is often pointed out that the peak of the stock price bubble in Japan in late December 1989 was excessive because the Price–Earnings Ratio (P/E ratio) was about 80 in the case of the Nikkei 225. The P/E ratio of the Nikkei 225 has since 2004 fluctuated within a range of 14–16—the level generally regarded as appropriate. Nonetheless, the fact that stock prices have—to date—not reached their maximum levels suggests that the profits of listed firms have not been strong enough to reach the maximum stock prices recorded in 1989, after the bubble burst. It also gives investors the impression that capital gains are unlikely to be large, which may deter new investors.

In addition, the P/E ratio based upon the Nikkei 225 has declined (to about 13.5, as of early August 2018) and current earnings per share (EPS) have risen steadily since 2017 (Fig. 8.6). As a result, the gap between the Nikkei 225 and P/E ratio has widened. A similar pattern can be observed in the case of the TOPIX. These features indicate that stock prices have not caught up with the current favourable corporate profits. On the one hand, this could indicate that *Japanese stock prices have become somewhat under-priced*, despite the BoJ's monetary easing, including the ETF purchases. On the other hand, this could be associated with market participants' negative outlook on future corporate profits, as compared with current profits. Corporate profits began to rise steadily in 2013, reflecting the yen's depreciation and the associated higher yen

[6]The Joint Comprehensive Plan of Action, known as the Iran nuclear deal, was signed between Iran and P5+1 (the five permanent members of the United Nations Security Council—China, France, Russia, the United Kingdom, the United States—plus Germany), together with the European Union, on 14 July 2015. The United States withdrew on 8 May 2018.

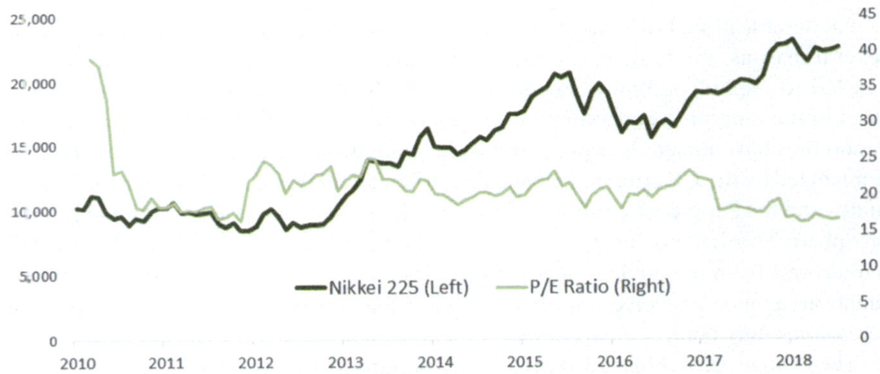

Fig. 8.6 Nikkei 225 (¥) and P/E ratio.
Source Bloomberg

value of foreign profits, public investment mainly related to the 2020 Olympic Games to be held in Tokyo, real estate development activities and lower oil prices since the fiscal year 2014 (Fig. 8.6). Corporate profits recorded the highest level in the fiscal year 2017, although the pace of the increase relative to the previous year moderated. The level of corporate profits for the fiscal year 2018 is widely expected to be lower than that of the fiscal year 2017. Thus, the sluggish P/E ratio may reflect such an expected slowdown in corporate profits. Some market participants hold the view that the BoJ's expected unwinding of ETF purchases—expected to begin with a decline in the number of annual purchases from about ¥6 trillion—may have discouraged active investment.

8.4.3 Greater Impact on the Stock Prices of Small-Cap Companies

The BoJ's holdings of ETFs recorded about ¥21 trillion upon a book value basis as of August 2018. The BoJ could be the second largest shareholder of listed shares after the Government Pension Investment Funds (GPIF), which hold Japanese stocks worth about ¥41 trillion as of June 2018. GPIF manages about ¥163 trillion of the Reserve Funds of the Government Pension Plans, making it one of the largest sovereign wealth funds in the world. Out of ¥21 trillion held by the BoJ, about ¥12 trillion and ¥7.8 trillion are estimated to have been allocated to TOPIX-related ETFs and Nikkei 225-related ETFs, respectively. Some concerns have been raised by market participants over the BoJ's substantial purchases of ETFs, since the central bank has become one of the largest shareholders of listed stocks upon a *per* investor basis with no voting rights being exercised—together with the GPIF. As the BoJ and the GPIF do not exercise voting rights, the presence of a public entity as a major

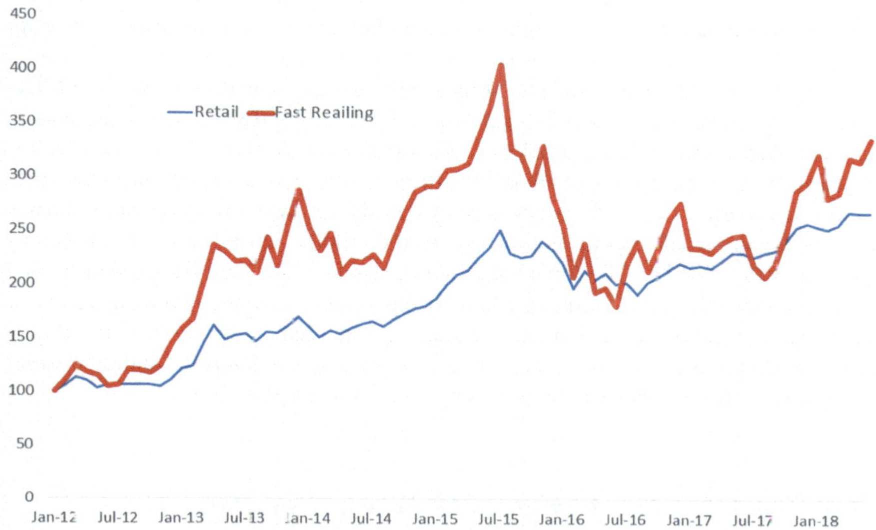

Fig. 8.7 Stock prices of the *Fast Retailing Co.* and retail sector. *Source* Bloomberg

silent shareholder may delay Japan's much needed corporate governance reform. Furthermore, concerns continue to be raised with regard to a possible over-valuation of the stocks of some small-cap firms, particularly those included in the Nikkei 225.

Figure 8.7 depicts the movements in the stock prices of the *Fast Retailing Co.* as well as the retail sector (to which the *Fast Retailing Co.* belongs). It shows that the stock price of the *Fast Retailing Co.* has been higher than the retail sector trend since 2013, especially when the retail sector stock prices (also the overall stock prices) have been on a rising trend. Moreover, the P/E ratio of *Fast Retailing* is around 38 as of August 2018—much higher than the 13.5 in the case of the Nikkei 225 and the 18 in the case of Tokyo Stock Exchange Sect. 8.1. Such seemingly over-priced stocks may face a sharper fall when the BoJ unwinds its monetary easing stance. While there may be other firm-specific factors contributing to this gap, the stock price could be over-priced, partly as a result of the BoJ's purchases of the Nikkei 225-related ETFs. The difference between the weight in the Nikkei 225 (7.5%) and in the TOPIX (0.3%) is one of the highest among other stocks. This indicates the BoJ has been purchasing this stock heavily, as compared with the outstanding number of stocks issued.

The Nikkei Newspaper reported, on 17 June 2018, that the BoJ had become—*vis-à-vis* the US dollar—one of the top ten largest shareholders in about 40% of listed firms as of the end of March 2018. Of these, the BoJ had become the top shareholder in five listed companies including the *Fast Retailing Co.*, when only floating shares are taken into account. For example, the BoJ holds about 17.5% of the total number of shares issued, but this ratio becomes much higher, to wit, 70%, in terms of floating shares.

In response, the BoJ attempted to improve the situation by buying more TOPIX-related ETFs and fewer Nikkei 225-related ETFs in July 2018, as mentioned above. This had been very much expected by market participants. Nonetheless, the continuation of the ETF purchases of about ¥6 trillion annually is likely to intensify stress in the stock market since price distortions would be likely to continue and intensify not only for the small-cap firms included in the Nikkei 225 but also for all stocks included in the TOPIX. The longer the BoJ continues with the ETF purchases, the more turbulence the stock market is likely to experience when the BoJ makes a major step towards normalisation. This might make it much harder for the BoJ to adopt a smooth exit strategy. The dilemma between achieving the 2% price-stability target and coping with the various side effects may become amplified.

8.4.4 Stock Market Dominated by Foreign Investors as a Group

Foreign investors as a group were the largest shareholders of listed firms including first, second, Mothers and JASDAQ Sections. They hold about ¥200 trillion upon a market value basis or 30% of the total as of the fiscal year 2017. Business corporations (non-financial firms) were the second largest investors as a group, with ¥146 trillion or 22% of the total. The third largest investors were "trust banks," with ¥136 trillion or 20.4% of the total. Trust banks' stockholdings include stocks held by the BoJ, the GPIF, other pension funds and investment trusts. Individuals were the fourth largest investors as a group, with stock holdings of ¥113 trillion or 17% of the total (Fig. 8.8).

8.4.4.1 Rising Foreign Investors' Presence as the Largest Shareholder

In addition, foreign investors increased their presence over the period between the fiscal years 2012 and 2017, with the ratio of their stockholdings to the total market value of stocks rising from 28.5% in fiscal year 2012 to 30% in fiscal year 2017. Next, business corporations and trust banks also increased their stockholding ratios over the same period from 21% to 22% and 18% to 20%, respectively. The stockholdings of business corporations include own stocks purchased through a buy-back strategy. An increase in the ratio of trust banks reflects an increase in the BoJ's ETF purchase as well as the 2014 reform of the GPIF with regard to the basic portfolio guidance. The GPIF reform increased the stockholdings and reduced the holdings of domestic bonds including JGBs. With effect from the end of October 2014, the allocation of domestic bonds dropped from 60 to 35% (with a pemissible range from ±8 to ±10%), while the allocation of both domestic stocks and foreign stocks rose from 12 to 25%, respectively (with a permissible range from ±6 to ±9% for domestic

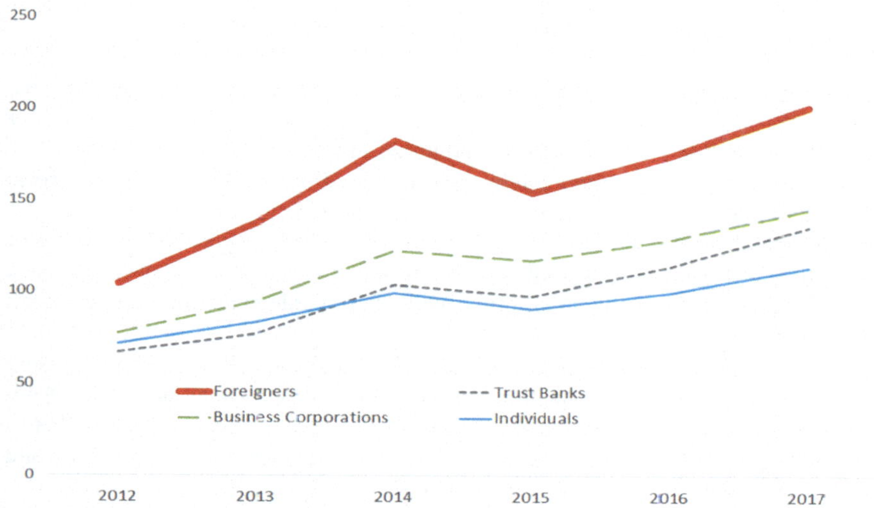

Fig. 8.8 Stockholdings at market value (trillions of ¥).
Source Japan Exchange Group

stocks and from ±5 to ±8% for foreign stocks). The allocation of foreign bonds also grew from 11 to 15% (with a permissible range from ±5 to ±4%). Some of the other public pension funds changed their asset portfolio in line with the GPIF reform.

By contrast, individuals—as a group—were not very enthusiastic investors over the same period, as their share dropped from 19.5 to 17%, in spite of an increase in the number of individual investors from about 46 million in fiscal year 2012 to 61 million in fiscal year 2017. The increase in the number of individual investors is attributable to a series of government tax exemption initiatives (with regard to a 20% levy on income from dividends and capital gains) to encourage individuals to invest in stocks and diversify their financial assets. The initiatives include (1) Nippon Individual Savings Account (NISA) adopted in 2014, which enables individuals of at least 20 years of age to open a NISA account (for a maximum investment of ¥1.2 million a year, up to ¥6 million for 5 years); (2) Junior NISA adopted in April 2016, which enables individuals under 20 years of age to open a Junior NISA account (for a maximum investment of ¥800,000 a year, up to ¥4 million for 5 years); and (3) Instalment-type NISA adopted in 2018 for a maximum investment of ¥400,000 a year, up to ¥8 million for 20 years. In addition, the government promoted an individual-type *Defined Contribution Pension Plan* (iDeCo) or a private pension plan with all contributions being tax deductible for virtually all individuals aged between 20 and 59. Notwithstanding these measures, together with BoJ's monetary easing and GPIF reform, individuals have not become enthusiastic about investing in Japanese stocks.

8.4.4.2 Foreign Investors Have Become Active Trading Players

In addition to being the largest group of stockholders, foreign investors have been the most active players in both selling and purchasing transactions. They accounted for over 60% of the total value of selling and purchasing transactions as of June 2018, respectively—both rising moderately from below 60% in 2012. The next largest selling and purchasing amount was achieved by individual investors. However, the ratio dropped from around 15–19% in 2012 to around 15% in June 2018, in terms of both selling and purchasing transactions, after a temporary increase to over 20% each in 2013, when strong rising stock prices and the yen's depreciation had generated momentum.

Transactions by trust banks—with the third largest selling and purchasing values—were much smaller than those of individuals, despite their large-scale holdings of stocks. This could suggest that most of the stocks managed by trust banks are maintained without active trading—a buy and hold approach. Their selling and purchasing transaction values have remained stable after a moderate increase in 2013. Meanwhile, investment trusts increased the values of selling and purchasing transactions over time, since some individuals increased investment in stocks directly through investment trusts. Nevertheless, these values of selling and purchasing transactions were much smaller than those of individuals.

Figure 8.9a, b show the value of selling and purchasing transactions of the two largest trading players—foreign investors and individual investors. These figures show that foreign investors were dominant and that they actively increased both selling and purchasing transactions over time. This is in contrast with the behaviour of individual investors, which remained inactive except in 2013.

8.5 Conclusions

This chapter has highlighted the ETF purchases conducted by the BoJ under the current monetary easing policy. This policy is unprecedented in terms of both scale and duration among major central banks. Stock prices began to rise from late 2012 together with a sharp depreciation of the yen in anticipation of the BoJ's aggressive monetary easing. Stock prices rose due to various domestic and foreign factors. Domestic factors include the BoJ's monetary easing (through a decline in short- and long-term interest rates, ETF purchases and the depreciation of the yen) as well as favourable corporate profits, which are also partially supported by the BoJ's policy. Foreign factors include higher US stock prices and the appreciation of the US dollar against major currencies.

The purpose of the BoJ's monetary easing was to increase aggregate demand and thus inflation (and inflation expectations) as well as to promote portfolio re-balancing among individuals and other entities. Regarding individuals, their outstanding amount of stockholdings rose only moderately and lagged behind that of

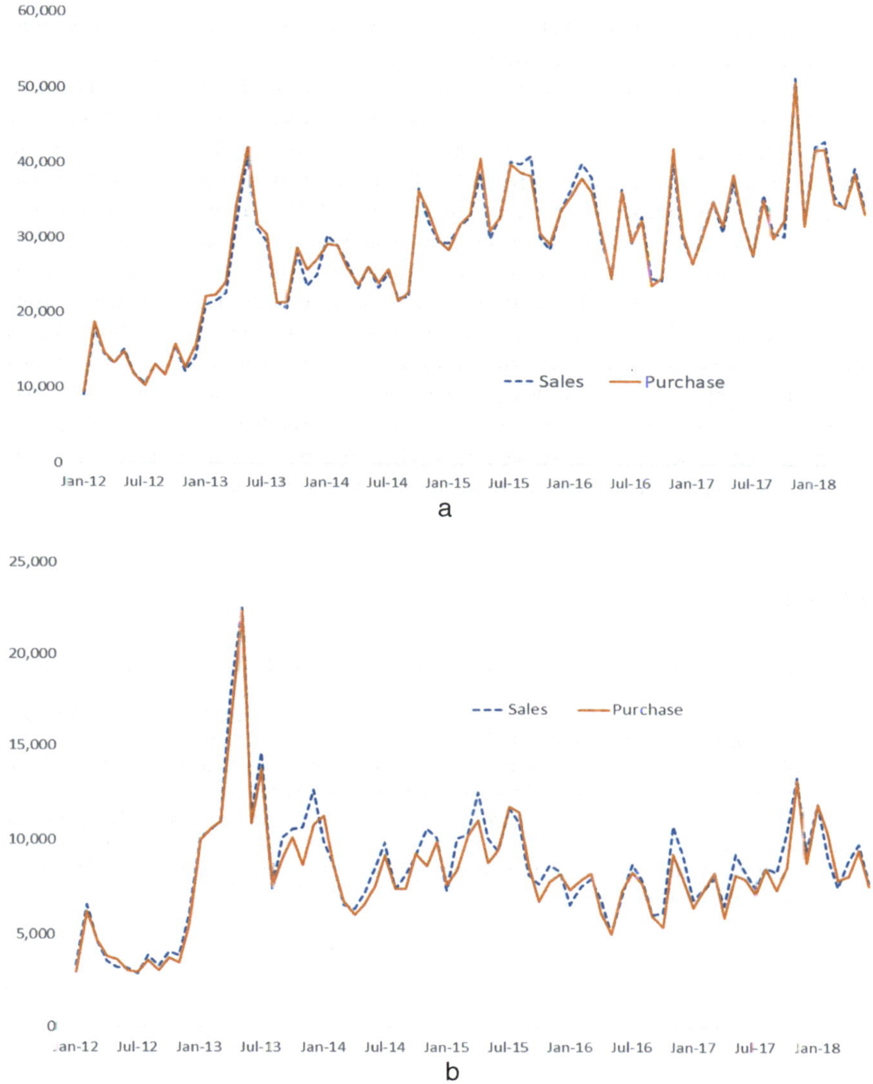

Fig. 8.9 Individual investors selling and purchasing transactions (billions of ¥). *Source* Japan Exchange Group.

foreign investors. In addition, the value of transactions in the stock market by individual investors did not reflect this rising trend. In other words, individuals remained largely risk-averse and did not actively re-balance their portfolios in favour of risk assets. This was despite the BoJ's policy, the GPIF reform that increased stockholdings, and a series of government tax incentives to promote stock investment for

The manufacturer's authorised representative in the EU is Springer Nature Customer Service Centre GmbH, Europaplatz 3, 69115 Heidelberg, Germany. If you have any concerns regarding our products, please contact ProductSafety@springernature.com

Printed and bound by CPI Group (UK) Ltd, Croydon, CR0 4YY
05/10/2026
02228069-0002